Life and Death on the Greenland Patrol, 1942

New Perspectives on Maritime History and Nautical Archaeology

5-21-15

For Dave —
with best wishes for
Fair winds —

Pete

Florida A&M University, Tallahassee
Florida Atlantic University, Boca Raton
Florida Gulf Coast University, Ft. Myers
Florida International University, Miami
Florida State University, Tallahassee
New College of Florida, Sarasota
University of Central Florida, Orlando
University of Florida, Gainesville
University of North Florida, Jacksonville
University of South Florida, Tampa
University of West Florida, Pensacola

New Perspectives on Maritime History and Nautical Archaeology
Edited by James C. Bradford and Gene Allen Smith

Joshua M. Smith and the National Maritime Historical Society (2009)

Voyages, The Age of Engines: Documents in Maritime History, Volume II, 1865–Present, edited by Joshua M. Smith and the National Maritime Historical Society (2009)

H.M.S. Fowey Lost . . . and Found!, by Russell K. Skowronek and George R. Fischer (2009)

American Coastal Rescue Craft: A Design History of Coastal Rescue Craft Used by the United States Life-Saving Service and the United States Coast Guard, by William D. Wilkinson and Commander Timothy R. Dring, USNR (Retired) (2009)

The Spanish Convoy of 1750: Heaven's Hammer and International Diplomacy, by James A. Lewis (2009)

The Development of Mobile Logistic Support in Anglo-American Naval Policy, 1900–1953, by Peter V. Nash (2009)

Captain "Hell Roaring" Mike Healy: From American Slave to Arctic Hero, by Dennis L. Noble and Truman R. Strobridge (2009)

Sovereignty at Sea: U.S. Merchant Ships and American Entry into World War I, by Rodney Carlisle (2009; first paperback edition, 2011)

Commodore Abraham Whipple of the Continental Navy: Privateer, Patriot, Pioneer, by Sheldon S. Cohen (2010; first paperback edition, 2011)

Lucky 73: USS Pampanito's *Unlikely Rescue of Allied POWs in WW II*, by Aldona Sendzikas (2010)

Cruise of the Dashing Wave: *Rounding Cape Horn in 1860*, by Philip Hichborn, edited by William H. Thiesen (2010)

Seated by the Sea: The Maritime History of Portland, Maine, and Its Irish Longshoremen, by Michael C. Connolly (2010; first paperback edition, 2011)

The Whaling Expedition of the Ulysses, *1937–1938*, by LT (j.g.) Quentin R. Walsh, U.S. Coast Guard, edited and with an Introduction by P.J. Capelotti (2010)

Stalking the U-Boat: U. S. Naval Aviation in Europe During World War I, by Geoffrey L. Rossano (2010)

In Katrina's Wake: The U.S. Coast Guard and the Gulf Coast Hurricanes of 2005, by Donald L. Canney (2010)

A Civil War Gunboat in Pacific Waters: Life on Board USS Saginaw, by Hans K. Van Tilburg (2010)

The U.S. Coast Guard's War on Human Smuggling, by Dennis L. Noble (2011)

The Sea Their Graves: An Archaeology of Death and Remembrance in Maritime Culture, by David J. Stewart (2011)

Life and Death
on the Greenland Patrol, 1942

---

by Thaddeus D. Novak, edited by P. J. Capelotti

Foreword by James C. Bradford and Gene A. Smith, Series Editors

University Press of Florida
Gainesville · Tallahassee · Tampa · Boca Raton
Pensacola · Orlando · Miami · Jacksonville · Ft. Myers · Sarasota

First cloth printing, 2005
First paperback printing, 2014

Library of Congress Cataloging-in-Publication Data
Novak, Thaddeus D., 1919–1997.
Life and death on the Greenland patrol, 1942 / by Thaddeus D. Novak; edited
by P. J. Capelotti; foreword by James C. Bradford and Gene A. Smith.
    p. cm. — (New perspectives on maritime history and nautical archaeology)
Includes bibliographical references and index.
ISBN 978-0-8130-2912-2 (cloth: alk. paper)
ISBN 978-0-8130-6028-6 (pbk.)
    1. Novak, Thaddeus D., 1919–1997—Diaries. 2. World War, 1939–1945—
Naval operations, American. 3. World War, 1939–1945—Personal narratives,
American. 4. World War, 1939–1945—Campaigns—North Atlantic Ocean.
5. World War, 1939–1945—Greenland. 6. United States. Coast Guard—
Biography. 7. Coast defenses—Greenland. 8. Greenland—History, Military.
9. Sailors—United States—Diaries.
I. Capelotti, P. J. (Peter Joseph), 1960– II. Title. III. Series.

D773 .N68 2005
940.54'293'092—dc22
[B]   2005053161

The University Press of Florida is the scholarly publishing agency for
the State University System of Florida, comprising Florida A&M University,
Florida Atlantic University, Florida Gulf Coast University, Florida International
University, Florida State University, New College of Florida, University of Cen-
tral Florida, University of Florida, University of North Florida, University of
South Florida, and University of West Florida.

University Press of Florida
15 Northwest 15th Street
Gainesville, FL 32611-2079
http://www.upf.com

All royalties from the sale of this book benefit
the Foundation for Coast Guard History.
Please visit their website at www.fcgh.org.

I shall sell life dearly to an enemy of my country,
but give it freely to rescue those in peril.

from the Creed of the United States Coast Guardsman

This true story is dedicated to the crew of the U.S. Coast Guard vessel *Natsek*, whose lives were claimed by the sea, and to the crew of the U.S. Coast Guard vessel *Nanok* and its one-of-a-kind skipper Magnus G. Magnusson, and, finally, to all others who comprised the Greenland Patrol during World War II.

Contents

Foreword

Water is unquestionably the most important natural feature on earth. By volume the world's oceans compose 99 percent of the planet's living space; in fact, the surface of the Pacific Ocean alone is larger than that of the total land bodies. Water is as vital to life as air. Indeed, to test whether the moon or other planets can sustain life, NASA looks for signs of water. The story of human development is inextricably linked to the oceans, seas, lakes, and rivers that dominate the earth's surface. The University Press of Florida's series *New Perspectives on Maritime History and Nautical Archaeology* is devoted to exploring the significance of the earth's water while providing lively and important books that cover the spectrum of maritime history and nautical archaeology broadly defined. The series includes works that focus on the role of canals, rivers, lakes, and oceans in history; on the economic, military, and political use of those waters; and upon the people, communities, and industries that support maritime endeavors. Limited by neither geography nor time, volumes in the series contribute to the overall understanding of maritime history and can be read with profit by both general readers and specialists.

Life and Death on the Greenland Patrol, 1942 is an intriguing six-month diary account (June–December 1942) of an ordinary seaman serving on board the Coast Guard vessel *Nanok*—a small fishing trawler converted to Arctic service—on the Greenland Patrol during World War II. The existence of this diary is remarkable because the Coast Guard forbade the keeping of such memorials; Thaddeus Nowakowski (Novak) kept his account in secret and in violation of standing orders. Moreover in December, when Novak's chief (George Talledo) learned of the diary, which could have led to an immediate court-martial and destruction of the memoir, the chief spared the young seaman, instructing him to get rid of it as soon as possible. Novak disregarded those orders, and the journal survived the war as well as another six decades. It now offers us a glimpse of a remote, barren, and frozen land that was important in 1942 for the production of cryolite (used in the production of aluminum) and as a refueling stop for planes flying between North America and England.

Novak's diary rarely mentions larger geopolitical issues involving strategy, tactics, or the course of World War II. Instead, it focuses on the day-to-day life of an average sailor. It describes the inner feelings, the loneliness, and homesickness of men at war, as well as the personal conflicts, sexual humor, foul language, and obsession with gambling that preoccupied their existence. The diary also provides insight into the wartime encounters between sailors and native Greenlanders, enlisted seamen and their officers, and between men from different branches of the American armed forces. Perhaps most important, this diary chronicles a young man's inner struggle to make sense of his surroundings and the growing conflict that seems so far removed from his existence. Ultimately, Novak wants peace, a promotion, and to go home to his bride; the latter remained an undercurrent driving him to survive.

Ted Novak survived both the arduous duty in the Arctic and the war. He received a medical discharge because of a back injury and missed the 1943 cruise of the *Nanok*; the vessel was decommissioned in July 1944. Novak later returned to Michigan, took a job with the state, and built a life with his bride, Lucille. Three years before his death in 1997, Novak sent his diary to the U.S. Coast Guard Historian's Office, where P. J. Capelotti came across it. A senior enlisted member of the Coast Guard stationed at the Historian's Office, Capelotti is well suited to edit this diary. He has written about the Greenland patrol, led a 1993 archaeological expedition to Svalbard, and has experienced firsthand the pounding Arctic seas that Novak encountered.

At its basic level this book is but the diary of a Coast Guard seaman on an isolated station, a backwater of a war that ranged over much of the rest of the world. Yet this is a story of introspective growth and maturation as well as an epic account of survival against the battling elements of nature. This is a story of friends and their trials and tribulations—their loneliness and the ways they battled depression and boredom. Moreover, there are very few autobiographical accounts of the early crisis era of the Greenland Patrol; this is the only account from the perspective of an enlisted seaman. And while several naval historians have focused on World War II at sea, there are few who focus on the role of the Coast Guard. As such, this manuscript offers us another important perspective on the contributions of the "greatest generation."

James C. Bradford and Gene A. Smith, Series Editors

Editor's Note

When war brings a young man to a cold and remote place, and his youthful longings lead him to record his experiences in a forbidden diary, what might that diary, if it ever surfaced after the war, reveal?

When great opposing forces train their weaponry, their local tactics and global strategy, on an Arctic shoreline thousands of miles long and populated by unconnected hamlets sheltering at best perhaps a few thousand people, what events transpire? When the young seamen and old chiefs of a small naval force come into contact with the natives of an alien Arctic landscape, what memories do they take with them?

Such questions are considered almost daily in the small ground floor office at United States Coast Guard Headquarters at Buzzard Point in Washington, D.C., where the office of the United States Coast Guard historian is located. Throughout its polyglot history, an almost bewildering variety of Coast Guard roles and missions have taken its petty officers and chiefs, its officers and seamen, through all of those "locked drawers and hideaways" that Melville wrote awaited them across the seas of the world. Only occasionally have glimpses of what these men saw and felt during these times away from their homeland emerged, and even less frequently do such accounts find their way to Buzzard Point.

Thaddeus D. Nowakowski, "'ski," diligently kept a diary during his six crucial months as a seaman on board the *Nanok*, a small fishing trawler converted to wartime Arctic cutter on the Greenland Patrol. That such a diary surfaced half a century after the conclusion of the war is little short of remarkable. No other such extended diary, kept by an enlisted man, has survived this Arctic war, and with good reason. Nowakowski kept his diary in almost unforgivable ignorance of standing orders forbidding such memorials. In fact, six months of loyalty to a seaman's memories was almost wiped out in a trice when his chief discovered the diary's existence in December of 1942. (Such was the least of his worries, however, since the

Greenland and the locations of some of the prominent points
mentioned in Novak's diary.

very existence of the diary could have led directly to Nowakowski's court-martial.)

But the chief—as chiefs are wont to do—only flew into a temporary rage, then turned his back and spared both the seaman and his transgressional diary of a Coast Guard wartime patrol in Greenland. So the diary exists, and beyond the expected undercurrents of fisticuffs, foul language, sexual humor, mordant military humor, obsession with nicknames, gambling, and almost universal homesickness and crude loneliness of men at war and men without women, the diary goes much deeper.

It offers a striking account of the wartime encounters between native Greenlanders and enlisted sailors, between various branches of American services in the far north, and between enlisted men and their chiefs and officers. The latter clashes are rarely recorded, and when they are the incidents are invariably related from the viewpoint of the officer. Not here. When he sizes up his officious new executive officer, Novak is hardly a gentleman. He simply thinks: "Where did this asshole come from?"

There is herein little mention of geopolitical strategy, great military maneuvers, or pivotal naval engagements; the diary instead is a young man's attempt to make sense of his immediate surroundings. This is a sailor caught amid storms he can barely comprehend, wishing, at base, for peace, for an end to all injustice within the hearts of his fellows and, at the end of his cold Greenlandic rainbow, for the golden promotion to petty officer and the loving and welcoming arms of his bride.

Evincing every bit of the fable of the adaptability of the American enlisted man, Nowakowski learns more from his first brief encounter with a Greenlander than all the Viking, Danish, British, and American explorers and officers had learned in a thousand years of exploration, exploitation, and colonization: "No longer must I wonder what I may teach these uneducated natives, but what they will teach me."

That he could shed his previously unquestioned cultural superiority so rapidly and strikingly is a testament, if in miniature, to the open-mindedness of the enlisted soldiers and sailors that the United States sent to every corner of the globe during World War II. Such open-mindedness is extended to revealing glimpses of a solitary seaman in Greenland, a newly married man suddenly and harshly separated from his bride, a stranger in a strange land if ever there was one. At one point Nowakowski yearns to communicate with a native Greenlander if for no other reason than to attain some rationale in his otherwise completely alien surroundings. He ponders, thinking: "I would like to tell them how very lonely their land and environment makes me feel. I would like to ask them how they manage to tolerate loneliness if indeed they do."

To add to this burden, fate conspired to place Nowakowski and the *Nanok* side by side for six months in Greenland with the *Natsek*, the only one of the ten Arctic trawlers lost during the course of the Greenland Patrol. The *Natsek* drifts briefly into and out of Nowakowski's diary, as if reminding him subconsciously that they share a fateful rendezvous. Nowakowski and Captain Magnus Magnusson, more than sixty years ago, shared the bridge of the *Nanok* during that long December night and day in the Strait of Belle Isle when the *Natsek*'s lights vanished in the swirling snow, never to be seen again. In fact, Nowakowski's account of those horrendous seventeen hours on December 17, 1942, provides the only glimpse extant of what might have transpired on the bridge of the *Natsek* before that vessel went down. To this day no trace of the vessel or its crew has ever been found.

*   *   *

Although the Greenland Patrol was formally organized on October 25, 1941, the U.S. Coast Guard had long experience in both Greenland and Arctic waters prior to formal American entry into the Second World War later that year. This experience included a more than a half century of Bering Sea patrols in Alaskan waters, a quarter century of International Ice Patrols following the sinking of the *Titanic* in 1912, and episodic forays north such as Edward H. "Iceberg" Smith's scientific expedition to the Davis Strait with the cutter *Marion* in 1928.

This body of experience had created a cadre of Coast Guard officers who were expert navigators in Arctic conditions. Such experience was called upon almost two years before the formal entry of the United States into the Second World War.

Germany invaded both Denmark and Norway on April 9, 1940. The Danes capitulated soon after; the Norwegians held out until June. The Danish North Atlantic colony of Greenland thereafter loomed as a potential advance base from which Hitler could stage an invasion of North America.

With lines of communication severed between Copenhagen and Danish colonial offices in southwest Greenland, and Oslo and Norwegian weather stations in northeast Greenland, the Danish governor in Greenland, Eske Brun, recast the island as independent of occupied Denmark. In May, Brun asked the United States for protection, and such an agreement was formalized the following April. The U.S. Coast Guard would provide protection, and in return the U.S. would receive the mineral cryolite from Greenland.

The cryolite was mined from deposits located at Ivigtut on the island's southwest coast. This quartz-like mineral, used in the electrolytic production of aluminum, was essential for construction of aircraft. The mine's production quantity dwarfed the total production of the only two other known mines in the world, one in Colorado and the other in the Ural Mountains of the Soviet Union. Greenland cryolite had been a cornerstone of the U.S. aircraft industry since the 1920s and accounted for practically all of Greenland's exports. It would become an essential element in the production of more than a quarter million combat aircraft in the United States and Canada during the war.

The Ivigtut mines are less than a mile up the Arsuk Fjord from the sea and vulnerable to enemy attack. Vessels transporting cryolite from Greenland to the U.S. were also in grave danger, particularly when southbound through the narrow Strait of Belle Isle. In May, 1940, an American consul—the first in Greenland—was transported to Ivigtut by the U.S. Coast Guard cutter *Comanche*, then delivered farther up the west coast to Godthaab, where a rudimentary American consulate was established. To safeguard Greenland's (and America's) neutrality, ex–Coast Guard sailors were sent to Ivigtut in August, armed to defend the mines.

Throughout 1940 and 1941, a number of Coast Guard cutters equipped with aircraft began to cruise both the east and west coasts of Greenland, in search of sites for naval, air, and weather stations, and to create new charts to replace the former Danish charts now in occupied Copenhagen. The U.S. Coast Guard cutter *Northland*, under the command of "Iceberg" Smith, cruised from New York to Greenland in the late summer of 1940, charting both eastern and western coastlines.

In northeast Greenland, *Northland* met with the free Norwegian navy inspection vessel *Fridtjof Nansen*, under the command of Norwegian Ernst Ullring, itself in the process of destroying Norwegian radio stations and removing Norwegians suspected of collaboration. At Ivigtut in October, Smith drew up a defensive scheme for the Arsuk Fjord, emplacing a 3" gun left there earlier by the cutter *Campbell*.

These many and various activities—charting; defense of undefended Greenland; protection of the cryolite mine at Ivigtut; denial of the Greenland fjords to German submarines, weather stations, and patrol aircraft; blocking European ambitions in the Western Hemisphere—was one of the most closely guarded secrets of the war. By the end of 1941, it was designat-

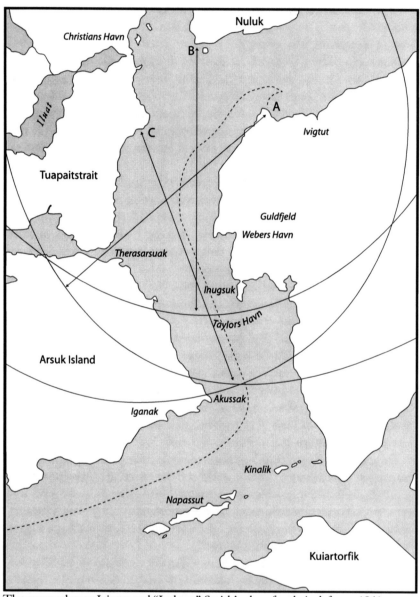

The approaches to Ivigtut and "Iceberg" Smith's plans for their defense, 1941.

ed as Task Force 24.8 and attached to the commander in chief of Atlantic naval forces. Most called it the Greenland Patrol.

*   *   *

In addition to its cryolite, Greenland was strategically desirable in several other ways. It provided a refueling stepping stone for short-range, England-bound U.S. military aircraft and served as weather observation outpost for North Atlantic convoys.

In early 1941, the United States passed the Lend-Lease Act and, defying German sea blockades, began supplying the British with large amounts of munitions and other war materials. These shipments transited Greenland waters. At the same time, a South Greenland Survey Expedition on board the U.S. Coast Guard cutter *Cayuga* searched for appropriate locations to site airfields, seaplane bases, aids to navigation, and radio and weather stations. In April, the United States formalized its agreement with the Danish ambassador that placed Greenland under the protective custody of the United States.

The U.S. Army used the data gathered by the South Greenland Survey Expedition to propose thirteen sites as potential bases, code-named "BLU-IE." The most promising of them, Bluie West One, near the village of Narsarssuak in southwest Greenland, was located in the same area identified as similarly promising nearly a thousand years earlier by one Eirik Raude, the Norse explorer Eirik the Red.

Throughout the summer of 1941, army freighters escorted by U.S. Coast Guard vessels carried enough soldiers and supplies to Narsarssuak to construct eighty-five buildings, three miles of roads, and, eventually, one of the most important air bases of the Second World War.

On June 14, 1941, President Franklin Roosevelt ordered the American-held assets of Germany and Italy and the countries occupied by them to be frozen. Less than a month later, U.S. troops were moved into Iceland to shield it and Greenland from possible German invasion and to safeguard the seaways between Iceland, Greenland, and the United States. The United States then closed all German and Italian consulates in the United States.

On September 4, a U-boat launched its torpedoes against a U.S. Navy destroyer, the *Greer*, as it passed Greenland bound for Iceland with mail for the new American base there. Less than a week later, Roosevelt issued his "shoot-on-sight" order, declaring that German or Italian war vessels that entered waters deemed necessary for the defense of the Americas did so at their own peril.

One day later, *Northland* seized a sealer flying the Norwegian flag, the *Buskø*, which was carrying a German radio station to northeast Greenland for the Nazis. The Coast Guardsmen from the *Northland* destroyed the radio and captured the *Buskø*, the first American naval capture of the war.

On December 11, 1941, four days after the Japanese attack on Pearl Harbor, Germany and Italy declared war on the United States, and the U.S. Congress quickly responded in kind. The Greenland Patrol under the command of "Iceberg" Smith was now faced with the task of insuring the safe transport of shipping to and from Greenland, traffic that had suddenly increased by a factor of three.

Smith was suddenly desperate for escort vessels to convoy the increase in Greenland-bound shipping and to supply the outposts and weather stations of the Greenland coast. Most U.S. weather observation outposts in Greenland were now manned by small numbers of U.S. Army meteorologists, and mail to these outposts could only be delivered by ship during the brief Greenland summer. Otherwise, only if they were fortunate and weather conditions not too fierce or dangerous, could aircraft parachute in additional mail or supplies. The army meteorologists were a special breed, able to tolerate isolation and privation, with their radio transmitters and receivers as their only lifelines. These outposts were responsible not only for providing weather observation data, but also to assure that no enemy presence would function in their vicinity for similar purposes.

So when Commander Smith located ten 120-foot fishing trawlers in Boston, he immediately recognized their strategic potential and cabled Vice Admiral Russell R. Waesche, commandant of the Coast Guard. Waesche commandeered the trawlers for the Greenland Patrol and manned the vessels with handpicked crews.

Both Waesche and Smith knew this to be but a temporary expedient, but more appropriate vessels would not be on-line for more than a year. Until then, this small fleet of ten vessels had to fill the yawning breach in American naval strategy that stretched from Boston to Narsarssuak and supply remote outposts flung along the length of a hostile and forbidding shore.

The ten vessels converted into expedient Arctic cutters were all in the 120-foot, 225-ton class. They were assigned Greenlandic names: *Aivik*, *Aklak*, *Alatok*, *Amarok*, *Arluk*, *Arvek*, *Atak*, *Natsek*, *Nanok*, and *Nogak*. These vessels, as Thaddeus Novak writes, looked not unlike

> huge wooden shoes, and were needed because they were capable of snaking-through narrow Greenland fjords, dense fields of icebergs and cake ice. Their maneuverability could not be equaled by larger,

freighter-sized vessels. For the most part, large freighters were to bring supplies from the U.S. to Greenland, but the wooden shoe trawler fleet would do most of the distribution to the many small installations. Despite being relatively petite in size the trawlers were capable of ferrying some 90 tons of hold cargo and many more tons on deck. It seemed most probable that enemy submarines would so treasure their secret location that they would even refrain from surfacing to deck-gun a tiny trawler into oblivion, which of course they could. The wooden shoe trawler's true enemies were the elements. In all but one instance, they would prove to be more than worthy adversaries.

* * *

My feeling of kinship with the young Nowakowski (now Novak) stems in part from my own service as a senior enlisted member of the U.S. Coast Guard Reserve, head of a minute staff of enlisted reservists who perform their national service at the Coast Guard Historian's Office. This affinity was also prompted both by my having written, in 1992, an anniversary article on artist and *Natsek* skipper Lieutenant Thomas Sargent La Farge and the sinking of the *Natsek* and by a compelling desire that took me to St. Matthew's Cathedral in downtown Washington to see La Farge's mosaic there. An archaeological expedition to Svalbard in 1993 also gave me some experience in the Arctic (not to mention an incapacitating bout of seasickness as our small icebreaker was pounded by rough seas for twelve miserable hours) as well as with the prevailing style of command on board Norwegian merchant vessels, the same tradition which nurtured Magnus Magnusson.

Thus when this wartime diary made its way to the Coast Guard Historian's Office in early 1994, I felt drawn to undertaking the task of editing Novak's diary and bringing it to publication. This has been accomplished with much encouragement and support from Robert Browning, Coast Guard historian, Scott Price, assistant Coast Guard historian, William N. Still Jr., former director of the Program in Maritime History and Underwater Archaeology at East Carolina University, and Susan Barr of the Norwegian Cultural Ministry. Wynne Caldwell once again came to my aid during the exacting editing process. Ted Novak himself, before his death in 1997, was gracious in responding to and answering numerous requests.

Obvious typographical errors have been silently corrected, but most stylistic variations and grammatical errors have been allowed to stand. Bracketed material indicates instances of unclear handwriting or presumed omissions.

The diary that follows is one of the few firsthand accounts to survive from the early crisis period of the Greenland Patrol and the only such firsthand account from the perspective of an involved young enlisted seaman. Therefore, it occupies a unique place in the history of the U.S. Coast Guard, of U.S. naval operations in the Arctic, and of the Second World War.

Abbreviations

AG   Auxiliary (U.S. Navy)

AM   Minesweeper (U.S. Navy)

IX   Coast and Geodetic Schooner

SC   Subchaser (manned by U.S. Coast Guard)

VP6   Patrol Bomber Squadron (PBY Catalina-equipped, U.S. Coast Guard)

WAG   Icebreaker, Heavily Armed

WAGL   Icebreaker, Aids to Navigation

WPG   Gunboat, Icebreaker, Convoy Escort

WSC   Subchaser, Convoy Escort

WYP   Arctic Trawler, Patrol Type

WYT   Harbor Tug, Icebreaker

Life and Death
on the Greenland Patrol, 1942

Author's Preface

This true story is an expansion of my wartime diary. While in boot camp's long weeks of quarantine, for need of something to do, I purchased the diary from the base's small stores outlet. It was impossible to keep the diary chronologically perfect aboard ship for several reasons. At times the weather was so bad the ship's rolling and pitching made it impossible to guide pen on paper. Thank goodness my bunk had a sideboard to prevent me from rolling out onto the deck while asleep. The other side of my bunk was the ship's outer skin.

Other times when the workday was long and the chores extra heavy, I was happy just to flop into my bunk and fall asleep before reaching the pillow. Yet other times my mental attitude was in such a state of depression I considered giving my diary to the sea. During times of comparable activity, there was little to record. Therefore as many as five days might pass before I bothered to catch up on "dear diary."

The reader should know that wartime ship movements, arrivals, departures and schedules are rarely mentioned in any of the crew's presence. Therefore we crew members only caught snatches of such detail, and only when the skipper conversed with our executive officer or some visiting dignitary. What made keeping a diary even more difficult was that ordinary crew members never got to see maps or charts, and we had no radio to listen to. The radio shack was taboo for all but radio operators.

Whenever names of Greenlandic places were mentioned, they were always tongue twisters. In my diary I spelled them as they sounded phonetically to me. Example, "ah-ma-sa-leek" later proved to be Angmagssalik. In putting this story together, much backtracking had to be done. There were old, obsolete maps to be found and examined, Greenlandic village names to associate with military base code names, etc. There were copies of ships logs to obtain and many facts to verify. The pieces were gathered and roughly assembled in 1944, but then my enthusiasm waned. Now there is need for haste if any of the remaining crew is ever to see the completed story. I know of only four of them still alive. [1]

Conversations between crew members are not verbatim, but are as accurate as memory and diary-keeping can make them. Attitudes of characters are my interpretations as I witnessed them and as factual as I perceived them to be.

*   *   *

I am from a family of eight boys and four girls. There was a thirty-one-year age difference between Benjamin the oldest and Edward the youngest. I was the second youngest. Ben was twenty-five years old when I was born. He was a volunteer infantry man in World War One. Seeing him, I often wondered if one day I would become a blood-and-guts, mud-spattered, Yankee doodle, dog-faced yard bird in the same trenches of France's Argonne Forest where the Germans mustard-gassed Ben while trying, fortunately without success, to shoot holes in him.

When war came to my generation, three options were open to me. I turned 21 on June 3, 1940, and in September of that year the U.S. created its first peacetime conscription, called "the Selective Training and Service Act." Men aged twenty-one to thirty-six were to be first on call and qualified for military training. My first option was to wait until drafted into whatever branch of military service the system selected for me. (After draft was instituted, I was assigned a draft number and thereafter awaited President Roosevelt's summons [one that always began—humorously, so I thought then—with the word: "Greetings."]) Secondly, I could voluntarily enlist in any branch of the service that I qualified for (but then I would have to remain in that service for the entire preestablished enlistment period for that branch of service—perhaps even well beyond the war's end). Three, I could run off to some nearby country where the U.S. could not get its hands on me. Truth is, the third option never crossed my mind.

Ultimately, I decided on the second course of action and joined the U.S. Coast Guard, known as the Mickey Mouse Navy by some. During several summer vacations from high school I worked as kitchen help aboard a Great Lakes ore carrier, *Norman J. Kopmeir*. There I saw the Coast Guard in action several times and thought they never left the Great Lakes or the lighthouses they maintained. In other words, a safe place to spend the war if it were to come—beyond the range of enemy bullets. I had been laid off from my job as a laborer on the automotive assembly of Chrysler Motors Dodge main plant in Detroit. On Monday, August 25, 1941, I stopped off at the factory and bid farewell to my friends there. I returned my employee identification badge and later that day was sworn into the U.S. Coast Guard.

Besides myself, World War II captured my brother Joseph, a south seas U.S. Navy Seabee, Raymond, an Army yard bird, and Edward (Duke), a PT boat torpedo man. Soon after we all enlisted, we lost track of one another for the duration of the war. Although we all survived, we all became casualties.

* * *

After a three-day train journey, I arrived on Thursday, August 28, 1941, at the U.S. Coast Guard Training Station in Algiers, Louisiana, just across the river from New Orleans. After six weeks training, I was transferred to the Coast Guard Lifeboat Station at Jackson Park on the South Side of Chicago, Illinois. From there, to the Lifeboat Station at Frankfort, Michigan, then back to the old Chicago Lifeboat Station near the navy pier. So far, all as I had expected. Then I was transferred to Curtis Bay, Maryland, where I boarded the *Sea Cloud* as a seaman 1/c. At the time, the *Sea Cloud* was the largest sailing vessel in the world, and we busied ourselves rerigging this beautiful, white, gold-trimmed vessel from a peacetime luxury vessel into a wartime Coast Guard cutter.

Marjorie Merriweather Post, the Battle Creek, Michigan, cereal heiress had the *Sea Cloud* built at the Krupp Works in Kiel, Germany, in 1931 at a cost of $900,000 American, a fantastic sum at the time. The *Sea Cloud* was 316 feet long, had a beam of 49 feet 2 inches, and a depth of 24 feet 10 inches. She weighed 2,300 tons and flew 86,000 square feet of sail when underway. Her bowsprit was a magnificent 21-foot-long gilded maiden. The *Cloud* boasted nine refrigeration units and a walk-in electrically heated clothes drying room. After most masts and all canvas had been taken off ship and stowed, her auxiliary plant became her main power. There were two giant electric motors to turn twin propellers at the tail ends of 90-foot-long stainless steel drive shafts. Diesel engines turned several electric generators that powered the motors. In peacetime there was a crew of seventy-two to serve a maximum of thirty guests in seven large air-conditioned bedrooms below main deck. A wide circular stairway led down to them, the stairway banister a heavy, stiff, three-stranded silk, red, white, and blue rope handrail supported by gold brackets.

Ms. Post's bathroom was very large with walls of large, square, beautiful slabs of pink and black marble. The toilet seat was inlaid with white, yellow, rose, and green gold oriental flowers, and the toilet paper was printed with colorful, scenic, oriental patterns. The main deck salon had very thick glass walls with protective steel outer walls. They slid open silently at the touch of a button. Every oil painting in the salon was secured onto the face of a wall-cabinet door which, when opened, exposed wall-wells filled with fine, bottled wines.

The vessel was so designed for guest privacy that none of the crew would have any casual occasion to cross through the guest area. From the forward crew quarters, crew members were required to step down below main deck, follow a passageway aft, then climb back up to main deck beyond the guest area. Ms. Post leased the *Sea Cloud* to the U.S. government for $1.00 per year and supposedly for the duration of war hostilities, and it was probably the best financial bargain Ms. Post had ever received. During the wartime, fuel was rationed and not available for pleasure craft. The *Cloud*, therefore, would have had to remain idle at a maintenance cost of some $200,000 per year. When no longer required, the ship was to be returned to its owner, completely refurbished, free of charge. If the vessel were destroyed by the enemy, its value would be replaced. This type of lease agreement was extended to anyone willing to allow the government to borrow vessels suitable for governmental use. [2]

The *Sea Cloud* became very useful for weather observation patrol in the far North Atlantic. From her and vessels like her came the weather data General Dwight D. Eisenhower would use to calculate the date for the invasion of Normandy.

Thaddeus Novak wrote this preface and the additional notes for his August 18 and October 23 entries before he sent the diary to the U.S. Coast Guard Historian's Office in 1994.

June

Captain Magnusson (if not an enemy in disguise), is the most encouraging piece of equipment on board. The man is a tough, powerful, stubborn-looking Norwegian (so we hear). He is said to have been born and raised in Iceland. We would later learn he owns a fleet of fishing trawlers similar to the Nanok. *He has some thirty-seven years of North Atlantic sailing experience built into his medium-sized frame. . . . Brine sea spray has rimmed his eyes with white circles around blue, tempered-steel pupils. He has a square, cast-iron jaw that juts forward of his chest. The sea must be made of his salt.*

June 8, Monday; U.S.C.G. Cutter *Sea Cloud.*

Damn!

I have been transferred from the beautiful U.S.C.G. cutter *Sea Cloud* to the Coast Guard Receiving Station in Boston, Massachusetts. The station is the ancient Brunswick Hotel on Boylston Street, around the corner from the elegant Copley Plaza Hotel.

The Brunswick is so old, toilet flush water tanks are mounted high on the wall behind the sit-on poop buckets. To flush, one must pull on a chain that hangs from the bottom of the tank and *voila!* you get a superb flush with suction enough to make a giant hickey out of your entire backside. The flush also thrashes your behind with some of your own dirt. You soon learn to get up off of the seat before pulling the chain, and quickly jump away after the chain is pulled.

I will not miss the North Atlantic weather patrol duty of the *Sea Cloud*, but I already miss the camaraderie of the buddies I had acquired. Weather patrol duty consists of wallowing in the ocean somewhere far out in the North Atlantic, thirty to forty-five days at a time. Every hour or so, a helium filled balloon is sent aloft with a box of weather-sensitive devices attached. The device radios back high altitude weather data that is invaluable to American warship and plane movements on both sides of the Atlantic. All large scale military actions require accurate weather information.

June 9, Tuesday; Brunswick Hotel.

Boston overflows with servicemen, mostly sailors. Bostonians are kind to us. The ladies seem to adore us. Someone said, "whenever a Boston damsel's eyes light up, they glow red, white and navy blue."

Boston, where so very much of America's march toward independence began. I am in awe of the many historic landmarks that still stand, and I feel I must touch everyone I am allowed to. I pause at various places and ponder the events that had taken place there. From my youth I recall Faneuil Hall, "the cradle of liberty," the Market Place and Public Hall of early Boston. It is a mere eighty by one hundred feet and just three stories high, once the home of "the Ancient and Honorable Artillery Company of Massachusetts." I spent at least ten minutes standing at the March 5, 1770, site of what is known as the Boston Massacre, where a squad of British soldiers [was] struck by debris thrown at them by a crowd of demonstrators. The soldiers fired into the crowd killing five men. Without having been there when the incident had taken place, I had to conclude the punishment hardly fit the crime. The soldiers were tried for murder and were defended by John Adams and Josiah Quincy. Two were convicted of manslaughter and were branded on the thumb. The others, including their officers, were acquitted.

It is a moving experience for me to stand within the tiny cemetery called the Granary Burial Ground surrounded by towering buildings in the middle of downtown Boston. Progress does not disturb the sleep of those who lie here. Many of those I met in history books lie beneath my feet, including Paul Revere, Ben Franklin's parents and three signers of the Declaration of Independence. There are the great and remembered and the not so great and mostly forgotten lying side by side.

I love beautiful Boston Commons, a greenery of flowers, trees, shrubs and grass in the heart of the city. In the year 1634 it was purchased from one Reverend Blaxton. It was to be the militia's training area and a hanging place for pirates who were hung from the branches of an elm tree by the frog pond. Too, this was where the red coats began their journey to join the Battle of Lexington. The first public school originated here in Boston, and its first schoolmaster was Philemon Pormort.

Boston, the capital of Massachusetts, is the seat of Suffolk County. It encompasses over forty-seven square miles and houses more than 801,000 people. It has a fine thirty-five-foot-deep channel and some forty miles of ship berthing space. It is one of the largest dry-docks in America. Here occurred the 1773 Boston Tea Party, the 1775 ride of Paul Revere, and the 1775 Battle of Bunker Hill.

I minutely examine the Old North Church and study every outside architectural feature. It is difficult to imagine this neat little church has been here since 1723. It still has the tower where warning lanterns were hung for Paul Revere to see. Bostonians, accustomed to the church's presence, hurry by its portal without a second glance. It is the transient soldier or sailor that is taken by this historical shrine of liberty.

I am familiar with Paul Revere, but find myself wondering about the identity of whoever hung the lanterns for him to see. Perhaps he or she is one of the many who lie uncelebrated in the Granary. Possibly history records the name or names somewhere.

Several soldiers and sailors stop and join me to study the church that is, on occasion, illuminated by candles. We stand on historic ground. It is another time, another time of war, World War II, the great war of my time. I wonder if any of these men will be a hero of the future. Is there an Adams, Washington, Webster, or Jefferson amongst them? Do they wonder if I am one of such?

Will any of us ever live to pass this way again? I hope so, but I for one am not of heroic tendency.

June 10, Wednesday; Brunswick Hotel.

They say loafing can be great here. That is, if you can avoid being selected for a work detail headed for the shipyard to scrape black oil, scum, and slime from stinking ship bilges. They cornered me today, but I vow, never again! I had to throw away the clothes I wore.

Boston has declared today to be Hero Day, honoring thirteen heroes. Perhaps they were bilge cleaners.

June 11, Thursday; Brunswick Hotel.

The *Sea Cloud* shoved off today. Me and two new-found buddies went and got smashed at the Cocoanut Grove Lounge. It's not easy to enjoy drinking drinks you really cannot afford. Somehow we managed.

June 12, Friday; Brunswick Hotel.

I am reading everything I can get my hands on. Anything to distract me from thinking about Lucille, my wife of just four months.

June 13, Saturday; Brunswick Hotel.

Got eye-tired of reading so I took a leisurely stroll through Boston Commons. For the first time in my life I was approached by a very pretty young lady of perhaps seventeen years of age, who asked me outright to have sexual intercourse with her. I must be somewhat abnormal for I blurted a "no!" loud enough for other strollers to hear. I was strangely afraid yet sexually aroused. My sailor trousers do not hide an arousal but emphasize it instead. I hurried back to the Brunswick and tried desperately to focus my thoughts on Lucille. No luck.

June 14, Sunday; Brunswick Hotel.

Just moped around all day, haunted by yesterday. I miss Lucille more than ever.

June 15, Monday; Brunswick Hotel.

Good Lord! I have only been here seven days and have been given the assignment of marching a company of men from the Brunswick to Boston Commons, down Boylston Street. I know little about marching or drilling a company of one hundred. After all, I am only a seaman l/c. The only experience I have had is when we horsed around in Algiers. We used to take turns drilling a squad or two just to pass time.

The chief boatswain in charge marched silently alongside of me. I am sure he has done this as a joke. If I were to fail, surely he would take over . . . so I hoped.

I wanted to deliberately fail so he would excuse me and take over the task. On the other hand, I knew if I fouled up I would be too embarrassed to face any of this group ever again.

The chief wore a coon-dog-eatin'-crap grin on his face as we marched along. He, however, did not assist me in any way. After my initial fear and nervousness subsided, I began to enjoy the experience and surprised myself by doing very well.

Crowds of people stopped along curbside and some even cheered as we marched smartly by. I had the men sing in cadence as we marched along:

Sound off . . . sound off,
in cadence count,
won, oop, dree, fohp,
won, oop, dree, fohp.

Left, left, left right left,
I had a good home
But I left.

The Waacs and Waves
Will win the war
So what in the hell
Are we fighting for?

Won, oop, dree, fohp.

June 16, Tuesday; Brunswick Hotel.

Routine, eat, sleep, and cuss the fact that a war is going on.

June 17, Wednesday; Brunswick Hotel.

What do you know!?

My old tub *Sea Cloud* picked up eight survivors from a Portuguese schooner called the *Marie da Gloria* that was sunk by a Nazi submarine on June 6. She was merely fishing off the Grand Banks and was unarmed. The poor devils on board a small lifeboat were adrift for ten days and were half starved. One man died while another went berserk, jumped into the sea and was gone. Lifeboats with thirty-four others simply disappeared, adrift, only God knows where. It looks like the Nazis do feel that small vessels are worth torpedoing after all.

June 18, Thursday; Brunswick Hotel.

During early a.m. a dozen of us swabbies were taken to the shipyards to scrape stinking bilges once again. After three red-hot showers I picked up a ticket at the Buddies Club to see Fred Waring and his Pennsylvanians. Later a few beers at Steubin's Bar.

June 19, Friday; Brunswick Hotel.

Getting bored with keeping dear diary. Nothing interesting or exciting to write about. . . . At least not yet.

Slept in and missed a.m. muster. Got myself chewed out by the angry chief boatswain that made me march to Boston Commons.

June 20, Saturday; Brunswick Hotel.

Got several letters from Lucille. Sat around, listened to radio, washed clothes, and went to see a dumb, boring movie.

June 21, Sunday; Brunswick Hotel.

Days drag for me, too long, induces homesickness, especially since I have a young, beautiful bride awaiting me.

The Coast Guard upsets me in that long-term, close friendships are not encouraged. They are often broken up when known by a superior to exist.

When transferred from boot camp to the old Chicago Lifeboat Station, I first learned of the practice. Our skipper Olander learned that I buddied with Clare (Clarence) Boike, my boot camp buddy, and he immediately split us up. I was retained at the old Chicago Station while Boike was sent to the Wilmette, Ill., station. Captain Olander had a sensible but unpopular theory. Whenever two men became close buddies and one or the other gets himself maimed or killed, it often causes the other to suffer the loss too much mentally and reduces his effectiveness as a combatant. I have no quarrel with the theory, but still hated to lose Boike's camaraderie.

Now I hear a familiar voice. I turn around in the chow line and come face to face with Boike!

We both are overwhelmed and hug hell out of each other while others in the line make uncomplimentary female-sounding comments about lovers. It has been a hell of a long time since Clare and I have seen each other. We did not care a pot of piss what anyone thought. Our meeting proved to be a super morale booster for both of us. After getting free tickets at the Buddies Club, Boike and I go to see Fred Waring and his Pennsylvanians. A great orchestra and show. Sitting in the front row reserved for servicemen, we are quite content.

June 22, Monday; on board U.S.C.G.C. *Nanok* at Constitution Wharf.

After 22 long days comes a transfer at last! From bad . . . to possibly worse! From the Brunswick to the U.S.C.G. cutter *Nanok*, an ex–fishing trawler that reeks of rotted fish!

All of those on board are given an allowance to temporarily purchase meals from restaurants. The *Nanok* has no cook as yet, and no food provisions. Who could eat on board with the foul stench anyway? Our allowance is $1.20 per day.

Buddy Boike and I are separated once again. He has been transferred on board the U.S.C.G. trawler *Atak* that is also tied up here, just forward of the *Nanok*. Old Ironsides, the forty-four-gun frigate that figured so prominently and heroically in America's early history berthed here during times of warfare long ago.

One of only three surviving images of the U.S. Coast Guard cutter *Nanok* (WYP-169), shown here in Greenland in 1943. (Photo courtesy of Russell C. Clark, private collection.)

The tiny wooden shoe *Nanok* is a product of the Snow Shipyard in Rockland, Maine, and launched but a year ago. Though she is very young, she looks very old. She wears no makeup. She is but 120 feet long overall, has a modest 24 1/2-foot beam and a maximum draft of 12 feet. Her U.S.C.G. identity and call letters are WYP-169. When fully manned, she is to carry a complement of twenty-one men and two commissioned officers.

The east end of Constitution Wharf protrudes into Boston's inner harbor. Its west end terminates at Atlantic Avenue which runs roughly north and south. From the west comes Hanover Street which ends here at Atlantic Avenue and Constitution Wharf's front door.

I find the historic wharf disappointing. I expected Old Ironsides' berthing place would be a magnificent and elaborate dockage. Instead, the wharf's structure is somewhat in decay. There are numerous barrels indoors. A sharp, mouthwatering pungent odor suggests they are filled with vinegar and some are leaking.

We must walk the partial mile from Atlantic Avenue, up Hanover Street to our favorite fun place, Scollay Square. The square is a notorious knock-em-down and drag-em-out bar and dancehall area that is "off limits" to all servicemen. That's probably why servicemen gather there in droves.

Our skipper is not yet known to us and is not on board the *Nanok*. An old sourdough, fuzz-faced chief boatswain's mate about sixty-two years old is temporarily in charge. He hails from Stapleton, Staten Island, N.Y. He never talks, he always shouts. He was about to be retired when the war came along and he was compelled to continue in service for the war's duration. Chief Talledo is mostly American Indian. [3] He is a squat figure about as wide as he is high. His dark, deeply lined face makes him appear as if he is about to attend a very unpleasant tribal meeting. He is obviously a man of great physical strength, extremely muscular. As old as he may be, I would not choose to test his strength. I am wondering how anyone can manage to stay out of his path for any great period of time on board so small a vessel as the *Nanok*. He is a steamroller and practically steps over those in his path.

I meet and become immediate buddies with Sullivan (Davy) Jones, a seaman 2/c from Yonkers, N.Y. "Sully" is a massive, shy, twenty-two-year-old with a bass drum in lieu of a voice. He wears a perennial blush-red face. Talledo says the blush comes from playing with himself too often. I doubt that. Sully's shoes are more like pontoons. The guy laughs easily from cavernous depths. His "haw, haw, haw" carries half a mile. He is the only one I know that still shaves with a straight razor. My nerves shatter every time he trims the hair on the back of his neck with just two or three fast swipes of the sharp blade. Whenever we try to harmonize in song, he sounds like a bullfrog with a hangover.

June 23, Tuesday; *Nanok.*

I try to locate Boike but he is not around. Jonesy asks me to accompany him to Scollay Square for drinks and laughs so away we go. On Hanover Street near the square we stop at a rundown theater to see Charlie Chaplin in *Gold Rush*, then to an upstairs drink and dancehall on the square. We converse with a few lively girls. Sul's face is afire but I know he enjoys every minute. After a dinner we drink too much and enjoy a laughing jag. We wander into the subway and take a long ride just for the hell of it. We have no particular destination. Somewhere we wander into a cemetery. Jones keeps yelling that it is the day of resurrection and that everyone should "rise and shine." It is probably after midnight and we have dared one another to steal a floral wreath. We both do so. We haul it back to the *Nanok* on the subway whose passengers all seem to have extra large eyes.

On board the *Nanok* we lay it gently atop Pete Petrenko's sleeping body. Everyone else in the forecastle is asleep also. I take a large pan and a wooden spoon and crawl into my sack. Jonesy is already in his. It is fairly dark and silent except for snoring here and there. I suddenly smash the wooden spoon into the pan. Silence is shattered! I quickly hide pan and spoon under my blankets. Everyone in the place sits upright like a bunch of zombies with wide staring eyes. As Petrenko sits up, his head and upper torso rises through the center of the wreath like a finger through a donut hole. His arms are pinned to the sides of his body. Even in the semi-gloom he realized the wreath was a cemetery thing and lets out a blood-congealing scream! The fearful sound raised hair on the nape of my neck and prickled my ears!

Pete is a rawboned giant with basketball sized hands. I realized instantly we could never, ever tell Pete who encased him in the wreath. There are numerous more pleasant ways to die. Pete leaped out of his sack, ran topside with the wreath and threw it overboard along with another frightening roar that I could hear even below deck. I doubt that anyone fell asleep again that night. I swore Sully to secrecy about the wreath, pan, spoon, and the drummer. He kiddingly threatened to tell. I kiddingly promised to bury him if he dared.

June 24, Wednesday; *Nanok.*

Hot diggidy shit!

We got our skipper today! He is Lieutenant (j.g.) Magnus G. Magnusson (Res.). [4] Immediately and automatically he became "Maggie" to everyone.

We guess Maggie to be around sixty years of age. He mentions that he has a wife and several children and hails from Winchester, Mass. Some of the crew say they met him yesterday. Staneczak said Maggie had called to him from the wharf and was wearing civilian clothes at the time. He had asked Stan the whereabouts of the *Nanok* and Stan replied: "This is it."

Looking disdainfully at the wooden shoe, with a foreign accent and curled back lip he muttered a disgusted, "Jeezusskryst!!" He did not come on board or identify himself. He spun around and left.

Today he returned. In just minutes the guy takes over. His arms are loaded with fresh, brand new, tag-filled G.I. clothing, including several skipper hats piled atop his head. We wonder if he has had any Coast Guard training whatsoever. It was common knowledge that any serviceman wearing anything other than his official uniform could get himself locked up in the pokey. How come he arrives twice wearing civvies?

As there was no one to introduce him to the crew, and since he showed no proof of identity, spoke with a foreign accent, and didn't even wear a uniform, I had a fleeting thought that, *good Lord*, he could be the enemy! Since Talledo accepted the man "as is," who was I to think such thoughts?

Maggie (if not an enemy in disguise), is the most encouraging piece of equipment on board. The man is a tough, powerful, stubborn-looking Norwegian (so we hear). He is said to have been born and raised in Iceland. We would later learn he owns a fleet of fishing trawlers similar to the *Nanok*. He has some thirty-seven years of North Atlantic sailing experience built into his medium-sized frame. He is said to be a lifelong personal friend of Rear Admiral (Iceberg) Smith. [5]

Maggie is thin of face. Brine sea spray has rimmed his eyes with white circles around blue, tempered-steel pupils. He has a square, cast-iron jaw that juts forward of his chest. The sea must be made of his salt. He impresses me as being damnably strong of will, demanding, clever and intelligent. I feel I have known him a long time and like him.

We hurry to dress the *Nanok* in wartime costume. At the same time we try accustoming ourselves to our new environment. We also work at trying to acquire new buddies and most everyone is trying to become one. None of us has ever met any of the others previous to our gathering here.

Nanok is pronounced "nahnook" by the Eskimos and means "polar bear." I believe some Coast Guard name-assigner goofed and "*Nanok*" should have been "nahnook." My early impression of the *Nanok* is that she is a puny wooden shoe from a dirty foot. . . . An undernourished tugboat, ugly and without grace. She is cramped, damp, and tired, and the rotted fish odors are built into her thick, wooden skin. Compared to the beautiful and graceful *Sea Cloud* I served on board, the *Nanok* is an outhouse.

We flush out her entrails, scrape out her bilge barnacles, dust her hold and paint her whatever. It should not be overdone because she may demand a coming out party.

Shore liberties are most liberal. There is much more liberty than liberty spending money. For the most part, the deck crew's quarters and galley combined are in the fo'c's'le (forecastle), on the level below the main deck. Directly above crew's quarters and at main deck level is the "head" (toilet, shower and laundry room) and the locker room. The fo'c's'le floor plan is shaped like the head of an arrow, its point being the ship's prow.

The gun deck tops the entire fo'c's'le. On it is mounted port and starboard 20mm antiaircraft guns. Between them and slightly forward of the 20mms is a World War I, 3" cannon. It is probably not worth the scrap iron it is made of. The aged blunderbuss has to be aimed like a bazooka. It may be an accurate weapon under certain conditions, but on our small vessel it would be worthless. The tiny *Nanok* would roll and pitch too much to properly aim it. Fairbanks says the gun is just for show. With its gun covers off it should probably scare the hell out of some Eskimo in a kayak. "Guns," our Third Class Gunner's Mate Wilbur Owens, says the big gun will come in handy only if we are to fight enemy army tanks at sea. He strongly suggests we do not dispose of any slingshots we may have. I feel the gun will prove invaluable if we are ever forced to scuttle the *Nanok*. Its weight would help sink her quickly. "Guns" is an ex-farmer from Harbinger, N.C. He is of medium height and build, has a heavy North Carolina tar heel drawl, an infectious grin, and eyes so pale blue they are almost transparent.

No end of excitement today. We hear Tobruk, city and port of Libya on the Mediterranean Sea, has fallen to the Nazis on June 22. Germany claims 25,000 prisoners. I wonder who counted them.

A long, black, two-masted schooner pulled into our slip with the intention of tying up just ahead of the *Nanok*. Its pilot house apparently lost its communication with its engine room. We see a crew member dash from the pilot house towards the engine room ladder aft (we later learned he was attempting to order "reverse engine"). The vessel fast approached the end of the wharf and the building that joins Constitution Wharf with the adjacent wharf. Too late! The wayward vessel crashed some twenty or more feet into the building! The structure partially collapsed onto the bow of the nameless vessel. Much effort is expended trying to extricate itself, and finally manages to do so.

June 25, Thursday; *Nanok.*

We take on board a hell of a lot of Arctic clothing. We receive full-length heavy woolen stockings, pull-over-the-head stocking caps with tails that become wrap-around-the-neck mufflers. The caps are hood-type that have slits for the eyes, nostrils, and mouth. There are heavy woolen gloves by the dozens. All of these things have been handmade by elderly lady Salvation Army volunteers. I have a sneaking hunch we are going to be more than grateful to these unknown ladies. God bless all of them.

We now know the direction the *Nanok* is to sail. I shiver at the thought. The idea of Arctic duty displeases me. I am of cold blood and very compatible with warm weather. Were it not for the "joke" of Mr. Armstrong, my boot camp company commander, I might have enjoyed some South Pacific tropical paradise.

Just before being shipped out of boot camp, Armstrong mustered company "V" and informed us we were about to leave. "Which of you swab-jockeys want to go to the South Pacific?" About half of the company raised their hands, including me. "Okay," said Armstrong, "move over to this side. The rest of you galley punks want to go to the Atlantic, right?" There was a loud yell, "yeaaaahhh!" "Okay, those of you that want to go South Pacific are going to the North Atlantic. Those of you that want to go to the North Atlantic are going to the South Pacific instead." Our load of protests were laughed at. "I know you guys want to go as close to your homes as possible so that you can continually pester your skipper for short and long leaves of absence. We're gonna make it a bit undesirable for you to do so."

We were all furious, but Armstrong was the law. He had his favorite brownnoses strong-arm many of us individually at night for "voluntary" gift contributions. We were told it was customary for a commander's company to provide such a gift when parting company. . . . Sure!

Even worse, several days before being shipped out, he offered us low-cost photographs of ourselves in uniform so we could mail them to our loved ones back home. In the evening after dark, we were loaded onto a stake truck and were driven to what we were told was Armstrong's photo studio. Instead we were herded into his basement. Since we all had paid in advance, there was no choice but to follow through.

There was a plain, dark-colored bed sheet hung from the overhead joists to serve as a backdrop. A very small camera was mounted on a tripod some distance in front of the background curtain. We were singularly paraded between backdrop and camera. The camera would click and the next guy moved into the vacated position and the camera clicked again, again, again, etc. I knew very little about sophisticated cameras then, but I did know that film had to be inserted once in a while. This was never done. Suspicion grew in me but I was not about to accuse my tough company commander of anything. After all, I did not know how much power this guy had. If I were to accuse him of anything, he might have had the authority to send me to any rotten place on earth.

The evening before we were to ship out, the pictures were "not ready yet," but they would be mailed to us as soon as they were. To my knowledge no one ever received a single photo. (Much later I was to learn that several months after I left boot camp, Armstrong accidentally shot himself to death while cleaning his pistol. He will be missed by a lot of people.)

Reason for cheer!

The *Nanok* welcomes its cook. He is the personable Russell "Rusty," "Cookie" Clark. He is handsome, tall, slender, wears a small moustache, infectious grin, and has a pleasant, enjoyable, New England accent. Clark's dishes don't get "washed," they get "warshed." Clark is not too happy about where the *Nanok* is "pahked."

The trawler *Belmont* flies into Constitution Wharf's slip. I can't believe my eyes!! They apparently lost communication with their engine room the same as the two-master did yesterday. The vessel went slamming into the same hole that the two-master made yesterday. Now the hole is at least thirty feet deep! Maggie too is astounded! His eyes are opened wide as possible in disbelief! He asks Talledo: "Do you know the odds of such an accident happening to two different vessels two days in a row in exactly the same place? "No," Talledo replies, shaking his head negatively. Maggie asks him again and Talledo says, "no," and Maggie asks him the same question several times more until Talledo gives him an odd look and walks away. I ask Lindsay Jordan if he knows of a captain asking a man the same question five or six times in succession. Jordan says, "no." I ask him again and he gives me a grin and a hell of a shove.

Several summers during my high school years I worked on the great lakes ore carrier *Norman J. Kopmeir*. There I learned quite a bit of seamanship. Somewhere over time I'd forgotten much about knots, splices, rules of the road, etc., so I began to read my *Bluejackets' Manual* in earnest. [6] Boot camp helped a lot but not enough for me to earn promotion to coxswain, petty officer 3/c. This rating I was determined to acquire as soon as possible. I'm not sure whether it was because of the increase in pay or to make my wife Lucille and my family proud of me. I intend to speak to Maggie about my desire tomorrow. I want very much to learn what he expects a coxswain (coxs'n) to know and to be, then I'll work my ass off to meet his standards.

June 26, Friday; *Nanok.*

After he enjoyed a satisfying breakfast, I decided it was a good time to approach the skipper about elevating me to the position of coxs'n. He invited me into his cabin to talk in private. He sat on the edge of his bunk, listens intently to my request as his steel eyes look through me. I tell him of my Great Lakes sailing experience, perhaps exaggerating a bit. I also point out the fact that I am leading seaman on board the *Nanok*, and the only seaman l/c. He seemed surprised and confused about my "leading seaman" inference. I mention it because I find no reference to "leading seaman" in *The Bluejackets' Manual*. It was taken for granted that a leading seaman was automatically considered to be next in line for whatever deck force petty officer's position he and his superiors agreed upon. I requested that the skipper consider me to be a striker for a coxs'n rating.

Maggie questioned me at great length, asking me many things about ships. Luckily I had answers for all of the questions put to me. He appeared very impressed. He led me to believe my promotion would not be much more than a formality, that we have no coxs'n on board and that we could make good use of one. I was so elated I wrote and told Lucille that when I come home on leave, she might have to salute her husband.

We worked like slaves today.

The *Nanok* has an upper level superstructure just aft of amidships. The forward part of top level is the pilot house, and rear of the pilot house is the skipper's quarters. He is therefore able to walk back and forth between pilot house and his cabin without going outdoors. In another structure at same level and a short distance behind the skipper's quarters is the radio shack. On the same deck portside, just aft of the pilot house, is a deck-level flat hatch cover. It is the entrance to the executive officer's cubicle cabin. The cabin protrudes downward. Looking down into it, there are no portholes, just a dark void and a semi-visible top surface of a bunk. I cannot imagine how this dungeon is ventilated, and there is no air-conditioning on board the *Nanok*.

Beneath the pilot house and below the main deck are quarters for the entire "black gang" as well as for the chief bos'n, motor machinist mate, radioman, carpenter, and yeoman. The companionway also leads forward to the engine room.

For power, there is a trustworthy diesel engine that rattles the *Nanok*'s bowels. Only a magician such as Chief Motor Machinist Mate Nelson (Mack) McClay and his black gang crew can squeeze eleven knots of speed from the bulky monster. At full throttle, Madam *Nanok* throbs in tempo of a trolley car. How anyone aft can ever get a full night's sleep with the engine pounding away is beyond imagination.

June 27, Saturday; *Nanok*, **still at Constitution Wharf.**

Took liberty alone, feeling melancholy. I experience such feeling too often I fear.

Went to pick up some special items of laundry from a Chinese hand laundry. I happened onto a scene at a most humorous time. After the incident I would learn the details. The mister has a weakness for gambling. The moment his hand wraps around a few customer dollars, he is off to a nearby bookmaker and promptly loses it in a bet on a dog race.

At the time of my arrival, the man's missus has him cornered and cowering in a far corner of the shop. She pounds on him with a small ironing board. He is screaming, for mercy I suppose. The woman apparently never heard of mercy. The ironing board splits down its length. She drops it to the floor and grabs a giant pair of tailoring scissors and beats on him with the handle. He pulls the scissors away from her. Both scream unpleasant Chinese words. He makes for the front door. She grabs the back of his thin, white trousers at the waist. His momentum carries him through the wooden screen door, minus the top portion of the back of his pants that have been torn off almost to the knees. The man has no underwear. . . . Probably lost it gambling. His bare buttocks are exposed. He dashes up the street, shouting. Terrified onlooker pedestrians scatter. The missus returns to the shop to service me. She explains the affair in high-pitched Chinese which I do not understand a word of. I nod in agreement, I need my clean laundry. She cools down, speaks broken English, and I learn the entire story which I did not choose to know.

My melancholia has been alleviated by the incident. I pop into the Silver Dollar Bar and hoist a few brews, then off to see the movie *Reap the Wild Wind*. It is very good and so are my spirits.

Roamed through the open-air fruit and vegetable market. It is very large. I understand bits of the Italian language and it sounds like that is the only language spoken here.

June 28, Sunday; *Nanok.*

John Petrenko, Jr., "Pete the tramp."

Pete does not like being called tramp. Because of his massive size and strength, nobody ever does so in his presence. . . . No one except Norman "Elmer" Comer, who does so whenever agitated by Pete.

Pete is taller than me and I am six foot two inches tall. His weight must top two hundred and fifty pounds. His face is that of a Roman gladiator, large and broad across the forehead. He has very dark, deep sunken eyes and strong, jutting chin. His dark hair is ever awry. His heavy, black whiskers make him a frightful-looking antagonist. He could use a shave every hour. Added to this are high cheekbones and protruding ears. In repose, Pete is a dark, fierce looking giant, hence, Pete the tramp.

Pete invites me to join him for a home-cooked Sunday dinner at his girlfriend's house. I jump at the opportunity. Not just for the dinner, but because I was curious to see the lady who found Pete attractive. I find it difficult to understand that any woman can find anything attractive in any man. It is obvious, however, that women do so. Perhaps women all have poor eyesight.

Pete's girlfriend lives in far-off Malden, Mass. We travel there by rail to the end of its line, then we walk a long way. The family Fitzgerald lives at the top of a tall hill. As we walk up it, Pete tells me of skullduggery that, if told to me earlier, I would not have come along.

Margaret "Peggy" Fitz., the younger of two sisters, was the one who first invited Pete to the Fitzgerald home. According to Pete, Peggy was wild about him, but he preferred the older sister Mira. Pete just wanted me along to distract Peggy so he could spend time courting Mira. I reminded him that I was a happy, newly-married man. This mattered not to Pete. He insisted "I don't want you to make love to her . . . just keep her occupied." As the damn fool that I sometimes can be, I reluctantly agreed.

I married Lucille Edna Ketelhut on February 10th of this year and I am very much in love with her.

The Fitzgeralds proved to be a very fine, close-knit family. It was their patriotism that prompted them to invite servicemen to their home for Sunday dinner. Mister was somehow related to a Mrs. Joseph P. Kennedy, wife of a strong Mass. politician I know nothing about.

After dinner Peggy, Mira, Pete and I attended a movie. On the long walk back, I learn much from Peggy that Pete should have told me but did not. We walked in pairs, Pete and Mira in the lead. Peggy and I spoke of many light things. Peggy was very outgoing and vivacious, a temptation for any young man. I mentioned Pete's obvious affection for Mira and Peggy laughed. She then told me that Pete was first attracted to her. He had become quite obnoxious and she had to tell him that her friendship toward him was platonic and nothing more, and never would be. If he has any romantic notions toward Mira, he would get the shock of his life because Mira disliked him intensely!

So that was it!

Pete was rejected by Peggy and was having a go at Mira! "That tramp!!" I muttered. I immediately felt ashamed for thinking so because I liked Pete a lot. After all I could not blame him for trying to find affection. He is an unmarried man and either sister was a prize.

What was disturbing me more than Pete's using me for his romantic purposes was Peggy's seeming affection for me. She gently kneaded my hand in hers and snuggled as close as she could as we walked. I must confess I felt something more than just casual friendship at the moment. Perhaps I was misinterpreting her action. At any rate, no damage done because I had already made up my mind to see the Fitzgeralds no more.

We stayed late, missed the last train from Malden to Boston. We hitch-hiked part way, found a taxi, and arrived at the *Nanok* just in time for my midnight to 4 a.m. watch. Physically, I was a total loss but the dinner and company was worth it.

June 29, Monday; *Nanok*, **still at Constitution Wharf.**

Before parting yesterday, Peggy insisted I promise to return today. I phoned her home and told her mother I could not make the visit and could not tell her when I might do so again. Mrs. Fitzgerald sounded very disappointed. I believe both parents enjoyed my visit. All the more reason for a married man to stay away.

Worked hard all day. Old buddy Boike's trawler *Atak* left, supposed-ly bound for Portland, Maine. The vessel *Belmont* and another rusty tub tagged along with them.[7]

During wartime even the uppermost ship's officers did not always know their specific destination. This was for security purposes. This secrecy was accomplished in a variety of ways. When I sailed on board the U.S.C.G. cutter *Sea Cloud*, it was said the skipper received sailing instructions in the form of a large stack of sealed and numbered envelopes. Envelope number one had a time and date printed on its face. On that time and date the en-velope was to be removed from the ship's safe and opened in the captain's presence and that of his top officers. The envelope's contents instructed the captain of time of departure, course to steer, distance and or time to do so, and sometimes even speeds at which to travel. It could even con-tain instructions as to what time, date and location envelope two was to be opened. Thus very few on board would ever really know where they were going, time of arrival or duty to perform. It follows that each enve-lope would also contain emergency instructions. In [the] event the ship was about to be taken by the enemy, there would be instructions for quickly destroying the balance of envelopes, possibly by shredding. Whether such procedures were fact or fiction is unknown to me. It is obvious the proce-dure would have merit at least under some circumstances.

Ashore for a few beers with Pete.

June 30, Tuesday; *Nanok*.

I can't imagine why I did it, but from the *Nanok* I phoned Peggy just to say hello. She sounded quite excited and insisted that I come to visit immediately. I told myself it was just the home cooking that beckoned me.

Even as I spoke to her, I heard some of the crew were being sent to a place called "Price's Neck" near Newport, Rhode Island, for gunnery practice. It was to be on 20mm anti-aircraft and .50 calibre machine guns and other such weapons. I also heard I was in the first group to go. Peggy reluctantly excused me. Bos'n Robbins, Schafer, Charlie Rolston, "Guns" Owens, Petrenko, and I received our pay, caught the train to Newport, then by open truck to Price's Neck.

July

There are no longer any doubts. Rumor is now fact. We are bound for Greenland!

July 1, Wednesday; Price's Neck.

Schafer is a radioman 1/c. He is of medium height, slender, rather dark-skinned, near bald. A very nervous, excitable, and introverted individual. He reminds me of a cowed dog being kicked into a corner. I am very surprised when he begins one of his very rare conversations with me. He suggested just he and I go into town in the evening for a few drinks. He strikes me as being lonesome as hell and in need of someone to talk to. Not many of the crew pay any attention to him or converse with him. Probably because he makes no attempt to be friendly. I tell him "OK," I would join him later in the day.

Spent first half of day assembling and disassembling 20mm guns until we were able to do so in total darkness. A very useful talent we are told.

Second half of day is spent firing the guns. The pilot of a small, slow-flying military aircraft tows a very large, cigar-shaped air sock, tethered to the rear of his plane with a very long line. He flies from left to right for a very long distance, then reverses his course and passes before us from right to left. We all fire away at the sock but tracer shells show we never come close to hitting the damn thing except for once or twice. After several passes the pilot lands somewhere. Our instructor receives a phone call telling him that the pilot refuses to fly anymore. He claimed our missiles were scorching the back of his neck instead of hitting the sock towed far astern. What is the use of being able to disassemble and reassemble 20mm guns in the dark when we can't hit a bull in the ass in broad daylight!? We need much more practice.

From then on, large helium-filled balloons are released one at a time and we fire at them. They ascend skyward and drift away in the distance, most of them untouched. It is obvious that our gunnery training is necessarily speeded up far beyond practicality. We are merely being taught fundamentals. The war cannot wait for us to become proficient. In all probability the tiny *Nanok* will become a target. As mentioned before, it is doubtful that any valuable torpedoes will be wasted on her. If, however, the *Nanok* should ever meet a couple of enemy canoes or rowboats, we'll show them!!

Schafer and I enjoy several copies of a new cocktail called "the zombie." They consist of many layers of various colored liqueurs, gently floated atop one another in a tall glass. The drink was said to be so potent that bartenders were advised not to serve more than one per customer. Our bartender must not have been informed of this rule. Schafer and I enjoy two each and would like more but they were too expensive (but delicious).

The more Schafer gets, the more he rambles on about his mother. I'm not sure whether he misses her badly, or if she cannot bear it without him. I understand that he is her only son and sole support and she is quite ill. There is no doubt that he is very worried about her. His elephant tears flood the channels between nose and puffed red cheeks. At one point my eyes become watery too. I decide to leave him but discover I have lost my wallet. A young waitress finds it and returns it to me. I reward her with a wet kiss diluted with a tear or two. She seemed sorry to have returned the wallet.

I stay long enough to have a couple more drinks, play a few cards, win a few bucks and spend it on a sheath knife and a taxi. I really hadn't the slightest idea where I lost Schafer but didn't give a rat's ass. He depressed me and I am homesick enough without worrying about his mom too. Homesickness has been visibly growing aboard the *Nanok* since day one. There are signs of it on many faces.

July 2, Thursday; Price's Neck.

Talk about homesickness, wow!!!

Maurice (Robby) (Bos'n) Robbins relates to me a tear-filled story of his Mom's situation. In addition to his Mom being quite ill and elderly, she lives alone. Her only company and assistance is Robby's wife who happens to be pregnant. She has no auto and has to walk a great distance almost daily to look after Robby's Mom. I don't understand because if Robby explained his situation to our superiors, I believe he would be given home-base duty. Radioman Schafer's situation is almost a carbon copy of Robby's.

I break away from Robby because my sympathy is upsetting me. I converse with Radioman 1/c Charles A. (Rolly) Rolston. He too is homesick and lays his sorrow onto me, yipes!! I now have an idea how my Catholic priest feels when listening to confessions. Only Guns Owens manages to stay dry-eyed out of all I have spoken to. He must not be married, has no sweetheart, and is an incubator person without parents.

I work on .50 calibre machine guns and fire two of them. One jammed but I managed to hit a balloon anyway. We are all experiencing some degree of accuracy now.

The aircraft carrier *Ranger* passes nearby. She is a super magnificent piece of hardware! She blots out the entire horizon. I would take a pay cut just to serve and scramble across her decks! What beauty! What class! What awesome power! [8]

Guns keeps us awake half the night telling joke after joke, embellished with his delightful tar-heel-twang accent. He continues to drawl on as I fall asleep.

July 3, Friday; *Nanok*, **at Constitution Wharf.**

Spent early morning firing guns until my ears turned inside out. We caught the truck and train back to Boston and the *Nanok*. Flirted with four pretties on the train and received invitation for weekend house party on the beach.

Been stationed aboard the *Nanok* twelve days now. Getting restless to move on and hopefully find something to help obliterate homesickness. Got cleaned up and went to visit my good friend Howard (Howie) Fox, the bartender in the Brunswick Hotel's basement bar.

I enjoyed a chat with Howie and had a couple glasses of beer at the bar. I sat near an outer corner, around the corner sat an older man that was probably in his late fifties. I don't feel like conversing but he does so we converse. After learning I am of Polish decent, he said he was too, but his family came from Russia rather than Poland.

"What a small world, eh?" he says.

I didn't think both of us being of Polish descent made it a "small world."

There are people one takes on an immediate dislike to. To me, this is one of those people. I did not care for his shifty, furtive, back and forth, crafty glances, nor his know-it-all attitude. He had a fat, squat, dumpy body, black clothing with much old food rubbed into the lapels. He claimed to have very recently painted President Roosevelt's portrait at the Whitehouse. I could not imagine F.D.R. sitting in the same room with this man for long periods of time. His body odor was terrible. We got around to discussing the war and try to guess how long it might last. I guessed and hoped it would not last very long. He guessed it could go on forever, or until the last human on earth was dead. His guess annoyed me very much because it tended to destroy my hope for the war to end while I am still alive. We began to argue about it. Since I was quite worked up, he decided to back-off some. He pouted because I refused to believe his guess. He was silent for about two minutes, then said, "it makes no difference anyway. When this war ends, the United States will have to go to war again!"

"With whom!?" I demanded.

"Russia!" he said, a crafty smile on his face.

"You must be a fool!" I replied, "Russia is our ally!"

"Now, yes!" he said.

"I think you're crazy, mister!" I reply.

"Am I?! Oh am I!?" he blurted. "You're not only going to war with Russia, you're going to lose!" he said, stabbing a forefinger into the bar's surface for emphasis.

Something inside me shook with anger.

"What makes you so sure?" I asked.

"Because America has no guts, that's why!"

I was on the verge of losing complete control of myself. I wanted to beat the man's face into pulp. Then he added, goadingly: "You're mad as hell at me, aren't you!?"

"You damn well know it!" I am almost shouting now.

"Well, why don't you hit me!?" he demanded. "If I was as mad at you as you are at me . . . I'd hit you! That's why America will lose the next war which will be with Russia, no guts, like you!!"

We now had the attention of everyone in the bar, including Howie. He sternly asked us to, "keep it down for crissake!" I was embarrassed, and even though this hateful man was possibly three times my age and obviously of very little physical strength, or perhaps because of it, I could not prompt myself to hit him. I had no doubt whatsoever that I could destroy him in two or three punches, and I did not fear being hurt by him. Instead of fighting, I chose to leave the bar. I spun about and headed for the exit. He was still shouting!

"Americans have power but no guts!!"

I knew I would never forgive myself for walking away from him. The incident would surely begin a long period of self examination. Was I a coward? Something in the outer me said "hell no!!" At the same time, something very deep in me asked, "Are you sure? Are you? Why didn't you hit the bastard?! 'cause he was so old? Shouldn't there ever be justification for hitting a person just because they are older? Of course not. You should be ashamed of yourself for thinking so. . . . But why should I feel ashamed, dammit!? Would I have enjoyed a feeling of victory if that old man ended up lying flat on the floor at my feet? Would the bar patrons have applauded me?"

I knew I would retain conflicting thoughts for a long time to come. I hurried back to the bar to do what I should have done. I wanted much to kill him! But why did I experience such relief when I learned no one had noticed his leaving?

The incident did something awful to my self confidence. From now on I would wonder and fear that maybe I am a coward. Worse, that while being a coward, I would become a laughing stock. I would be ridiculed.

I began to study the men who I was to sail with. Mentally I evaluated each of them. Were the big, tough-looking ones like Petrenko really as tough as they appeared or was toughness just a veneer? Were the meek and mild ones like Elmer Comer really just mice? Or was his exterior a veneer also? I know that I should not have, but I paid a surprise visit to Peggy's house. It helped lighten my mood.

July 4, Saturday; *Nanok.*

Independence Day!

Anniversary of America's independence since 1776 and here we are at war. Shame on all mankind.

I spend the first half of the day stowing ammunition into *Nanok's* hold. A tough, heavy chore. Schafer says it is to assure us of continued independence.

July 5, Sunday; *Nanok.*

We wear summer white uniforms for the first time. Nice and cool. Went to movie with Sully Jones, then food, then to Buddies Club on Boston Common. After a couple of dances, a pretty young miss talked my leg off. I excused myself, went to the head and snuck off to the *Nanok.*

July 6, Monday; *Nanok.*

Evening at the Fitz's for a light dinner. Peggy burned her leg pretty bad. Spilled hot grease on it. "Billy the kid," a sailor from Kent, England, played piano for a sing-along. He's here at Mira's invitation. Billy and I get a lift to the railway.

July 7, Tuesday; *Nanok.*

Worked hard all day, wrote letter to Lucille, then phoned her in the evening. I don't tell her about the Fitzgeralds because she is sure to get the wrong idea. I haven't mentioned Lucille to the Fitzgeralds either. I fear there would be no more homey visits or dinners.

A very young girl came to the small U.S.C.G. vessel tied nearby. She is looking for a sailor who told her his name is Charlie Noble. She is pregnant and Charlie is the father. This proves to be a humorous joke. Charlie turns out to be Chollie Noble which is the sailor's name for the galley stove pipe. The miss is told there is no Charlie Noble aboard. She leaves in a burst of tears. I wonder how many more like her are looking for their Charlie.

Albert (Stan) Staneczak argues heatedly with George (Fair) Fairbanks. Stan is an annoying know-it-all and believes he must constantly prove to himself that he indeed knows it all. Both men claim they know the amount of feet there is in a "shot" of chain. George insists it is one length and Stan insists otherwise. I don't offer an opinion. I don't choose to become involved. Besides, I don't know. One day I will ask Talledo.

Stan is much taller than Fair. He is considerably younger, stronger, hard, muscular and aggressive. His lips curl back and he speaks through clenched teeth. His square face seethes in anger. His forward-falling straight hair creates a Hitler image. On the other hand, Fairbanks is comparatively smaller in stature and somewhat frail. I cannot imagine how he managed to pass C.G. physical requirements. Too, he is the oldest seaman aboard. He has to be more than fifty years of age. The Coast Guard has never drafted anyone, and it is difficult to imagine why he would have voluntarily enlisted.

George has a thin, hatchet face. It is dark, heavily freckled, and at times his small eyes are invisible in their dark, deep canyons. His face quivers nervously and his straight-up hair quivers even more.

Stan tries to intimidate George but George is a man and refuses to be brow-beaten by the bully. Stan makes a move to strike George in the face, but Roach steps in between the two men and grabs hold of Stan's cocked, right wrist. The day is now ruined for everyone in the fo'c's'le. Elmer Comer whispers, "if he" (meaning Stan) ever pulls that sort of shit on me, I'll cold-cock him!" I have to smile. Comer is about the same size as Fairbanks. I felt sure Stan could devour Comer in two bites.

July 8, Wednesday; *Nanok.*

Stayed aboard, washed clothes, developing a summer cold, I think.

July 9, Thursday; *Nanok.*

Worked hard. Have cold and sore throat. Talked myself into going to the Fitzgerald's, for sympathy and pampering I guess, and I get it. The Fitz's insisted I stay overnight (hot dog!).

Rumor is strong that we may finally ship out tomorrow morning. That would be nice. I want to stop going to the Fitz's and can't get myself to do it. Shipping out is the answer.

July 10, Friday; *Nanok.*

Hot dog!

We got a washing machine today. No more having to wash clothes by hand! My head cold is so bad I find it difficult to concentrate on the most simple things.

We hear the Russians have torpedoed the giant German battleship *Tirpitz* yesterday in the Barents Sea. Unfortunately she was not sunk. She is Hitler's pride and joy. Sinking her would be a severe blow to the nutzy leader's ego and confidence.

July 11, Saturday; *Nanok.*

Comer, Jonesy, Chips and I go to a movie, then to Boston Commons for some dancing with sweet-smelling partners. Later to the Silver Dollar Saloon for beer, then back to the *Nanok.* I accidentally dozed off for a few moments while on watch in the pilot house. . . . Bad boy!! Never again.

July 12, Sunday; Portland, Maine.

We leave Constitution Wharf. *Nanok* bids Boston "goodbye."

Running alongside a large excursion-type vessel full of women, we wave "goodbye" at one another. Why are women so friendly whenever they are out of arm's reach?

Outside Boston Harbor we heave-to for four hours awaiting arrival of the U.S.C.G. cutter *North Star.* [9] We rendezvous and leave together but lose contact with one another later in the day.

We are carrying all sorts of machinery and parts thereof. We even have an airplane engine aboard.

We anchor outside of Portland, Maine, for the night. So far, very little "spit and polish" on board the *Nanok.* How nice . . . but could it be dangerous?

July 13, Monday; Portland.

The hook is pulled up, *Nanok* enters the harbor and the hook is dropped.

Had four to eight a.m. watch in pilot house. Saw the U.S. battlewagon *Massachusetts* and a dozen or so of the "can type" vessels coming in. It is one thing to see a movie of a battlewagon, but quite another to see one with your own eyes. They are awesome in all respects. You realize their gigantic size when you learn the tiny ants skittering across her decks are actually men. [10]

Liberty ashore. Wrote to Lucille at the U.S.O. (United Services Organization), then went drinkin' with Fairbanks and Guns Owens. Not a bar-room as such to be found. Danced and drank a bit at a second-story dance hall called Oriental Gardens.

Caught the last liberty boat to the *Nanok* at one a.m. Boat is chock-a-block full with drunks, half drunks, and just stupid-looking sleepy swabbies. Although he denies it, Petrenko missed the last boat and did what had to be done. He tied his clothes in his neckerchief and swam out in total darkness to the *Nanok*, about a quarter of a mile with the sack of clothes tied to the back of his neck. Who knows how he made it in the cold water with un-lighted, small, motorized boats dashing back and forth. If he was drunk, he was stone sober when Elmer Comer helped him on board.

July 14, Tuesday; Portland.

Son of a bitch! What a day!

It started off when I was assigned the job of red-leading the exec's cubicle. Cookie Clark is in a rotten mood and argues without reason. Then Talledo and I hit it off badly. I want desperately to please the man but find it impossible to do so. He hisses when he speaks to me. He is always gruff and speaks in caustic tones. He is a continual irritation to me and apparently I to him.

Al Staneczak is no help. He finds delight in goading the chief at my expense. He injects such things as, "I don't think he heard your orders, chief." Or, "Maybe that job is beneath his class, chief." Or, "Maybe he thinks he should have your job and you have his," etc., etc., whenever the opportunity to do so presents itself. Dammit, I'm learning to dislike Stan too! I ask him on several occasions to cease, but he gives me an indignant, hurt look, and says, "Geez, I'm only kiddin' around fella!" His "kiddin' around" I know, is costing me points with Talledo. Stan wants very much to become a coxswain too, and I can appreciate that. But maybe he feels that the *Nanok* can afford only one coxswain and wants himself to fill the position, I don't know.

Since I am the leading seaman on board, normally, the bos'n should consult with me when lengthy jobs are to be done. I would be expected to take care of the lesser details and minor instructions. I would thereby be in strong contention for promotion to coxs'n. No such recognition has been afforded me. Much of this problem, I feel, lies with the skipper. He exercises no visible chain of command which is normal Coast Guard practice. [11] So far, all activities on board the *Nanok* are informal. While this is a comfortable way for subordinates to live, it creates a multitude of other problems. Someone once said that familiarity breeds contempt and indeed it does. It may sound friendly for a senior officer to address his bos'n 1/c as "buddy," but "buddy" may rightfully be expected to address the senior officer as "pal" or some other such ridiculous designation. Such lack of discipline and formality could lead to subordinates ignoring authority and questioning commands.

Example, Bos'n 1/c Robbins is shown very little respect by the skipper and therefore Robbins receives but a minimum of respect from the seamen beneath him. Deck activities are often performed without informing him at all. Many on board the *Nanok* grumble about the captain's disciplinary looseness. Robbins, of course, Fireman Abe Brill, Petrenko, Jonesy, Fairbanks, Comer, and others.

As mentioned before, many believe our skipper received very little, if any, formal Coast Guard training whatsoever. Rumors remain that he is a close, personal friend of Admiral "Iceberg" Smith who supposedly coaxed Maggie into the Coast Guard. Possibly because of Maggie's vast North Atlantic experience. It is further rumored that Maggie agreed to enter the service only if he did not have to take foolish training. I must add that none of the crew have any proof of such allegations. From the onset, the skipper demonstrated nothing but disdain for formality, discipline, and chain of command. He mentioned on several occasions that ratings should be abolished and we should all simply be crew members. He was once asked by Talledo, how would we differentiate between crew members. The captain answered, "by the amount of pay they would be getting. Ratings are for boy scouts!" he said.

He often referred to Chief Boatswain's Mate George Talledo as "the bos'n." [12] On several occasions he had given me oral messages to convey to Chief Motor Machinist Mate Nelson McClay and said I should take them to "the mechanic." I did not mind too much because my rating was a minor one, but I did hope to wear a coxswain's "crow" on my right arm with a pride of achievement. Too, I fretted at the thought of being overlooked for a pay raise that was so important to my wife.

News of my poor relationship with Talledo would surely reach the captain and could well destroy my promotion possibilities. With hindsight it was easy for me to realize I should have never mentioned the possibility of my becoming a petty officer. It was very wrong for me to have done so. Something inside me said both Talledo and Maggie could become insurmountable challenges for me to overcome. I vow to prove my seaworthiness to both of them. It should be as easy as conquering Hitler.

July 15, Wednesday; Portland.

Oho!

Our executive officer has finally arrived. He is a reserve ensign named Dicastro. [13] He identifies himself thus, and does not mention his given name. Perhaps he has none? He is of medium height and weight and has sand colored hair. His face is round and has a frozen expression of a pampered, spoiled child. He immediately makes it clear that he is a tough, gung-ho, spit-and-polish yokel. Methinks rules and regulations may arrive in quantity.

Talledo still on my tail!

July 16, Thursday; At sea, northbound.

Took on a load of fresh water from a large freighter in the harbor. I do not learn its name. We tie up alongside of it and pump water directly from its tank into ours. Maggie promises we will not always get water this easily.

Wrote a letter to Lucille but did not mail it because I am not on shore liberty today. Washed clothes, practiced semaphore with another ship that is at anchor. Also sculled a skiff around the harbor. There are a great many seals frolicking in the harbor. When the tide is low, a number of hulls of very large, concrete, World War I vessels can be seen. They were built to be used as open barges to be towed laden with war materials. These were possibly leftovers. They were expected to remain intact for just one ocean crossing. My mind could not accept that concrete vessels could be loaded and floated across the ocean intact. I was assured it was true.

Our diet of entertainment on board the *Nanok* consists of studying, dice-rolling, card playing, and group singing, take your choice, but no radio. My three harmonicas come in handy even though I don't play very well.

Since Dicastro came on board yesterday, Cookie Clark became restricted from any liberty until further notice because he was a fatal five minutes late serving chow. Can you believe that! Dicastro was meaner than hell with Clark! Too bad. Clark is one of the most conscientious workers on board. Privately, Clark tells me of four or five things Dicastro can do with his liberty. None of Clark's suggestions are practical or even possible. Dicastro, I'm sure, would have a most difficult time trying to do as Clark suggested.

I got the four to eight p.m. watch. The hook is hauled in and we leave Portland about 5:15 p.m. I wheel the *Nanok* out of the harbor. Bos'n Robbins assists because the *Nanok* controls are very stiff. We are one of a convoy of five vessels, the *Nanok* being the smallest. All of the others are at least three times our size. I'd give my left nostril to sail on board any of them.

July 17, Friday; At sea.

Passed Halifax, Nova Scotia, bound north and east. Saw many porpoises. Frisky and fun to watch. Reading *King's Row*, good story. Practiced firing 20mm anti-aircraft guns.

Saw whales spouting some distance away. Stan and Fairbanks thought they were periscopes and reported same to the bridge. A good laugh was had by all (except Dicastro). Breezes carried terrible odor of whale breath to the *Nanok*. Both whales and *Nanok* could use mouth wash.

Dicastro is a pain in the ass!

Believe it or not, he has done away with night lunches! Too, there is to be no more than two slices of bacon per man at breakfast. If we are to have jelly or jam, there is to be no desert at that meal! Where did this asshole come from? All American vessels, civilian and military, have always afforded night lunch to crew members when they complete night watches. Crew members grumble but none want to go over the head of Dicastro to complain to the skipper.

There are no longer any doubts. Rumor is now fact. We are bound for Greenland! Ye gads! That's the top of planet earth!

July 18, Saturday; At sea.

Saw flotilla of many vessels including a few submarines. They must be ours, we're not firing at 'em. Drilled on 20mm guns again today. Dicastro began cutting off the gun covers because, according to his calculations, we were a bit late in reaching our battle stations after "general quarters" was sounded.

No matter how quick we respond, he is not satisfied, and begins slashing away with his razor-sharp sheath knife! Whatever time it takes us, he reduces the time allowed by a few seconds off his stop watch. It mattered not that Fairbanks came directly from the toilet seat and holding up his unbuttoned dungarees as he climbed the gun deck ladder using one free hand. If Dicastro continues thus we will have to arrive before we start!

Some of the vessels with us are the *Driller*, a tanker, and the *Hydrographer*. Our two flanking escorts are the cutter *Mohawk* and the *North Star*. [14] We expect to be in Sydney, Nova Scotia, on the morrow.

July 19, Sunday; Sydney, Nova Scotia.

We arrive late in the p.m. and drop the hook. Steel mill furnaces light up the sky like a cloud of blood. Too late for shore liberty.

It grows very dark before Maggie decides to change our anchorage position, so it is "up anchor" for the move. My station is at the anchor-lift winch on the main deck just forward of the pilot house. In the now nearly total darkness I hurry to the narrow space between winch and pilot house superstructure and the man-height drum on which the starboard anchor cable is wound.

I bump headlong into someone in the darkness. The someone begins to cuss me. It is Dicastro!

"What in hell are you doing here!?" he demands.

"Chief Talledo assigned me to this station whenever the anchor is to be lifted or dropped now and in the future."

"Get your ass on the gun deck and help them cat the anchor," he growls.

"But sir, this is my station!" I protest.

"Your station is where I want it to be," he snarls. "And right now it's on the fo'c's'le head, now git!"

"Sir," I say, "winch is very tricky, sir."

"Go, dammit!!" he screams, so I go.

If the clutch control wheel is not turned very, very slowly, the clutch catches or grabs suddenly, and the anchor chain is yanked suddenly. Whoever may be handling the anchor at the time could be injured. As I get to the anchor catting station on the bow of the ship, Talledo asks: "What in hell are you doing here!?"

"Dicastro sent me," I reply.

Talledo mumbles angrily.

There is a six-foot-high davit on the *Nanok*'s bow. It has a rope falls hanging from its arched-down end. When the 500-pound Baldt-type anchor is raised from the sea-bottom, up to the shipside opening that guides the moving chain, the hoisting is stopped. The hanging rope falls is attached to the anchor's shackle. "Slack" in the chain is shouted for, so that the chain will slide back out of the guide (hawse-hole) making it possible for the anchor to be lifted with the rope falls and hand power, above the top surface of the deck. It is lifted high enough to clear the top of an eighteen-inch-high cable-rail that is intended to prevent personnel from accidentally sliding overboard.

It is very dark, and the anchor is still outboard of the ship. Dicastro has hoisted it smoothly. No sudden jerking, etc. As the shackled top of the anchor reached the height of the hawse-hole, the hook at the end of the rope falls is attached to the shackle. Robbins yells to Dicastro for "slack" and Dicastro responds. We commence pulling the anchor above the deck and the top of the safety cable-rail. We begin to swing the anchor inboard the several feet it takes to clear the safety rail and reach the anchor's on-deck cradle in which we are to tie the anchor down. There is not quite enough slack in the chain to permit us to pull the anchor inboard far enough.

Again Robbins yells for "slack."

Dicastro responds with "what?"

"Slack, slack off!" shouts Robbins.

Instead of slacking-off as requested, Dicastro takes-up on the chain and yanks the anchor back over the side! Because of the sudden, unexpected movement, we too were being pulled overboard! My left hand was in an unfortunate location, the middle finger was smashed between the anchor and one of the safety-rail's stanchions. The flesh was torn loose to the first joint on the palm side of the finger. The flesh was folded forward like an extended fingernail. I lay below while the others finish catting the anchor. I fold the torn end of the finger back over the exposed bone.

Soon Jones and Robbins come below. I feel no pain, only numbness. I do not experience fear, yet I feel about to pass out and say so. I am seated and Jones forces my head down between my knees. It helps and I remain conscious. Robbins, seeing the amount of blood I was losing, went to Dicastro for permission to take me to a doctor on board one of the larger vessels anchored nearby. Before leaving, he wrapped the finger in a clean white sock.

Robbins returned, looking dumbfounded. He said, "I told Dicastro about your finger and told him you should see a doctor right away. Know what he told me? He said 'tell him to put some iodine on it and wrap it in something.'"

Robbins ranted and raved, calling Dicastro's indifference every foul name that came to mind.

"He had no god-damned business at the winch in the first place. It's too tricky to operate without practice! You know that 'ski!"

I nodded affirmatively.

"I'm going to see Captain Mag," shouted the infuriated Robbins.

I cautioned him not to do so. Dicastro did not strike me as one who would ever forgive or forget anyone who might go over his head to see the skipper. The wrapped finger appears to have stopped bleeding. I go to bed but do not sleep well. The pain finally defeats numbness. My entire hand hurts like hell! It is a throbbing pain.

July 20, Monday; Sydney, Nova Scotia.

Ensign Dicastro caught hell from Maggie for not allowing me to see a doctor. I suspect Robbins told Maggie about my injury but he does not admit it. I am ordered to see the doctor on board the *North Star* anchored nearby.

John "Dreams" Connors is quite a fellow. His pink cheeks are chubby with fine, pinfeather fuzz. He appears to be sixteen years old but I feel sure he must be at least twenty. John is dubbed "Dreams" because of his ability to fall asleep anywhere at anytime at the drop of an eyelid. Even when pulling on his boots, he manages to fall asleep.

Dreams rows me over to the *North Star* in our smallest dory. I climb up to the ship's high deck by means of a Jacob's Ladder. Dreams chooses to wait in the dory even though the waves are quite high. The dory bobs like a cork. It appears to be hardly more than a barnacle on the side of the giant vessel. From the dory bow a light manila line leads straight up and its end is secured to the inboard side of the gunwale.

Under the fluoroscope we see the bone of my left, middle finger is broken off diagonally and there is a considerable separation. The doctor cleanses the wound and tapes the finger to a wooden tongue depressor that serves as a splint. Doctor says the finger will require a long time to heal because of the bone separation.

I am away a short period of time. When I return and look down at the dory, I see Dreams sitting wedged in its prow. His head rests on his forearms that lay across the top of his drawn-up knees. Waves are banging the dory against the side of the *North Star*. Dreams is in dreamland, fast asleep! Awake, Connors is hell-on-wheels when it comes to work. He is an excellent seaman. I let out a war whoop. Connors jerks awake. Obviously he is disoriented for a moment. My face is turned away so he cannot see me stifle a laugh.

Later in the day Talledo and Dicastro lock horns. Dicastro attempted to order Talledo to do some degrading, menial task. Talledo tells Dicastro to "shove it!" He's been around too long to eat crap.

Near evening I ask Dicastro if I could return to the doctor for some pain killer. He says I am a sissy and a little pain will help make a man out of me. I hope so, then I'll kick the shit out of him! Again he refuses to allow me to see the doc.

Skipper allows us evening liberty. I sure can use a few pain-killer shots. The only drinkin' place to be found is a sort of hall that is chock-a-block full of servicemen, mostly sailors. The hall is so large it is near impossible to see all four walls. I'm sure there are walls but most are hidden behind curtains of cigarette smoke. It is also near impossible to estimate the number of drinkers in the joint, or even the amount of tables. Waitresses are the only females in the place. Their backsides must be swollen from all the pinches and feels they get. Can't imagine how they tolerate it but they do—with smiles yet.

Maybe they are just super patriotic—of course they received many tips. They take your table's order, disappear in the distant smoke wall and later reappear with a tray full of quart-sized bottles of beer. The beer is lousy, but the bootleg hootch being sold by some half-drunk sailor for five bucks a bottle is quite an effective pain killer. It tastes much like the rat's urine my brother used to cook up. My finger feels much better.

At all times, somewhere in this cavernous joint, a fist fight is going on, way off in one direction or another. As soon as one battle is halted, another begins elsewhere. They are fun to watch—from a distance. It is a real-life series of comedies—especially since all contestants are hardly sober enough to stand.

At a table to my rear sat a group of the largest French submariners imaginable. They wear dark berets with shiny buckles. Their wide-open V-shaped blouse-fronts display horizontal, candy-striped undershirts. While my attention is focused on a scuffle some fifty feet away, mayhem explodes behind me. My chair is kicked out from under me, by accident I suppose, I fall to the floor. As I arose, I become aware that all of the submariners are fighting one another. It was none of my affair so I chose to leave. Before I could do so, one of them struck me an uppercut that landed just at the bottom of my rib cage. I swear, my six-foot-two inch body was lifted completely off the floor. I flew backward across the top of one table, on to the floor beyond and under the next table. I remained conscious but had to fight for breath. The fight raged on and expanded. I was kicked a number of times by swift, shuffling feet. As soon as possible, I crawled on hands and knees thirty feet or so, arising beyond the perimeter of the fight, and staggered out of the place. I caught the 0100 liberty boat back to the *Nanok* and had no problem falling asleep. My finger did not hurt anymore.

July 21, Tuesday; Sydney.

Once more my finger feels as though it has been slammed into the breach of a closing cannon. Because of my injury, Talledo told me to take the day off and relax. I lay in my sack reading. Dicastro finds me and orders me to "turn to" and do some chipping, scraping, red-leading, and painting.

I tell him that Talledo told me to take the day off.

Dicastro says, "I am your chief and I say 'move!'"

Rust forms on the *Nanok*'s steel fittings almost as fast as it can be chipped off, or so it seems. Someday someone will invent a ship that will require no paint and will win the undying gratitude of every man-jack that ever swung a chipping hammer or wire brush. It is too painful for me to use my left hand at all, and impossible to do the job with one hand.

The crew managed to offload the aircraft engine so we begin to secure for sea. Don't know when we may be near a doctor in the future so again I ask for permission to go. Dicastro again refuses to allow me to do so. I couldn't believe it. My entire arm throbs with pain. Dicastro said we hadn't the time to spare for "unnecessary sick calls." I don't dare go over his head to Maggie. I'll learn how to live with this son-of-a-bitch-bastard! In civilian life he was a mattress sewer—that figures!

We kiss Sydney "goodbye" and head north into the Gulf of St. Lawrence.

Coldest day to date. Porpoises are more abundant.

July 22, Wednesday; Northbound in Labrador Sea.

I attempt to work on a cargo net of manila hemp rope but pain in my arm forces a halt. Jonesy changes my bandage. Dicastro is on a rampage. He is on everyone like the seven year itch, finding fault with even the slightest everyday things.

We have two submarine alerts today. The cutter *Mohawk* takes off in pursuit. Something to brag about after the war—if still alive.

Nanok's course is a bee line north and east from the mouth of the Belle Isle Strait to the southernmost tip of Greenland. Greenland, the world's largest island, governed by Denmark, with more history than inhabitants. It is roughly 800 miles wide and 1,650 miles long. It's an area of 840,000 square miles of ice cap, and only 130,000 square miles of ice-free land. In some places the ice cap is 7,000 to 8,000 feet in depth, a whole bunch of martini coolant, I'd say.

Summer temperatures in the south are a mean of 48 degrees F. The island is home to seals, reindeer, polar hare, musk ox, wolf, lemming, and many sea birds. Farther north: polar bear, stoat, Arctic fox, and seasick sailors.

Can't wait to see the place.

July 23, Thursday; Labrador Sea.

Sight my first iceberg today. It is gigantic! About the length of a city block. I thought it to be an island. We skirt it widely. The sinking of the *Titanic* is recalled. Some claim icebergs lay 4/5 under water, some say 9/10, yet others say 5/6. I say, "a hell of a lot."

When the brand new ocean liner tore her side open on the side of an iceberg and plunged to the bottom of the ocean some thirty years ago it shook the entire maritime world. After all, the entire world knew the vessel was "unsinkable," but she sank—on her very first voyage!

I hope Maggie steers clear of these ice monsters.

The largest bergs are called "growlers." Bergs come mostly from some twenty glaciers on Greenland's east coast. Each year an estimated 15,000 giant bergs and millions of smaller ones travel south in the Labrador Current to meet the warm Gulf Stream and melt away. In their death throes they create thick fog banks that often hide them from even watchful sailor's eyes.

Arctic owls perch atop [a] few of the bergs that are estimated to be as much as 3,000 years of accumulating packed snow. Bergs come in colors from white to black with blue, brown, and shades of green in between. The giant berg that was struck by the *Titanic* had survived warm water melt to 42 degrees north. Berg colors depend on the sediment and plankton that stick to their bottoms when they were part of earth-scraping glaciers that spawn them.

We accidentally run into a cluster of three whales. One of them slaps our starboard bow with its tail as it begins to sound. *Nanok's* bow is pushed several feet to port by the blow. I am standing on the bow with several others when the impact occurs, and we near lose our footing. Very exciting!

Jonesy adds a bit of humor to the day when he reports to the bridge that a reindeer is floating by. It turns out to be the floating stump of a tree with roots six feet long. One had to admit the roots did resemble antlers. The entire crew take turns laughing at poor Jonesy. He will never live it down.

He stomps about, extra red faced the rest of the day. I'm happy it was not me that that first sighted the object. I might have reported it as a giant with long, tangled red hair.

The finger is numb and lifeless. Pain is awful. I try to forget by trying to work on the cargo net. Tying becket bends are not too difficult.

Days grow astonishingly longer.

July 24, Friday; Labrador Sea.

Drew more heavy duty clothing; a khaki-colored, fleece- lined, 3/4 length parka is great. It fits atop everything else I choose to wear. Its soft, fluffy interior makes it easy to fall asleep in this man-made cocoon. Also received heavy army shoes. Heavy but comfortable and excellent for walking. High-top rubber boots. All great stuff. I make immediate use of most of my allotment. Even my hair shivers when the air is cold.

Most of the world's weather is born north of here; the key to tomorrow's weather in the south. Off Greenland's west coast, even in mid-summer, there is a wide variety of weather from blustering storms to dense, blanketing fog, to bright warm sunshine. The ice cap temperature can vary from 50 degrees to minus 80 degrees. This is understandable since most of the island lies under thick ice.

Not much activity today. Maybe this Greenland Patrol will turn out to be the Greenland Gravy Train.

July 25, Saturday; Labrador Sea.

I awake to see icebergs to the glory! Big as mountains! I feel as though I am watching a travelogue movie. The sea is pitching and tossing something fierce! Up we go to the heavens, then downward we plunge into hell. Surprisingly, I am not seasick, but many are. The *Nanok* tosses and rolls at great angles. I wonder what it would be like for the old girl to be fine-ground between two of these giant bergs.

Grapevine says we should sight Greenland sometime tomorrow. It is supposed to be just over the horizon. Only Maggie has ever seen Greenland before. The thought of seeing honest-to-goodness Eskimos is very exciting. I feel like Gunnbjorn must have. He was the first European known to have sighted the island in about the year 900 A.D. He was a Norwegian blown off his course from Iceland. He chose not to explore the vast unknown country he called "White Shirt Land." [15]

The next European to come along was one "Eric the Red." Eric, like myself, had no choice but to do some exploring. I would guess our reasons differ. In my case, my government chose to send me to the "White Shirt Land." In Eric's case, Iceland's authorities pursued him with a manslaughter charge. To escape the iron arms of the law, he fled and landed in Greenland. He was "Eric the Red (because he had red hair) Thorvaldson." He renamed the White Shirt Land "Greenland," for reasons of his own. My idea is that the man had an enormous sense of humor and decided to call the land Greenland because it was all white ice, and Iceland happens to be all green. He should have named Greenland "springtime" because it presented a free and new life for him.

It is not likely that the redhead ever managed to explore the entire perimeter of his new ice-fouled homeland. An 840,000 square mile island with thousands of fjords would require a fanatically curious explorer to circumnavigate all. The island awaits the arrival of the *"Mayflower Nanok."*

I found nothing that explains how Eric managed to clear himself of Iceland's manslaughter charges. I wonder if a judge could be bribed in those days. It probably will never be known how Eric induced some 500 settlers to follow him from Iceland in 985 A.D. to establish a new colony with himself as leader. He and those followers settled on Greenland's southwest coast. About the year 1000 A.D., Eric's son Leif Ericsson is said to have brought Christianity to the island, the winter in which Eric the Red died. Ruins of his house are at Brattahlid and I hope to see them. [16]

Colonists brought by Eric the Red somehow survived and about the year 1348 A.D. were smitten by pestilence or plague. Few survived this also. These survivors later disappeared under unknown circumstances. There followed many explorations of varying magnitudes by men of many countries. Many are the records of Eskimo kidnappings and disappearing of exploratory ships and men. [17]

In the year 1721, Hans Egede sailed to Greenland with his wife Gertrud. Both were Norwegian and Hans a Lutheran priest. It was his intention to teach the ways of God to Greenlanders and search for signs of the missing settlers and explorers that preceded him. His vessel, the *Good Hope*, arrived on June 3, 1721. A stone house was built on Kangek Island, which he rechristened *Good Hope* after his vessel. He later moved to the mainland and established what became Godthåb, the capitol of Greenland. [18]

Greenlanders learned to love the kindly priest who brought and taught them goodness. His ability to live unaffected by sorcery practiced by some Greenlanders, immortalized him before their eyes. During his fifteen-year stay, Hans defied almost unbearable hardships and periods of near-famine. In 1736, when Gertrud died, he, in bad health, returned to Copenhagen.

Upon returning to good health, he returned to Greenland and served as superintendent to Denmark's mission to Greenland from 1740 to 1747. He retired to the island of Falster to die at age 73. His stone house still stands at Godthåb along with a giant statue of the priest on a hill overlooking the village.

Greenland continued to attract scientists and the curious from all over the world. Some names are legend and would fill volumes. Even America's flying ace Charles A. Lindbergh and his wife Ann Morrow Lindbergh were attracted to the White Shirt Land. Together in 1933 they made numerous flights up and down the west coast and over the ice cap in their seaplane. Eskimos named the plane *Tingmissartoq*, the one that flies like a bird.

I stand my bow watch and daydream this Greenlandic history. Wind is rising. It flings cold spray into my face and returns me to reality. My nostrils are dry and sting with puffs of my frosty vapor that reminds me of dragon's breath. How can anyone write with affection for the frozen wasteland? Soon I will know. It is said that everyone who visits Greenland is compelled to write about it. Perhaps I too may find some unwritten facet to write about. At the moment I long only to lay below in the warmth of my fo'c's'le sack.

July 26, Sunday; Labrador Sea.

Was awakened at 0330 to stand an 0400 to 0800 watch. He that awakened me left before my eyes had opened. I wondered why the ship's engine was silent. We were wallowing in sea swells. On deck the sun shone through slight haze lying low on the sea. It was a most beautiful morning. Cap Mag greets me with a gruff grunt and a nod as I begin my pilot house watch.

About a mile or so to starboard lies Gunnbjorn's "White Shirt Land." It appears as a colossal iceberg, fascinating but foreboding. It blends and fades into the distant horizon. The water's edge appears to be a jagged line of brownish-gray and red that is topped with white; white being the ice cap. It is not near enough to see in much detail. My first sense is similar to Gunnbjorn's. I feel very little desire to land here at the moment.

Cap Maggie says we await the arrival of the *North Star* to guide us into the proper fjord. Maggie and I are the only two awake above deck. All is peaceful and quiet. Air is surprisingly warm so I quietly open a shutter and lean outward to smell fresh sea air. It makes breathing so easy. I study the shapes of many great bergs around us.

The captain is unpredictable. Even in so short a time one learns to sense his moods. He watches one particular iceberg intently. It resembles a ten gallon Stetson cowboy hat except that where the crown should have been pinched with a crease there is a large hole completely through the ice.

There is a growing excitement in Maggie. His eyes shift quickly right and left. I am startled by the sudden sound of his voice: "'ski, wake up Guns." Curiosity bugs me but one does not ask the meaning of an order. But why a gunner at 0400 with no enemy about?

"Guns" does not want to leave the comfort of his sack. He thinks I am joking .

"C'mon, dammit!" I urge him. "The old man wants you in the pilot house on the double!"

"What in hell for!?" he demands.

"I think he wants you to fast-grease his pistol," I say, and duck as Guns swipes at me.

Maggie still stares intently at the berg that is now two points off our port bow. Goose pimples pop up on my arms. Could there be a camouflaged enemy ship or submarine out there that he does not want to lose sight of? I dismiss the thought as impossible for he would have sounded "General Quarters."

Guns Owens arrives several steps behind me. Sleep has left his eyes. He recognizes the expression on Maggie's face and knows I was not joking about summoning him.

"Guns," says the skipper, "this is a good time to see what serious damage our three inch twenty three cannon can do, don't you think so?"

Guns casts a quick, bewildering glance in my direction. I turn away a half-hidden smile from the skipper's view and tried to turn an involuntary laugh into a false cough.

"I guess it is, Cap'n, if you think so, sir," Guns replied.

"See that berg with the hole through it?" Maggie points at the Stetson hat.

"Yesser," Guns nods affirmatively.

"I wonder how it would sound if we split it with a shot?"

"I, I don't know, Captain," stammered Guns.

"We'll find out," says Maggie gruffly.

"Now, sir?"

"For God sake! Yes! Now!!"

"Aye sir," said Guns. "Give me a hand, 'ski, ok?"

"Okay."

The old man stayed in the pilot house while Guns and I dashed forward across the deck and up the ladder to the gun deck. Guns whispered to me that he was not sure if the gun still had recoil fluid in it.

"What if it doesn't?" I ask.

"If it hasn't, we're gonna get blown off this goddam deck!" he says. I helped him load the cannon and slammed the big gun shut.

"Okay," says Guns, "go ahead."

"Go ahead with what?" I ask.

"Fire the fuckin' thing!!" he blurts.

"Up your fantail!" I counter. "You're the gunner's mate, not me!"

Guns quietly and smilingly cursed me. I stepped back as far as I could possibly go without falling off the gun deck. Guns gets himself in position alongside the blunderbuss. The scrubby, rusty old hunk of iron has a curved shoulder brace and Owens fits his shoulder into it. The aiming apparatus is even more archaic. One has to align two separate cross wires with the right eye and also the spot being aimed at. Since the *Nanok* was on a gentle sea-swell roll, I felt that hitting even a battleship would be like trying to hit a running mouse in the ass with a sling shot.

Guns took aim, closed his eyes, held his breath and squeezed the trigger. There was a colossal "Boom!!!" that I am sure encircled the earth and came back to echo and re-echo off bergs and distant mountains. Up off the gun deck went Guns and me propelled by heavy marine plywood decking that had torn loose and popped us about a foot in the air! The "boom" was so loud it seemed as though someone had fired into my left ear through my right ear! Thank God there was recoil fluid in the gun!

In the shortest period of time ever recorded, the deck was filled with the *Nanok*'s entire crew. The faces looked sleepy but the eyes bulged, and every-one wore electrified hair. Maggie thought it was "jolly good fun." He was the only one who seemed to think so. Most of the crew were barefoot and in long underwear. A few were wearing their "Mae West" life jackets. All wanted to know where the enemy was. Guns pointed toward the captain in the pilot house. Dicastro appeared furious but wisely made no comment. Neither did Chiefs McClay or Talledo. Bos'n Robbins just stood muttering, clenching and unclenching his fists. Although there were always signs that Maggie had a weird sense of humor, no one now had any doubt.

My ears rang most of the day. I congratulated Guns. If the berg had been an enemy tank on the gun deck, he still would have scored only a near hit at best. The shot did however strike the giant berg just below its navel and only appeared as a small, black spot. Owens mumbles some profanity under his breath and returns, shaken, to his sack. Deck repair is left to Chips Delaney to worry about. Robbins said that hitting anything from the rolling deck of the *Nanok* would be like "hitting a raging bull in the ass with a pitchfork." Everyone is surprised to learn the gun deck is made of wood.

July 27, Monday; U.S. airbase at Narsarssuaq (BW 1).

Slept through breakfast but Cookie fed me anyway. My finger is festering under the nail. The aching pain is steady. I'm tired of hearing myself complain aloud about it so I cease.

The *North Star* makes her appearance and precedes us up a long fjord nearby. The fjord's jagged shoreline gradually magnifies into giant mountains on both sides of the fjord. As we proceed, the mountains rise higher and higher to breathless heights and from their crests hang giant icicles with peels of ice-cake frosting. The fjord is a narrow, water-filled, bottomless valley between snow and ice-crowned peaks of multi-colored rock. The mountainsides plunge downward at steep angles. Even small beaches are rare, and most have Eskimo villages atop them. Probably because fish and birds and seals abound in the vicinity in abundance enough to sustain life.

There is a majestic splendor to the mountains as we glide between them. Their magnitude fills me with awe, and their silence enhances a sense of loneliness. The *Nanok* is a mouse creeping into a crevasse. As we progress slowly up-fjord, we learn we are bound for Narsarssuak, a command center for the operation of naval patrol planes. There are at least 400 men including Army, Navy, Coast Guard, and civilian construction personnel. It is also the location of a large army base center. The installation's code name is BW 1.

It could not have been located in a more obscure area. I lay below for lunch and when I return topside, BW 1 lays two points off our starboard bow. There is much activity ashore and quite a number of vessels both at anchor mid-fjord and at dockside. There are a loud variety of sounds. There are men shouting orders, racing trucks and jeeps, engines and cranes. In from our portside, low overhead, glides an American Martin bomber in landing pattern. It passes overhead and causes the *Nanok* to vibrate.

When we are tied dockside, I go secretly to the cutter *Comanche* tied just forward of the *Nanok*. [19] My festered finger looks and feels worse than ever. My entire arm hangs almost useless. The *Comanche*'s doctor thinks I come on board with my captain's permission and I don't tell him otherwise.

Native Greenlanders wearing skin clothing and living in sod houses observe the transformation of their country by a massive American military operation. (U.S. Coast Guard Historian's Office.)

He smears the finger with some sort of salve and wraps it in gauze. He advises me to see the army base hospital doctor tomorrow, and that I would probably be hospitalized a few days.

Narsarssuaq turns out to be just a tiny Eskimo settlement on the side of the fjord directly across from BW 1. Both village and air base set in [a] sort of flat-bottomed valley that crosses the fjord at right angles. This low-lying valley may well be a trough worn into the rock by a glacier long forgotten.

I am disappointed to learn that Eskimo villages are out of bounds for everyone except Eskimos. If one does not have specific and official business to conduct, one is not allowed to visit with Greenlanders at their settlements. It should therefore prove difficult to accidentally or intentionally violate native customs as feared by Captain Magnusson. As matter of fact, it would be near impossible for land-based army or navy personnel to even reach any of the villages. There are no roads or even paths that lead from base to villages, or even from village to village or base to base. One would have to cross mountains and glaciers on foot, or travel by boat. Since land-based personnel have no access to boats or ships, they will never experience a one-on-one contact with natives.

But we on board the *Nanok* may. We on board the *Nanok* are privileged in that we have occasion and reason to visit various villages. There is bound to be some sort of fraternization.

Speaking of Eskimos, I am on deck and hear water splashing at the *Nanok*'s side. Peering over the portside gunwale, I get to see my first honest-to-goodness Eskimo face-to-face! We see one another simultaneously. He is startled and taken aback at sight of me, and I am of him! I conclude that he is not an enemy spy for he wears no disguising beard or handlebar moustache. No smoked glasses, or raincoat, nor does he carry a machine gun.

"Ahoy!" I say.

He answers with a smile and forms some sounds deep in his throat. I take it to mean "howdy."

His conveyance is a kayak some fourteen to sixteen feet in length, about two feet in width and perhaps eighteen inches in depth. It tapers fore and aft to pointed bow and stern. Its fuselage is a fragile-looking wooden skeleton covered with tautly-drawn seal skin. The cockpit is circular, precisely amidships, and is barely large enough to accommodate one person. It has a flexible, collapsible collar of the same type skin. A most uncomfortable appearing craft. Its pilot must wriggle into it as perhaps a woman might wriggle into a girdle. He must sit flat with his legs stretched straight forward, unbent. In a very short time the legs must become numb. Once inside the cockpit, its skin collar is raised and drawn tight around the passenger's waist with drawstrings, making the vessel watertight. Also, the passenger wears a waterproofed sealskin jumper that tucks into the cockpit's collar before it is tightened around the waist. The jumper has an attached hood that is drawn snugly around the neck with drawstrings. Another cord vertically encircles the entire face. Yet another cord horizontally encircles the forehead level of the head. The passenger thus becomes totally waterproofed within a sealskin cocoon.

My visitor laid aside his long, slender paddle that had a flat blade at each end and untied his cockpit collar. From somewhere inside his cramped quarters he withdrew a small codfish and held it up for my approval. I smiled and nodded approvingly. "Nice fish," I said, doubtful that he understood. He made a motion toward his mouth and away, and back to his mouth and away again. For a moment I thought he was trying to let me know the fish is good to eat. Then I recognize an old and common American habit. He slaps at his heart as if he is searching for something. Of course! He is trying to let me know that his inner blouse pocket is empty of cigarettes. Motioning the fish back and forth, to and away from his mouth, inhaling and exhaling, was his way of demonstrating the act of cigarette smoking! Damned clever of him.

To verify whether I was correct in my assumption, I pulled out a pack of smokes. I shook a cigarette part-way out of the pack and extended the pack toward the visitor. His golden-tan, moon face glowed when he saw the butts. Instead of taking one as is our custom, he grasped the entire pack and pulled it out of my hand and replaced it with the codfish!

"Hey!" I began, but away he went, bound for the village across the fjord. He paddled swiftly without a backward glance.

Standing in line with the rippled wake of the small vessel, I wondered if this was Greenlandic custom. There was no doubt I had been "taken" by this iceberg carpetbagger. He knew I was unable to pursue him. My spontaneous anger turns into laughter. No longer must I wonder what I may teach these uneducated natives, but what they will teach me. In the future I will be wary of welcoming committees.

The codfish has seen better days and emits an unpleasant odor. Something tells me it had been buried under rocks for some time to season. It (supposedly) then would become a delicacy. I've heard that Greenlanders did this with birds, but fish?! I bury it a second time, in the fjord. End of lesson one.

July 28, Tuesday; Narsarssuaq (BW 1).

Ashore for the first time except for my short walk on the dock to see the *Comanche*'s doctor. The base is very large in area including the air field. I stopped at an army recreation building and watched a few games of good old billiards and listen to a few phonograph records.

The base army doctor told me to keep my finger dry and clean and return in two days. He cleaned and rewrapped the finger and told me that if no healing is visible by the time I see him again, several finger joints may have to be amputated.

The thought of amputation infuriates me! I swear aloud at Dicastro's clumsiness at the winch and his refusal to allow me proper medical attention. The doctor questioned me about how the finger was injured. I told him the entire story. He thinks it incredible! He said he intended to make the incident known to Captain Magnusson. I ask him not to do so, that Dicastro would surely seek revenge. Doc said it was his duty to do so.

On my long walk back to the *Nanok* I experience another aggravation. Someone in supply must have goofed. Every man destined for Greenland duty should have been issued a mosquito net and a pith helmet! I wore none at the time. A small cloud of swarming darkness came swiftly toward me. The cloud consisted of thousands if not millions of tiny, pinhead-sized flies! They circled my head, landed on my eye balls, and entered my ears and nostrils. My open mouth became their garage. I swallowed many and others managed to crawl between teeth and inner cheeks. I ran! They follow! Thank heaven the little bastards did not bite. I spat up many and gag on others.

The doctor must have phoned Maggie. As I boarded the *Nanok*, the skipper summoned me to his private quarters and questioned me at length. Reluctantly I relate to him the entire story in detail. How the injury occurred and of Dicastro's refusal to allow me to receive proper medical attention except for the visit he knew about.

Skipper was infuriated! I lie and tell him that I harbor no ill feelings and wish the incident to be forgotten. Dicastro's wrath alone did not scare me as much as knowing the dirty bastard would take out his anger at all of the crew. Maggie chooses not to forget.

From inside the cabin closet he brought out a one gallon, flat, paint thinner can. He then poured out a half cup of green liquid that foams like soap. It turns out to be his own home-made cure-all medicine made from seaweed. He wrapped my finger in gauze and ordered me to "soak your finger in this." I protest: "But the doctor said I should just keep the finger clean and dry!" Impatiently he thrusts my finger deep into the green stuff.

"This stuff is good for everything," says the skipper, "even dandruff."

I wondered if he was not joking about the dandruff but he looks serious. He gave me a supply of the stuff and tells me to dip my finger into it whenever the gauze appears to be drying. I fear for the finger but have much faith in the captain so I accepted his recommendation. Besides, when Dicastro finds out I spilled the beans about him, I'm gonna need the skipper on my side.

As I leave the pilot house, he orders me to summon Dicastro and I do so. Dicastro orders me to accompany him but the skipper orders Dicastro to come into his cabin alone. The hatch is slammed shut. I hear Maggie begin shouting half in Norwegian and half in accented English. I make tracks beating it out of the area.

Truck drivers here get a whopping $1.56 per hour and all of the overtime they can handle! At Dodge Brothers Motor Car Company, I was receiving less than half that amount. In addition, all civilian workers receive free room and board. In return, the men must sign work contracts for periods of six months at a time. If, however, the worker breaks contract and quits work before the contract's termination date, his pay ceases immediately. Too, the company begins charging him an exorbitant price for food and lodgings. Those who quit early are informed that as soon as a berth on a ship returning to the states becomes available, the worker can leave. Coincidentally, or by design, the available berths fail to materialize. The worker's food and lodging bill skyrockets. The generous company then offers the worker an easy way out of the debt. If the worker would change his mind and finish his stint, his food and lodging debt would be forgiven. Not too many men who quit really go home.

July 29, Wednesday; BW 1.

Unbelievable but true! The pain is gone from my finger overnight! The pain has been with me for so long that I miss it. When I told Maggie about this minor miracle he said: "What did you expect? The finger to fall off?" He gave me another supply of the green stuff in a soup bowl. Stan says it looks like Cookie's fish chowder. Clark growls at him.

Good lord! What have I caused?! Already Dicastro is on a rampage! No one is excluded from his anger! It might have been better to have lost the damn finger. What the hell! This is the *Nanok*, not the *Bounty*! It seems the world always has more than enough pricks to go around!

Several of us walk to the civilians' PX. I feel like a pregnant mom in want of a chocolate bar and a coke. We cannot purchase anything at the post exchange. They do not accept cash, only coupons in ten dollar value booklets that are issued only to the civilian personnel by their employer. The PX is owned and operated by civilians. We learn civilian workers receive no cash wages in Greenland. It is either deposited stateside in a bank of their choice, or sent directly to next of kin, or both. Workers only receive the ten dollar value coupon booklets that are used to purchase their needs and wants.

Abe Brill says the PX stocks everything but lace panties.

"Why? Do you need some?" ask Chips.

Abe's face reddens. "Shit no!" he growls.

"They'd look great on your chubby little tush," Chips teases.

"Piss on you! Piss on all you guys!" says Brill as he stomps off.

"If they don't get paid cash here, where do all the crap and card game greenbacks come from?" I want to know. Fairbanks says many of the guys write home and receive cash in the mail. Besides gambling, cash is only used to pay for favors such as having someone do your chores. There is an army

PX here too, of course, but no one wants to tell us where. Most likely the army yard birds don't want sailors buying up all their goodies. We are told only our skipper is allowed to make army PX purchases. Even then, with limitations. What a crock of shit! The large C.G. and Navy vessels carry their own supplies but shit pots the size of *Nanok* do not. Because of space limitation?

Several of us stand in a group outside the civvy PX with hats-in-hand and beggar looks on our faces. We plead with all who enter to buy us a goodie or two. I want a bar of something sweet so badly I damn near drool watching civilians gobbling up the stuff as they walk by. We offer two and three dollars for a candy bar with no takers. We do not excel as pan handlers so we give up. Our lesson is that even the smallest luxury is gonna be hard to come by.

Each civvy is allowed to purchase two cans of beer per day. Some save them until they accumulate ten cans or so, then sell them for as much as $25 cash. I like to use a tiny bit of petroleum jelly to control my dry unruly hair instead of the more popular hair oil. The perfume odor of hair oil sickens me. Before leaving the PX, I make one more attempt to acquire a jar of the jelly. The civilian I ask is no gentleman. He finds it hilariously amusing to find a sailor in such dire need of a "jar of grease," as he called it. He implies I need the stuff for a variety of erotic sex purposes. I find his comments hilariously amusing also, and laugh along with him, until I learn he does not jest. There is only one way I know of to convince him that he is wrong. Since only my right fist is usable, I use it, and plant it on a laughing chin. He lay convinced, spread-eagled on the ground against the side of the building. His upper teeth have bitten through the flesh of two of my knuckles. I ask him if he still thinks his sex stories are true, but he doesn't answer. Several other civilians hurry out of the PX and demand to know who struck their buddy. My bleeding knuckles are thrust into my dungaree pocket and I say I never saw the culprit. Giant Petrenko steps to my side. He wears a fiendish grin and is spoiling for some exercise. Again I ask the comedian if he knows who struck him. Still no answer. Pete and I watch the comedian's friends half carry the guy off.

Before returning to the *Nanok*, we visit the paymaster. He is quartered in a corrugated sheet metal Quonset hut. We enter the front's only door. A few steps indoors is a waist-high railing that stretches from one side of the hut to the other. There is a small swinging gate for employees to enter. Just beyond the railing sits the paymaster at his desk. There are several other occupied desks also. Beyond the desks are bundles of American currency.

Two views of the U.S. Coast Guard cutter *Natsek* (WYP-170), leaving Boston in June, 1942. It would never return from its wartime journey to Greenland. (U.S. Coast Guard Historian's Office.)

(Later I would learn it was all one dollar bills, brand new.) The money is stacked from floor to near roof height. The bundles are about one foot square. Each bundle is sandwiched between thin wooden boards and bound with wire. In all my life I have never seen or been so near to such great amount of cash. It was all for service men, none for the civilians.

Mice must have gotten a greater share of the money than we did. Each of us received a small stack of America's finest greenery and carried it back to the *Nanok*. Jonesy sings, "I never thought I'd ever see a green thing lovelier than a tree." On board ship our small money bundles seem somewhat larger than when they were still on a stack in the hut.

The *Natsek* is here, tied up just astern of the *Nanok*. A half dozen of us board her and a red-hot crap game begins. The *Natsek* crew has gobs of money and we begin to separate them from it. Chet Benash and Norm White just look on. Before too long, they too are shouting "seven-come-eleven!"

The *Natsek*'s skipper La Farge is nowhere about. [20]

After several hours all hands experience hunger pains and the game ends. *Nanok*'s crew damn near cleaned out *Natsek*'s bucks. We are considerably wealthier. I hope the *Natsek*'s losses do not embitter its crew against us. Bob Repucci and Harry Baram are heavy losers but manage to smile. We are to work side by side with the *Natsek* quite often. Nice bunch of swab jockeys. It would not be the best of situations if we started out disliking one another.

Latest rumors are that we may be assigned patrol duty in Davis Strait. Hope not, sounds as dull and monotonous as my *Sea Cloud* weather patrol duty.

July30, Thursday; BW 1.

Went to see movie at army recreation hall with Chips Delaney. Saw *The Bugle Calls* with Wallace Beery. Chips is an excellent ship's carpenter and a sometimes member of the fo'c's'le choral (?) group. The guy is jovial and raucous, sometimes a tenor and sometimes half-assed baritone. Depending on his mood, I guess. He hails from New Jersey which he insists should be the capital of the United States. His body is thin with many protruding bones the same as his impish, ever-grinning face. After the movie, he and I walk a gravel road back to the *Nanok*. As we walk we clown around a bit. Chips lets out a loud, open-mouthed laugh and busts loose a body-shaking sneeze in the middle of it. An artificial tooth pops out of his mouth and lands somewhere amongst the road-gravel pebbles, or so he says. I had known he had lost most of his upper front teeth when accidentally hit by a ball bat when acting as a catcher in a childhood sandlot ball game. He had lost a large portion of the jaw-bone as well. As we searched for the tooth, I was never convinced that the search was anything more than one of his jokes. He showed a gap where the tooth had been, but it could be a tooth he could remove and replace at will. Since pebbles and an artificial tooth look similar, I was shocked when I found the tooth after an hour's search. Delaney grinned in toothless gratitude.

Gosh darn these endless days! I don't know whether to go to bed or to do my laundry. Daylight lingers around the clock! What a better way to end the day than opening a letter from sweet Lucy. Also received two postcards from Peggy Fitz. I no longer answer Peg's mail because of guilt feelings.

July 31, Friday; BW 1.

Maggie has told everyone about how pissed-off he is with Dicastro's antics and how he refused me proper medical attention. He mentions to McClay and Robbins that he'll "fix that mattress-makin' muskrat!"

Had 4 to 8 a.m. [watch] then spent the rest of the day as galley punk.

Oh happy, happy, happy day! Rumors are that Dicastro is about to walk the plank! Whoopee! Cookie Clark says if the rumor proves true, he will bake us the biggest friggin' cake we ever saw. There is no doubt the skipper wants Dicastro to shove off. The *Nanok* may still prove to be heaven.

Finger feels good dipped periodically in Maggie's *au jus*. No more red streaks up the arm or any pain in it. Dicastro has opened up all his meanest valves.

Eskimos appear in kayaks from time to time. They trade hand-made trinkets for candy, cigarettes, and for much desired "chew-gum." They are pleasant, happy people with concrete smiles that never disappear. We know naught of their customs and the why and wherefore of some of the things they do. We merely observe and try to interpret, and we do—I think—a fairly good job of it.

I would like to tell them how very lonely their land and environment makes me feel. I would like to ask them how they manage to tolerate loneliness if indeed they do. Perhaps I should keep my mouth shut and allow these happy people to remain happy. I yearn for the sight of trees and other greenery. Thus far all I have seen are ground-hugging, moss-looking carpeting in here and there patches.

Maggie says every village has its own overseer. They are called "governors." Wonder when we will get to see and meet one.

August

Cold weather is my enemy, but I must acknowledge a sense of gratitude for being stationed in an area relatively safe from enemy forces. While I complain of cold weather and petty discomforts, thousands of American soldiers in warmer climates are dying. I experience a feeling of guilt. We are away from the States slightly more than a month and already I am impatient to return. Time moves slowly and lies heavily on my morale. We are not busy enough. There is too much time to think and to feel sorry for oneself. Idleness brings on homesickness. I feel sure that World War II will go on forever.

August 1, Saturday; BW 1.

The U.S.C.G. icebreaker *Escanaba* arrives. Last time I saw and boarded her was on Michigan's northeast coast where she was known as a C.G. prison ship. Dexter, Jordan, Roach, Robbins, Elmer, and I go on board for a visit. Very few familiar faces on board so the visit was brief. [21]

Hope our duty doesn't amount to just lying here throughout the entire war. We've already been here five rather slow-moving days. The crew is obviously anxious to begin doing whatever it is we were sent here to do. It is boring and monotonous to chip away at loose paint, add red lead and Coast Guard gray paint.

Down fjord nearby we visit a scuttled foreign ship lying on the shore rocks. Very creepy. Cups and dishes were still on tables. Crew clothing and other personal belongings were left as if the crew were still on board somewhere. Abandonment was obviously hurried for I found one shoe in a compartment and the other was nowhere about. Comer suggests that the one shoe probably belonged to Peg Leg Pete or Long John Silver. We help ourselves to whatever we want to. Maggie says it is unlawful to take anything from this supposedly old Norwegian vessel, yet he leaves carrying a large sack of plunder. I find a beautiful set of clocks in a compartmented, felt-lined oak case, a solid silver-looking ship's bell about ten inches high, some exquisite fishing gear, sheath knife, fur-lined parka, binoculars, and a host of other goodies. Most returned to the *Nanok* loaded down. A few, including Jordan, chose to take nothing. Talledo, who carried off many articles, says the scuttled ship's crew will never get to see their ship again. The local inhabitants will strip it of everything of value.

It is rumored the ship's crew had mutinied. Other rumors are that a submarine pursued it, and rather than surrender, its skipper chose to scuttle it. He then surrendered himself and the crew to the enemy submarine commander. Whatever had taken place we would never know for sure. A variety of other tales were told but we would never even learn the vessel's true identity.

Dicastro growls at all of us. I hope the bastard will be gone as soon as the skipper finds a toilet to drown him in.

August 2, Sunday; BW 1.

Still awaiting orders from somewhere. Hope they are not from Paul Revere.

Shook Cookie out of his sack at 0500 but he fell back to sleep until 0730. Result, he faced the wrath of Chief Talledo. When Talledo finished, Dicastro took a turn at him. Clark grinned because he was already restricted and cannot leave the ship.

"What else can the bastard do to me?" asks Clark. "If the son of a bitch wants to keep eating, he'd better leave me the hell alone!" But Clark has been ordered to arise at 0300 from now on.

Dicastro is busy finding mean, dirty little things for me to do. Woe!

John "Balboa" Goncalves has sprouted a beautiful beard and moustache. Hair on his knuckle-head has grown fast and is shoulder length. John is of Portuguese decent and bears a striking resemblance to the Italian aviator Italo Balbo and is nicknamed after him. Someone added the "a" so we call him Balboa instead of Balbo. Very few men look good with a beard and moustache. Johnny is one of the few. He has also the powerfully impressing look of Benito Mussolini.

Balboa gives me a bald-head haircut. My entire head looks like something someone pulled out of the rear end of a very sick whale. Nick Vacar says he has seen better heads on a glass of beer. Dicastro says I look like shit. One of his close relatives, I suppose. McClay just grins like a coon-dog eatin' crap. Talledo has a laughing fit and is unable to voice his compliment.

Spoke to the skipper about my rating elevation from seaman to cox-swain. His "we'll see, we'll see" makes me feel my promotion prospects are dimming. I suspect that Maggie, Talledo, and Dicastro are unable to reach an agreement about promoting me.

Small luxuries are still hard to come by.

August 3, Monday; BW 1.

Great day in the morning! We are getting rid of Dicastro!! Skipper told Talledo that Dicastro is being kicked off the *Nanok* for numerous reasons, primarily for refusing a crew member proper medical attention, [but also] because he is ill-tempered, antagonistic, has aggravated every member of the crew, and deliberately acts upon orders as slowly as he possibly can. And probably about six dozen reasons equally as acceptable.

A number of the crew are on deck and are busy at work. Secretly we are there to witness this hateful person's departure. He has dragged his gear up out of his bird-nest quarters and down onto the deck just forward of the pilot house. He shouted—can you believe it!?—for me to carry his gear ashore! I turn my back on him and pretend not to have heard. Next, he calls to Balboa for help. Johnny spit down onto the deck in a demonstration of contempt and turned his back also. Dicastro shouted to Jonesy, but the skipper stuck his head out of [the] pilot house and bellowed, "Mister Dicastro, get off the ship, we are about to shove off!"

Dicastro was scheduled to serve on board the cutter *Blue Bird* which was tied just forward of the *Nanok*. [22] The *Blue Bird*'s stern [is] just forward of *Nanok*'s bow, but its deck [is] high above the *Nanok*. Many of the *Blue Bird*'s crew line her stern rail. They have heard of Dicastro's reputation and look on in amusement. Dicastro looked up at two of the men and ordered them to come on board for his gear. As if smitten by a giant hand, they turn their backs in unison, much like a chorus line. Again Maggie orders Dicastro to leave the *Nanok*. His voice sounds like a genuine order rather than a request. Without further ado, Dicastro picks up several of his bags and carries them onto the dock. Then he scrambled back on board, and in less than a few minutes he had all his belongings ashore. His face was purple with rage.

In exchange for Dicastro, we take on board a young ensign named Oscar Dillon. Oscar seemed to be a friendly, intelligent young man, looking much like a puffy-cheeked college freshman. We were told that Maggie thought highly of Dicastro's replacement and that was good enough for the crew. Oscar wears a brush-cut of hair. He is of medium build. His complexion is quite dark, smooth and flawless. I could see no whiskers whatsoever.

The first thing Oscar does is confiscate all cameras and lock them in the ship's safe. I hoped this was not a sample of his discipline. I had hoped to take many photographs. [23]

We leave BW 1 at last!

The *Nanok* strikes many small ice bergs and one quite large one. I lay in my sack daydreaming, idly scanning the overhead. We strike what surely was a sizeable berg because the ten inch square, overhead timber split through its entire length with a loud, tearing sound!

As usual, I turn to lay on my side, facing the outer skin of the ship and secretly fill in my diary entry. I feel a bit homesick, anxious for mail and missing the nearness of my wife. Memory of her remains ever-fresh, exciting, and damnably disturbing to my sleep. Her presence, even in dreams, is welcome.

The *Nanok* is expected to cross the Arctic Circle soon. The Circle, at latitude 66°33´N, circumscribes the frigid zone within which the north experiences twenty-four hours of sunlight after about June 21, and twenty-four hours of darkness after about December 22. Some of the crew wanted to get humorous certificate blanks on which to record the event. The skipper would not permit "such foolishness" and forbade the crew to bring any on board. The old grouch! The certificates are just for fun and supposedly have the blessings of King Boreas (whoever that is supposed to be). The document is awarded to initiate its recipient into the "Royal Order of Rugged Ice Worms," and "The Ancient Order of the Icebergs."

August 4, Tuesday; BW 1.

Been to Arsuk, Ivigtut, Julianehåb and several other villages, the largest being Julianehåb. [24] It is the largest by far and yet it can be traversed by foot in no more than twenty minutes. It consists of approximately fifteen brightly-painted wooden-frame houses. They are painted mostly in combinations of red with white trim, blue with red trim, and green with blue trim. The houses lay scattered across the gently-sloping, rocky hillside. Scattered between the houses are Eskimo huts. These are made of rocks, earth, scavenged old packing crate boards, pieces of tin, and many unrecognizable materials, [all] spackle-patched with chunks of moss. Along the lower edges of the village, close to water's shore are several storage buildings and workshops. There are no roads. There are no visible vehicles except small, man-powered pull-along wagons. Footpaths cross one another like spider webs.

The other villages are even smaller and less populated. We make deliveries to each of them, mostly medicines, clothing, and food stuffs.

In a quiet fjord we come across three U.S. Army officials in a broken down outboard motor boat. We take all of them on board. They are radio personnel. We drop them off at Julianehåb and return to BW 1.

The first Army WAAC nurses arrive by ship. One would think six Lady Godivas were landing. Every off-duty soldier, sailor, and civilian gathered at the dock to greet them. When I inquired about the crowd at dockside, someone jokingly said President Roosevelt [had] arrived on a tour of inspection. Gullible me, I believed it and joined the welcoming committee. I feel sure that Mister Roosevelt never enjoyed a more enthusiastic welcome than did the six blushing females. Officers found it near impossible to drag men from under the steep rising gangplank that the ladies were descending. They are average-looking women, but at the moment they were the most beautiful creatures the Lord ever created in heaven!! It was, without a doubt, their finest hour ever!! Catcalls and wolf whistles were deafening! With much difficulty two jeeps plowed slowly through the struggling mass of men. Scent of perfume and cosmetics hung in the air like the clouds of mosquitoes do. Traces of peek-a-boo lace are seen on several of the women and I feared a riot would begin! There are dozens of marriage prospects among the sea of lewdly grinning men. Base morale must have risen two hundred percent in a matter of minutes.

Almost immediately the base is stricken with a rash of minor pains and injuries. Most are treated with a cup of double strength Epsom salts. One soldier is fortunate enough to rupture his appendix. He is the only new patient to be admitted to the hospital this day. As suddenly as the plague began, it was eradicated.

August 5, Wednesday; At sea.

Arrival of the nurses prompted many men to write home for cheesecake photos of their sweethearts or wives.

We leave BW 1 once again and heave-to outside of an unnamed fjord and wallow in a heavy ground swell. We await a pilot launch to guide us to airbase Sondrestromfjord on a fjord of the same name. It is also known as BW 8, and lies above the Arctic Circle. As we await the launch, Maggie suggests we fish for fresh cod to take to BW 8 for they get no fresh fish from elsewhere.

Maggie proves to be an excellent fisherman. He uses 21-thread line and seven silver hooks, each about seven inches long. They are spaced some two feet apart and are baited with pork fat.

"Oops!," he says, "I've got one!" A bit more jiggling of his line, then,

"Oops! I've got two!," then, "Oops, I've got three! Oops! Four" until "Oops!" five, six, and seven. When he retrieves his line, sure enough, he has hooked seven codfish ranging from two to four feet in length!

I use the same kind of line and bait but only one hook. I never receive the slightest nibble, yet whenever I pull in my line to check my bait, I always find a giant cod hanging on to that single hook! I make it a habit to check my bait often, and regardless of how often I check, I have snagged yet another cod. They do not bite or yank. They do not fight. They are no fun to catch whatsoever. I've fished Lexington, Michigan's Great Lakes perch and received more battle than from these dead-assed cod.

As I pull them upward from an ideal forty fathoms (120 feet), something inside their body ruptures as the water pressure outside the body is lessened. They are more dead than alive by the time they reach the water's surface. Lifting the heavy beasts on board is a monumental chore.

Very soon we wade in fish several feet deep across the deck. The *Nanok* will smell her own self again. We filet the fish. Maggie cuts out their "cheeks" and "tongues." Both resemble scallops. Both are most tender and delicious. We have codfish chowder in the evening. Great!

Jonesy complains that I stand better watches than he.

August 6, Thursday; At sea.

Still awaiting pilot launch. Hope someone has told them we are here. They must be coming from Timbukthree or else they have lost their paddles.

Eating much more of the fish we caught yesterday. Finger feels fine but the blackened nail is about to fall off. Hair is growing back fast. Goncalves wants to clip me again. Forget it!

Dreams, Connors, Jordan, Roach, and Jones take turns crying to me about loneliness. Acute homesickness has infected us like the plague. I feel like my parish priest in his confessional. Makes me wonder, where does a priest go to find sympathetic ears?

I came across Abe Brill sitting on the crapper aft of the engine room, crying as hard as if his heart would break. As he comes out of the tiny cubicle, I give him a hug on impulse and he seemed to appreciate it. The thought crosses my mind that it is best none of the crew see me hugging Abe. Abe is the only one whose homesickness affects me. He erroneously feels that none of the crew likes him because of his frequent and lengthy seasickness spells. The moment the anchor chain rattles, Abe becomes nauseous. He remains that way until he hears the chain rattle again.

Small, improvised Arctic cutters were "Iceberg" Smith's solution to a defensive gap that stretched from Boston to Greenland. U.S. Coast Guard cutter *Aklak* (WYP-168). (U.S. Coast Guard Historian's Office.)

Abe is of medium height and somewhat overweight. For the most part, his dark eyes look downward, as if in apology for his existence. He walks in the somewhat furtive way a dog might when stones are being thrown at him. His shoulders hunch forward in unnecessary defense. The only reason he has ever upset me is because he too often kowtows to people. Of course some of the crew dislike him, but we all share various degrees of dislike toward people for one stupid reason or another. I prefer to see the guy walking straight up, smiling, and apologetic for nothing. [But] seasickness has taken its toll. Abe's face is gaunt and pale. His normally deep-set eyes are almost invisible in black, cavernous sockets.

I believe seasickness is uncontrollable and is nothing to be ashamed of. My quarters are forward and Abe's are aft, so I do not know whether Abe fails his engine room duties. I never hear complaints in this regard. Petrenko attempts to be amusing. He says Abe is a "gefilte fish fried in bacon grease."

Homesickness strikes me too today. I could use more mail and less crew tears.

August 7, Friday; BW 8.

A U.S. Navy launch arrives at last! Commanded by Captain Nemo no doubt. A pilot comes on board and guides the *Nanok* into Sondrestromfjord.

We cross the Arctic Circle at 1800 in latitude 66°33′ North and 55°0′30″ West while I am on bow watch. Most of the crew is on deck to experience the occasion. There are flags anchored on both sides of the fjord, marking precisely the invisible line of the Arctic Circle. The day is beautiful, sunny, and mildly cool.

Dark, multi-colored shades dress the high-rise mountains on both sides of the fjord. In some areas the mountain tops cannot be seen because they slope backward, inland. On our portside, ravine-creased mountainsides create giant, vertical shadows the sun does not penetrate. I have been trying to raise a moustache. Three weeks have gone by and I have hardly enough lip-fuzz to shape with a razor.

Bos'n Robbins asks, "What's that on your upper lip?"

"You could never guess," say I. "It is a moustache."

"I thought it was something crawling up into your nose," he says seriously. He comes over for a closer look. "By damn!," he grins, "It is a moustachio!"

I am irritated. "Wise guy!" I throw at him. "You just don't like moustaches," I say.

"Well, I'll tell ya," continues Robbie. "I wouldn't cultivate anything around my mouth that grows wild around my ass!"

That does it! I shave the fuzz off.

Since Maggie ordered there to be no celebration when we cross the Arctic Circle, none was planned by the crew. But after we complete the actual crossing, the skipper distributes individual certificates to each of the crew. That lovable old bastard! It was his private secret and he would not be denied the pleasure of surprising us. It was a wonderfully dirty trick! He must have spent many hours embellishing each document with fancy scroll work. As each of us was individually summoned to the bridge, the old man in fiendish glee would creep up from behind and shear us as bald as sheep! He didn't have much of a job on my short wool. The shearing is traditional, I'm told.

Spirits are boosted! An air of festivity prevailed. Clark baked a beautiful row of pies and [we had] tasty jello, and great coffee and triple portions of laughter, camaraderie, and singing.

August 8, Saturday; BW 8.

The *Nanok* is tied to the landing.

I go ashore to the army hospital to have my finger x-rayed. The bone still appears to be separated but is knitting.

This base airport lies eight miles from the base's center so we will not get to see it. We go to see a movie in the army recreation hall but are recalled to the *Nanok*. She has to be moved. Her space is needed to dock a large incoming freighter. On the way back we meet a stranded Coast Guardsman whose ship simply left without him. This occasionally happens when men do not return to their ship on time. No one is important enough to have a ship await his choice of time to return. Either his ship will have occasion to return, or some other vessel or plane that will some time rendezvous with his vessel may take him along. However he gets back to his ship, he can be sure never to step ashore in Greenland again.

We move the *Nanok* to center of [the] fjord and drop hook. BW 8 is very large. There are many tons of soldiers and construction. First in command here is Colonel Bernt Balchen who had once been chief pilot for Admiral Byrd in the Antarctic. [25]

August 9, Sunday; BW 8.

Because of my 0400 to 0800 watch, I cannot attend church ashore.

Carroll "Judas Priest" or "Jen" is the D'Artagnan of the *Nanok*. Rather than use profanity, Jenner uses the expression "Judas Priest!" Therefore, many refer to him as "Judas Priest." Others refer to him as "Jen" or "Jenner." Jen is by far the most handsome swab-jockey on board as well as a super radioman 2/c. He is in the six-foot-tall range and proportioned perfectly. With dark beard and moustache, he strongly resembles D'Artagnan of *Three Musketeers* fame. At one time two excited nurses point him out and ask me for his name. Of course I tell them it is D'Artagnan. Both sigh ecstatically.

Jen, I, and others go ashore in [the] afternoon to see *Ride 'em Cowboy*, a very bad Abbott and Costello movie. Then back to the *Nanok* for a quartet, Jen, Roach, Chips, and me. I particularly enjoy the occasions when Macon Leroy Roach joins the group I happen to be singing in. Roach is an officer's steward and the only Negro on board. If his color is different, no one seems to notice. He is golden brown, very handsome, and meticulously groomed, too much so. He constantly frets that his hair needs trimming. He often stands for long periods of time, scissor-snipping at imaginary, out-of-place hairs. His normal duty is to serve officers only. His personal attention seems to embarrass Maggie. He and Oscar Dillon rarely take advantage of Roach's special services. Instead, both officers choose to dine with the crew most of the time. Roach, for want of enough to occupy his time, assists Cookie Clark.

Macon is blessed with a beautifully plaintive voice, especially suited to the singing of spirituals, many of which he teaches us. When he is of mood, his singing comes from the depth of his soul. His voice carries deep emotion. I am easily moved by his sincerity and beautiful words. His singing transports me to peaceful, far away places. There is almost the scent of honeysuckle and mint in his voice.

August 10, Monday; BW 8.

I have to do some mess punk duty along with my regular watches.

This army canteen is good to us. I have a couple of cans of beer and get my cigarettes for forty cents per carton. I smoke them until they are so tiny they burn my fingers. Maggie threatens to abolish the seastores because the crew is buying so much ashore. I think the canteen ashore just happens to have a surplus. I took a turn at punching the heavy bag at the canteen's gym, had a soda-pop, and wrote a few letters.

Sullivan Jones says Maggie has promised him a coxswain's rating. How can that be?! He is still a seaman 2/c and must first become a seaman 1/c! I believe he is kidding me. I am, however, disturbed because Maggie has not said the same to me and I believe I have already earned the rating. In June, Maggie led me to believe the rating was on the way and I would be getting it "soon." I've been waiting to sew a coxswain's "crow" on my right sleeve ever since. I felt the need to verify my status so I broach the subject with Maggie once again.

He retreats, saying, "It takes time and much experience to warrant a petty officer's rating. And there is plenty of time and opportunity to demonstrate seamanship ability if one has it."

I cannot believe I heard him correctly! Something seems to have changed drastically! He says not a thing about Jones. I wonder if Mister Dillon or Talledo may have spoken in disfavor of me? Too, I wonder how Jonesy found time to have proven coxswain capabilities?

This is all a devastating blow to me. Maggie not only sounds discouraging, he also implies that I am incapable!

Nanok is stuffed with cargo and ready to shove off, but when? To where?

And for how long? Indications are that we will head up the east coast of Eskimo land. Oh well.

August 11, Tuesday; BW 8.

I stand the 0400 to 0800 watch alone. I let Jonesy sleep. Maybe because I'm too jealous to speak with him about the possible forthcoming promotion. I am also doing mess punk duty again.

Elmer Comer took my 1600 to 2000 watch, allowing me to go ashore with Fairbanks, Delaney, Vacar, and Robbins. Got a few beers from a friendly civilian and paid for a few myself. We saw the same damned movie we'd seen at BW 1, *The Bugle Sounds*. Back on board ship we sing "Stormy Weather."

August 12, Wednesday; BW 8.

Chipped and painted all day. Stan and Jones were promoted to seamen 1/c today. Sully must have been told about this promotion at the time the skipper spoke to him about the coxs'n rating the other day. I am happy for these two guys, but at the same time I feel depressed and perhaps somewhat sorry for myself.

I begin sewing a large, canvas ditty bag for Chief McClay.

I was awkward. Someone left a coil of heavy line lying on deck. As I walked along, I was looking ashore and stumbled into the pile of manila spaghetti. Pitching forward, I fell and sunk my front, upper teeth into the wooden gunwale. I could have bitten off my lip. Most embarrassing! Instant headache! No one saw me, thank goodness.

Scuttlebutt is that American forces have landed in the Solomon Islands.

August 13, Thursday; BW 8.

Painting the boom and winch.

Shifted position several times during the day. We were supposed to shove off at noon.

Went on board the U.S.C.G. sea-going tug *Arundel* to see its much talked-about super sanitary engine room. [26] Even though I saw it with my own eyes, I found it difficult to believe. The engine room officer must be some sort of fanatic I thought. It is said one can sleep in the bilges in a dress-white uniform without picking up a smudge of dirt. I believe it now.

Steel deck plates glistened as if chrome-plated. Handrail rods and stanchions glow as polished silver with a watchmaker's finish. All brass has been made to gleam like gold. Paintwork appeared to have been washed down hourly. There was no dust whatsoever. In only one obscure area was there a single copper pipe fitting that defied being sealed tight. It dripped one drop of oil every one minute and forty-seven seconds. To catch the drips, there was a highly polished, solid copper, hand-made pan.

As I had entered this sanctum sanctorum, I was instructed to remove my shoes and put on a pair of rubber soled sneakers. After my tour, I hastened to put on my shoes and leave the premises. Had I not seen the engine room with my own eyes, no one could have convinced me that such a spectacle could exist. Before leaving the *Arundel*, I had coffee with the cook. He does not introduce himself to me. Instead, he burdens me with his homesickness and some rubs off on me. I hurry back to the ugly duckling *Nanok*.

Cookie Clark amuses himself by singing two songs. Neither contains the correct lyrics.

August 14, Friday; BW 8.

Early in a.m., we leave BW 8 and come across a scuttled foreign freighter being salvaged by the American vessel *Iris*. We meet Knute, the *Iris'* 1st mate and drink a bottle of his aquavit (phooie!) and about a case of his beer. We are assisted by Cookie Clark and the *Iris'* steward. We return to the *Nanok* and BW 8 late.

Clark has a masterful knack of irritating our skipper. The two are enemies. Clark is my mentor and dear friend. Captain Maggie is not. I think highly of Maggie as a man's man and an exceptionally brilliant sailor, but I wish he knew more about Coast Guard customs, rules and regulations, [not to mention] chain of command and when and how to promote C.G. personnel.

August 15, Saturday; BW 8.

Shoved off about 0600. Perhaps we will begin to earn our salt.

We tow a flat scow about twenty feet wide and thirty feet long. It is loaded with a variety of cargo, machine parts, food stuffs, etc. At the mouth of the fjord we transfer the cargo onto a foreign freighter called the *Lap-lander*. On the way back to BW 8, all hands are called at 1330. The scow has parted its towing hawser. Despite heavy seas and occasionally knee-deep, frigid water, we recover the damned thing about 1500. About 1530 the scow falls to pieces. Its hawser is quickly chopped away and the scow disappears beneath the waves. Talledo claims the disaster is Robbins' fault.

If he had shackled the barge correctly in the first place, "We would not have lost her!" I wondered how shackling her differently could have prevented the scow from falling apart? Robbie and Talledo are not friends. What a colossal waste of time and energy! Robbie feels terrible but he need not.

At BW 8, several civilian construction officials come on board. We are to transfer them to the *Arundel*, wherever she is now. I hope all these guys remember to sanitize their feet before entering the engine room.

August 16, Sunday; Teague Field.

We leave BW 8 early and head down fjord and out to sea a short distance, then back toward shore a short distance north. Some of the civilians refer to our destination as "Teague Field," while others call it "Marrak Point." From Maggie, Dillon, and Talledo, I hear "Kangamiut" and sometimes "Sukkertoppen." All I can be positive of, is that we are somewhat south and east of BW 8. Since we are never told officially, our destination could even be Timbukthree. Stan calls the place "Frozen Asskimo Land." I choose to call it "Teague Field." I like the name.

Teague Field is really only an airfield. There are no native villages nearby. The field is of smooth, flat rock, a natural pool-table surface as far as the eye can see. We deliver a motor sailboat. It is swung over the side by means of our starboard lift-boom. Talledo guides it by hand and steadies it as it is lifted. Connors controls the lifting device which is a horizontal, slow-turning, engine-activated, barrel shaped drum. Several turns of the trailing end of the boom's hoist line are wrapped around the turning drum. Whenever Connors pulls the end of the line toward himself, the many turns around the drum tighten. Friction between drum and rope increases. As the rope is pulled, the opposite end of the rope begins to lift the boom's end. The rope tied to the outer end of the boom leads upward and through a pulley near top of the mast, then down to the turning drum. The base-end is secured to the mast's base by means of a steel axle. A pull on the rope by Connors lifts the far end of the boom and whatever happens to be secured to it, in this instance, the motor sailboat.

Connors is careless. He allows one turn of the rope around the drum to creep under another turn around the drum. The line jams. Connors yanks at his end of the rope and pulls the jam loose. The boom falls. Talledo is nimble and barely escapes losing his life! Talledo mouth-lashes Connors and teaches all of us some brand new cuss words, some in his native American Indian language.

One of the civilians on board is known only as "Tiny." He weighs over 300 pounds. His nose, eyes, ears, and mouth are buried deep in his oversized head. His runaway overweight immediately has my sympathy and that of most of the crew. Soon, however, his constant complaining becomes irritating at best. He cares about nothing but his personal welfare and comfort. He constantly begs extra food, offers to purchase our individual desserts, and hides his face to secretly devour whole chocolate bars in a single bite. He gorges himself while making noises like a flushing toilet. He offers to buy my half-eaten lunch plate. I thought he was joking so I force a smile and push my plate slightly toward him. He grasped the plate and literally shoveled the remains into his tadpole looking mouth. I am astonished and nauseated and refuse to accept his cash offer. The guy is a spoiled, pampered child. I can't wait to see him disembark. He gets easily and terribly seasick. He vomits wherever it is convenient for him to do so and leaves his mess. When the *Arundel* takes him on board, he better stay out of the engine room.

Captain Maggie sadistically delights in seeing Tiny seasick. He asks Tiny if he'd like some fried salt pork and over-easy eggs. Tiny was lying in one of the crew's bunk and vomits into it. I follow Maggie quickly topside for fresh air.

Bob Hollingsworth, one of the other civilians on board, carries a portable, windup phonograph and a pack of records. We play the records and sing along with the ones we know. Charles "Charlie" "Rolly" Rollston is a radioman 1/c. He is a married guy from Portland, Maine. He is about twenty-six years of age, medium build, and mostly wears a round-faced pussycat grin. Charlie does not get seasick often, but when he does, he makes everyone around him as sick as he has made me twice today. Bob Hollingsworth is one generous soul. He has given each of us a chocolate bar. Because of Rollston's presence, I save mine for a later time.

August 17, Monday; Teague Field.

This airfield is the bed of a long-gone glacier. Snow capped mountains line both sides of the field. *Nanok*'s landing sight is the beginning end of the field. The far end is beyond eyesight. Mother Nature, not bulldozers, made this field.

Nanok lies heavily in the fjord's water. She bulges with cargo as if she were in advanced pregnancy. There is much lumber and prefabricated building sections to be off-loaded. Skipper promises that should we somehow manage to complete the off-loading by sundown, we could all sack-in

U.S. Coast Guard small boat sailors faced difficult Arctic conditions in Greenland. Here a small boat laden with lumber is poled through coastal ice to a desolate landing. (U.S. Coast Guard Historian's Office.)

all day tomorrow. All hands accept the challenge and turn-to with gusto. We make rafts of the lumber, float and tow them ashore. By sundown, all rafts and miscellaneous gear are ashore!

The outboard motorboat awaits us at the shore to return us to the *Nanok* at anchor. Elmer the yeoman is so completely exhausted he cannot climb into the boat. No one can muster enough strength to help him. He bends his body over the boat's gunwale and tumbles himself on board. Never in my life have I seen a man so completely spent. Arrival at the *Nanok*'s side, Comer is lifted on board by means of a rope sling and the efforts of four men.

Maggie breaks out a double case of canned beer and distributes it amongst those of us who drink it.

"Fine fellow, the cap," says Fairbanks, raising a toast.

"Amen" is the echo.

The skipper has great pleasure naming much of the area after crew members. Maps of the area do not identify many of the area's objects with official names. Maggie has taken the responsibility onto himself to properly identify all that can be seen. He claims his identifications will eventually appear on future official maps. He is serious about this.

The bay becomes "Dillon's Bay" after our executive officer Oscar. An island that disappears during high tide becomes "Staneczak's Island." The mountains lining one side of the airfield now bears my name followed by the designation "rock." Most members of the crew are similarly honored.

After a rest and a belly full of food, we enjoy a songfest. Comer has re-entered the realm of the living. Norman Comer is a product of Danville, Indiana, near Indianapolis. His normal duties are to process all of *Nanok's* paperwork. His title is yeoman 3/c. A yeoman is a petty officer whose crossed feathers insignia inspired the nickname "feather merchant," but the crew prefers to call him "Elmer" because the name seems to fit him better.

Elmer is a slightly built, bespectacled tiger. His milquetoast appearance camouflages extraordinary strength in the fragile-looking guy. I have seen him work until muscle spasms set in. It is his display of manliness that endears him to me. We are close friends. He only annoys me when we vocalize together. His voice is so high pitched it reminds me of fingernails being drawn across a slate blackboard. This, plus his ever-sour, everlasting, screwed up facial expression grinds upon my nerves at times.

Cold weather is my enemy, but I must acknowledge a sense of gratitude for being stationed in an area relatively safe from enemy forces. While I complain of cold weather and petty discomforts, thousands of American soldiers in warmer climates are dying. I experience a feeling of guilt. We are away from the States slightly more than a month and already I am impatient to return. Time moves slowly and lies heavily on my morale. We are not busy enough. There is too much time to think and to feel sorry for oneself. Idleness brings on homesickness. I feel sure that World War II will go on forever. The grapevine has it that much sea and air fighting rages from Iceland . . . east.

August 18, Tuesday; Teague Field.

We sacked-in as Maggie promised. The civilians are still on board. Bob Hollingsworth's title is surveyor. His Dad is a high mucky-muck in the Greenland construction project. Bob is nicknamed "Buffalo Bill" and is an excellent replica of the original BB. Bob wears a World War I cavalry campaign hat with the wide brim. His jacket is of deer skin embellished with long strands of fringe. His somewhat curly hair is shoulder length and is sandy brown. He sports a full, well-trimmed beard and moustache. Wherever he goes his portable phonograph goes with him. As is his father, Bob is extremely generous and is well-liked.

Tiny has become ill over the fact that he is unable to purchase all of Bob's supply of chocolate for himself. He offers me a ten dollar bill for my share. I refuse in disgust. I pretend to offer him my share free. He snatches them from me before I am able to react, and without a word of thanks! The glutton has made me ill.

Maggie has been ashore and bagged two ducks. Talledo claims Maggie found them tied to a tree.

We secure the *Nanok* for return to BW 8 in the a.m.

After a session of *dupa* band music (a kazoo, Jew's harp, harmonica, and teaspoon drumsticks beating on a wooden table—*dupa* means rectum in Polish), I have a one-on-one conversation with Dilly. He strikes me as somewhat immature. We speak about my desire to become a coxswain. His cherub cheeks sort of puff up. In a most serious manner, his forehead wrinkled from port to starboard. He said, "Well, 'ski, there's an awful lot of seamanship you still have not learned about but must know."

I asked for an example and then wished I hadn't.

Oscar pursed his lips, frowned in deep thought, then asked, "Well, what is a traveling lizard?"

I guessed Oscar was right. I was not prepared to become a coxswain. Time could come when the life of every man-jack on board could depend on my knowing what a traveling lizard was!

Note: At a much later time, I searched my *Bluejackets' Manual*, dictionaries, encyclopedias, no traveling lizard!! I even questioned all of the net-hauling old salts I met. Asking them about the lizard brought forth everything from baffled stares to uncontrollable guffaws! Finally, at Martha's Vineyard an old-timer smiled at me and wanted to know where I had heard this "quaint expression," for he hadn't heard it since he "was a kid." I told him I once feared my future depended upon my knowing what the lizard was. "Well now," he harrumphed, "supposin' you had a necessary tow line that was strung across a deck hatch, and you needed to enter that hatch. You would probably loop a short piece of thin line around the tow line and pull the tow line away from atop the hatch. This would not only clear the hatch for entry, but would allow the tow line some degree of forward and aft movement." "Yes, yes!" I said excitedly, "Then what?" "That's it," the old salt replied, "the short line you would have used and the way you used it would make it a traveling lizard." I was astounded! At last I knew what a traveling lizard was! Yet, for the balance of my Coast Guard career, I tried to find a single instance where this knowledge could be used but failed to do so. I often wondered if Maggie knew what a traveling lizard was. If he did not, do you suppose he would never have become a skipper!?

August 19, Wednesday; Teague Field.

Very early in the a.m., several of the crew go ashore to construct guide markers for future incoming vessels. In the meantime, the *Nanok* with half its crew, glides out to sea to guide in the *Arundel*, which radioed she was nearby. At sea we heave-to, and fish for and catch a large number of cod for dinner before the *Arundel*'s arrival. She comes towing quite a large scow she had lost and recovered twice at sea.

I squeegeed down the pilot house and Maggie rewarded me with a can of beer. We left the *Arundel* where she had met us and went to explore a series of small bays having tiny islands, reefs, and fjords. I sip my beer while wheeling the *Nanok* with one hand. We had only rough maps of the area, hand-sketched by the natives to guide us. They showed islands where there were none, small coves that did not exist, and so forth. Where the maps had shown open water, there were shallow reefs. It was constantly "hard right, hard to the left and hard right" again. We were trying not to strike reefs that were only partially visible. My wheeling arm tired quickly so I hurried to down the beer in order to have both hands for steering.

The skipper looks forward through the port shutter window and Dilly through the starboard. It is quite cold. The seas were not very high, but they were choppy. The throb of our diesel was quite loud in the pilot house. Dillon can be heard faintly humming to himself. No particular tune, just some melodious, open-mouthed, "Aaaaaah, aaaaaah, aaaaaah, aaaaaaah," and so on.

Staying on course was quite a chore. Choppy waves slapped at the *Nanok*'s large rudder. There is no power steering device. The pounded rudder jerks at the chain leading from quadrant to wheel, and from wheel into hand and arms. Dillon's humming grew ever louder and attracted occasional side glances from Maggie. Dillon was unaware that we heard him humming. He was in a sort of dreamy trance.

I noted the skipper's glances grow ever more frequent and angry toward Dilly. The throb of engine and ship vibrations caused Dillon's hum to become staccato in nature. Broken "aaaaahs" reminded me of "My Old Kentucky Home." It is too much for the skipper to bear. With a disgusted-sounding Norwegian accent he snorted, "Geeeezis Khrist!!" Turning swiftly he disappeared into his cabin aft.

Dilly was startled at the skipper's action. He looked questionably at me and returned to semi-consciousness. Obviously he had no idea of what set the skipper off, nor why I was wearing a big grin. Maggie returned, carrying his favorite drink, a can of beer usually laced with a large slug of dry gin. He appeared to have calmed down. Both Maggie and Dilly looked out their shutters again.

A few minutes later, I couldn't believe it . . . Dillon began to hum loudly once again! I'd give anything for a couple large gulps of Maggie's beer. Dillon's humming became louder than an evangelist's admonitions. Quite casually his eyes had turned toward me. My sardonic grin caused Oscar to snap out of his reverie. His face sobered and he swallowed with much difficulty. He blushed profusely.

"What course are you steering?" he asked, as if it mattered.

After watch I tell Vacar about the humming incident. He laughed so hard he said he feared his bowels would move. Nicholas Vacar is a motor machinist mate 2/c. Nick sums up Greenland precisely to the taste of many crew members. He says it is a "cold, damp, snowy, rainy, lonely, intimidating, terrifying, insect-ridden, fascinating, favorite cuss subject." Nick would like to explore the "White Shirt Land" under different circumstances. He finds it to be a fisherman's paradise. A wonderful place to get close to our creator because "it instills a sense that man is indeed a grain of sand."

Vacar is a rugged looking fellow from Salem, Ohio. He is stocky and powerfully built. His appearance is deceiving in that he is also a deeply sensuous person and eloquent of thought. Nick should have been a writer. He is a florist that assembles beautiful words into bouquets. For amusement and for want to convert otherwise lonely hours, Nick composes love letters for several of our less eloquent but love-struck crew members. They copy Vacar's romantic words to send to their loved ones. I believe his writings will be influential in bringing about a certain marriage when we return stateside.

August 20, Thursday; Teague Field.

The *Nanok* crew assists the *Arundel* crew into maneuvering the scow to the shore tie-up. They demonstrate very little seamanship knowledge. Chances are none of them have ever known a traveling lizard either.

Several Eskimo men come on board to trade four dead ducks to Clark for some biscuits and candy. We prepare for shore liberty but first we must listen to Maggie's clack-clacking about how and why we shouldn't dare to get intimate with any of the Eskimo women. He is scared as hell that one of us guys might run a hand down into the front of some woman's pants. The idea isn't bad, but opportunity seems remote. Per Maggie, the Eskimos are uneducated for the most part, [and] therefore should not be taken advantage of, especially sexually. I'm not sure how a lack of education and sex are related, but at the moment I choose to heed the skipper's warning.

Ashore we met up with an Eskimo family and have an amusing hour or so grinning at one-another. Later, around the bend of the beach, we came across a group of Eskimo women. They must have been from a village nearby, or else had an *umiak* (a large sealskin boat) beached somewhere.

Bob Hollingsworth and his phonograph are with us. He cranked up the machine and it grinds out a scratchy tune. Without too much effort we recruit the women into dancing in a snake-like conga chain. This allows female hips to be felt. The ladies take to the game gleefully, but not as eagerly as did the crew.

When we reach near exhaustion, we sat on large beach rocks and just listen to the music. The women loved the sounds. They are a varied age group. There were seven of us and nine women. It is apparent that someone has played music here before. Bob played "The Isle of Capri" and "The Beer Barrel Polka." The women have heard these tunes before. Eskimo lyrics are added to the music. They had sung the tunes in the past. Results are delightfully strange and pleasant.

One of the women was a midget. She attaches herself to me. I bounce her on my knee as a ventriloquist's doll. She loved it. The doll was about forty-two inches high and weighed probably seventy pounds. I am six-foot-two inches tall and weigh 176 pounds. We must have made a strange-looking pair. She wanted me to carry her off somewhere amongst the giant rocks. Her breasts were like small chicken eggs. I am twenty-two-years old. She must have been in her late thirties. She pulled my hand to her tiny breasts. I pulled it away, I was embarrassed. I had never before known an aggressive female. Too, it had been a long, lonely time away from my wife and I feared temptation. She spoke soft words that were repetitious. They are the first words other sailors had taught us in Greenland. The words have a spine-tingling ring to them when spoken by a female.

A familiar excitement stirred within me. I am weakening. Stench of urine in the woman's clothing helps clear my head as ammonia fumes might. I pulled her arms from around my neck. She smiled but was obviously disappointed. I was too, in a way. I noticed for the first time that her teeth were horribly decayed. Her breath was not much better than the odor from her clothing. Nausea overcomes me. I arose and she slid off my knee.

Too late!! Captain Maggie has rounded the bend in the beach! I and some of the others had been seen with the ladies! Maggie pretended not to have seen too much. With only a touch of anger in his voice, he ordered all of us to return to the *Nanok*. Some of the crew had successfully scurried away among the larger rocks and had been unseen by the skipper. They were fortunate. Maggie chastises me as though I had married the midget lady for an hour or so.

I return to the *Nanok* as if returning from my first teen-age date, frustrated and hurting in a certain area of my lower body. I might be feeling much worse if the skipper had not come along, but in a much different way.

August 21, Friday; At sea.

Maggie made a snide remark that I tried to have sex with the Eskimo midget, and that he felt that I should have my "ass kicked!" I responded with a foolish burst of anger and told him my affairs were none of his business! Surprisingly, he backed off.

The skipper does a turnabout and renames the bay after himself instead of Dillon.

Shoved off at 0730. Seas are rough as we head back toward BW 8. I am very tired.

August 22, Saturday; At sea.

0400 to 0800 bow watch was an ordeal. Solid, heavy, blue-green waves fly back over the bow and knock me to my knees a number of times. I was cold and wet. Water managed to trickle into my parka, around my face and around my neck front. We wallowed outside the fjord leading to BW 8, waiting to enter the fjord with the tide. Some try doing a bit of fishing; I do a bit of sack time. Maggie has apologized to me for making his unfair statement about me and the midget lady. I am very surprised at this, and grateful.

I am quite depressed today. Melancholia has set in. I tried to brighten up by joining a songfest. Sullivan Jones' deep bass vibrates pots and pans on the stove. A couple of sad sounding ballads bring on homesickness. Songfest ends.

August 23, Sunday; BW 8.

Surprised to see the flag at half mast. We learn two men have burned to death the other day. They chose to wash grease off the closed garage floor with gasoline. Gas fumes caused an explosion. A third man is near death with brain damage. A flying plank struck him in the head.

Life goes on.

Ashore we see movie *Babes on Broadway* starring Mickey Rooney and Judy Garland. A fine picture. In evening we shoot craps.

August 24, Monday; BW 8.

The army has given me and others new army shoes. I love 'em.

We install an antenna extension on our forward mast. The *Nanok* is loaded with food, water, drums of high octane gasoline, black powder, and dynamite. Ye gads! All civilians have disembarked, including Tiny and his body odor. Thank the Lord for small favors. In exchange we take on an army major.

August 25, Tuesday; At sea.

We leave BW 8 behind. Feel "salty" as hell! I have exactly one year in the U.S.C.G. today, a year too much!

Ran smack-dab into a heavy gale. One quarter of the *Nanok* is under water at all times. Army major promptly becomes seasick.

August 26, Wednesday; Teague Field.

We arrive and offload drums of fuel all day. Stan is in his glory. He is desperate to precede me into the coxswain's rating. So long as he earns it properly, it's gotta be OK, right?

Tiny and Buffalo Bill are here. How in hell did they beat the *Nanok* here!?

Maggie tells Cookie to "throw it out!" And he does. What a terrific meal!

Talledo dashes about as though he has lost his tail somewhere. His damn shouting is loud to the point of splitting ear drums. It is difficult to bear and impossible to hide from.

Did my laundry by dragging it in the sea astern of the *Nanok* and near lost it in the howling gale and heavy seas. Got seasick but no one knew it beside myself, thank goodness. Prospective coxswains, like skippers, are never supposed to get seasick.

Schafer has been acting very strange lately, moreso today. He talks aloud to himself, asks himself questions and answers them. The poor guy needs a doctor.

August 27, Thursday; Teague Field.

Dilly took over Connors' and Stan's watch last night and awakens me to take over the midnight to four watch. He had to give me two calls. I was so tired I half dozed through my watch. Rained all through the watch. Our radio works quite well since Schafer picked up a few parts for it recently.

Only Buffalo Bill is with us, no Tiny, thank God! Bill, Cookie, Robbins, and myself had a bull session on the fo'c's'le head. We depart Teague Field, bound for BW 8, then what?

August 28, Friday; BW 8.

We arrive and lay at anchor. Tug *Bridgeport* came to pump fresh water on board. We did an about face and headed back out to sea. As we are leaving the freighter *Lapwing* arrived with supplies for the base. Our mail was supposed to be on the *Arundel* with whom we were to rendezvous at the mouth of the fjord. We crossed the Arctic Circle for the umpteenth time. No one pays any attention any more.

Scuttlebutt has it, that we will head north on the east coast, for a change, to BE 2. From the way they describe weather conditions along the coast, I don't care to go.

Buffalo Bill and Robbins join our sing-along in the evening. Robbie is an emotional second tenor. For some reason he cannot sing with open eyes. It is amusing to watch the eyelashes of this rugged man flutter when he sings. Robbie wears a continual expression of worry. He is a sympathetic listener, a competent, likeable, hard working bos'n.

August 29, Saturday; At sea.

We arrive and drop hook at mouth of BW 1 fjord. *Nanok* drifts aground stern-first and the anchor is stuck fast. There are many anxious moments until the winch pulls the anchor that seemed to be stuck some fifty miles beneath our keel.

We are off and running and enter a fjord where the *Arundel* is found anchored. We rendezvous but she has no mail for us. Very disappointing.

Clark and I exchange tall tales on the gun deck during my evening watch.

August 30, Sunday; At sea.

Half chicken per man for dinner. Yeah man!! How Clark got some of this stuff we may never know and he will not tell. He is some kind of a finagler.

I sack-in most of the day, just reading. Very rough seas in the evening. Hope there's mail at BW 1 by now but I doubt it.

August 31, Monday; BW 1.

At anchor just inside of BW 1 fjord until foul weather forces us to head toward the base. On the way we narrowly miss running into reefs but old eagle-eye Fairbanks spots them in time to prevent a catastrophe.

George does not appear well but he does not complain. He converses less and less. I am too weary to see if he needs cheering up.

At BW 1, several of us visit on board the U.S.C.G. cutter *Algonquin.* [27] She escorted nine freighters up from Sydney, Nova Scotia.

Still no mail.

There are endless rumors of war activities, but they are only rumors. Being so far removed from the areas of heavy warfare, we will probably never learn of current, factual activities. It is just as well. If we were told of great Allied victories, we would probably not believe them. If we were told of severe Allied losses, depression might set in. All I care to learn one day is that the war has ended and the allies are victorious.

September

We still don't know the fate of the three men on the scow. We can only hope the cabin latch of the motor-sailor on the scow is unlocked. If not, the men will have to break out a pane of the shutter glass to gain entry into the tiny cabin for refuge. If this should be necessary, water would spill into the cabin and the men could freeze to death, providing they have not already been swept overboard.

September 1, Tuesday; BW 1.

Hot dog!

Received letters from sister Joann, the Fitzgeralds, and Lucille. Total thirteen.

Letters from home are read, reread, reread, and reread. Some we exchange with one another. It is possible to learn more about one's shipmates than about one's brother. Sometimes I feel that I am a member of a half-dozen families.

Worked hard all day trying to avoid the blues. Jonesy and I do some cable splicing on deck just forward of the pilot house so the skipper up in the pilot house can witness our expertise. I splice a thimble in a two inch cable in my quickest time ever. I use only a marlin spike, cutting pliers, several short lengths of 21-thread line, and an old broom stick, no vise. I surprised myself as well as Maggie who witnessed it from above.

Maggie demands that every seaman be capable of doing this, yet he is astonished that I did so! Maggie's logic is good. Says we need cable and rope splicing only when the ship is in some sort of trouble, and trouble only occurs during bad weather and emergencies. At such times there is no time to set up a vise. Besides, the *Nanok* has no splicing vise on board. Hoped my display will impress the old man that I just might be able to handle a coxswain's duties.

Met a number of the crew outside the civilian canteen. Some are drunk as hell and loaded with cans of beer. They paid some civilian workers high dollars for the stuff. It came about because Connors knew somebody who knew somebody. All Connors would do for me is to help me get a bit of pogey bait (candy).

One day some time ago, I had been in the pilot house temporarily relieving Mr. Dillon, who was having stomach cramps. I stood looking out the forward port shutter opening. Maggie was at the starboard. Connors was steering. His position was several feet to our rear, and at the ship's center. We three were in a period of silence, just studying icebergs in the distance. Through a side glance I happened to see a tell-tale flutter of Connor's eyelashes. I knew the flutter well. The guy was about to enter dreamland while standing and tending the wheel. I was amused and cleared my throat quite loudly to arouse his attention. There was no response.

The *Nanok*'s wheel is very large; its top curvature is chest high. There were no heavy seas to whiplash the wheel. It was steady and did not have to be moved more than an occasional inch in either direction to hold the *Nanok* on course. There was no sound other than the lulling throb of the diesel engine below deck, under foot. Connor's eyes were closing. He comfortably draped his left arm over a wheel spoke, then the other arm. A few moments later, he draped his left leg over a lower spoke. He stood like a stork on one leg, a tired scarecrow.

"Get up Dreams! Get up!!" I muttered under my breath.

Dreams did not move. He was comfortable and relaxed. He soon cradled his head on his right shoulder and fell asleep!

An iceberg, two points off our starboard bow, began moving exceptionally fast across our bow and off to port. Maggie watched it go and seemed to be amazed at its speed of travel. He was not yet aware that the berg was not moving, but that the *Nanok*'s bow was turning slowly to starboard. Suddenly he turned to look at Dreams who appeared to be impaled on the wheel. The skipper shouted with his Norwegian accent: "Schteady, Dreems! . . . Gah-gahnitt! . . . Schteady!!"

Dreams let out a sharp, involuntary snort and came alive.

Requested photos have been arriving from the states to the menfolk at BW 1 who had written home for them after the nurses' arrival. It was apparent that most requests were for cheesecake-type poses and many of the recipients kept theirs selfishly hidden from hungry male eyes other than their own. Even the most elderly men were receiving photos of their ill-proportioned women in shorts, skimpy costumes, and brief bathing suits. One oldster, overly proud of his wife, insisted on sharing her photo with me. She resembled a five-pound sausage in a three-pound casing. Her poor legs were a road map of varicose veins. To her husband, she was all that is beauty, sex personified. Who was I to judge?

Several men became embattled over pictures of their respective amour. Each had stolen the other's photo. Somehow I did not feel my short term of marriage so centered on sex. I wondered if I were normal.

September 2, Wednesday; BW 1.

Worked all day like a dog, no, two dogs!

More mail from home, hot spit!!

Spliced a steel thimble into one end of a four inch diameter rope hawser and a few other jobs.

Schafer has been assigned to permanent detail ashore here. He has been acting strangely lately. One cold morning he walked in his underwear, grasping the starboard quarter gunwale and yelling, "man overboard, man overboard!!" His eyes were popping out of his head as he appeared to be climbing the horizontal gunwale. He is tremendously homesick and still broods over the fact that his aged mother has to live alone. I will miss the guy.

Saw the scow we are to tow off to somewhere distant. It is more than twice as long and twice as wide as the *Nanok*. It is a flat, rectangular lump of floating steel. It has no superstructure whatsoever. Entrance into its hollow hull is via the removal of several, bolted-down manhole covers. The hull is partially filled with cargo, from precision tools to small electrical equipment, to 250 double cases of canned beer. We are not allowed inside. Atop the scow, there is a large wooden cradle fastened to the deck. It holds a motor sailboat of some twenty-two feet. The boat has a tiny cabin with glass shutters around its perimeter. Because of the scow's large size, Maggie anticipates difficulty if we encounter heavy seas. The steel thimble (eyelet) I spliced into the hawser's end will be used with a shackle to secure the hawser to a chain bridle at the front end of the scow. The opposite end of the hawser will be secured to a chain bridle in the *Nanok*'s stern.

Dexter is a radioman 3/c, a Mormon from Salt Lake City, Utah. We harass him by insisting that all men from Utah are cowpokes who tote two guns each. Therefore Dexter is called "Two Gun." Dexter is a quiet, medium-sized bookworm. His general appearance is that of a true cowpoke. Whenever he is not reading, he is constantly badgering Vacar to join the

Mormon faith. Why only Vacar? Who knows? I tell Vacar it is because only he on board ship looks like he could handle more than a few wives at a time. Vacar protests, but not vigorously.

News: Nazi Field Marshal Erwin Rommel has launched a vicious new attack in Egypt.

September 3, Thursday; Julianehåb.

We depart very, very early and arrive very late at Julianehåb with scow in tow. Half the crew get liberty ashore.

We trade candy, chew-gum, and cigarettes for sealskin cushions, wood and bone carvings, and miniature sealskin kayaks. I want to acquire a few of these hand-made souvenirs for Lucille.

Trading with the Eskimos is a trial of patience. An aged gentleman eases himself toward me as I am encircled by a group of younger Eskimos. I show him a cigarette and he grins at me as he comes closer. I put the cigarette into my mouth, pretend to puff on it, then return it to my shirt pocket. This lets him know I want more than a grin for the cigarette. He tries to appear disinterested. I turn my back on him and slowly move away into the crowd. He shouts at me! He is grinning broadly now and is holding up a miniature kayak for me to see. It is beautiful and perfectly detailed. It is edged with fine, delicately-carved fowl bone. There are several tiny wooden spears with barbs of bone. To the trailing end of the spear is attached a thin, long string of rawhide. The line is coiled in a basket-like rack atop the kayak and just forward of the passenger's cockpit. If the barbed spear is thrown at a bird, even in flight, and if the spear's point misses its target, one of the six-inch-long barbs sticking out the sides of the spear may impale the unfortunate bird. When the spear is thrown, the rawhide line plays out of its holder and is used to retrieve the spear. Spears used in hunting seals usually do not have the side barbs. When a spear enters a seal, the front, pointed end of the spear is designed to come loose from its long handle. The handle of wood will float and can be retrieved easily. The point of the spear will remain in the animal.

Usually the injured seal will dive deeply, but will remain attached to the spear point. After the animal's strength has been spent, or after the animal has died, the rawhide line, still attached to the spear point, is used to pull the animal up from the water's depths and to tow it to shore. Its blood is immediately drunk and I become immediately ill.

The kayak model held by the aged Eskimo even has a miniature hunter in the cockpit. It wears a tiny leather jumper. It must have taken weeks to create this model! I try to hide my excitement. I want the hand-crafted masterpiece desperately! I offer the man one cigarette. His smile is gone. The model disappears into the man's clothing. He resumes the pretense of not being interested, but he is not leaving.

My patience is being tested. An eternity passes. I pull out a full pack of cigarettes (which cost me forty cents a carton.) The brown-skinned huckster pretends not to notice. Another eternity passes. He must sense my impatience and rising anger. A faint grin of impending victory appears for a flashing moment on the man's face.

I am angry but try not to allow it to be seen. I am not successful. Without further ado, and to hurry the annoying procedure of bartering, I produce a packet of chew-gum and a large tootsie roll and add them to the two full packs of cigarettes.

The old beggar laughs at me!

"Go to hell!!" I shout and turn away.

He shouts back at me. Neither of us knows what the other says, but the tones of our voices speak an understandable language. He hands me the kayak . . . we have struck a deal!

I grasp the kayak with my free right hand, but he does not let loose of it! I understand. I allow him to grasp my goodies in his one free hand. He nods and we simultaneously relinquish the hold on our goods. The kayak is mine! It is a bargain! I am, however, still angry! Since the huckster cannot understand me, I shout at him. "You're a stinkin' thief!" His smile broadens and he stuffs his goodies inside his clothing. Then, he pokes the index finger of his right hand into a circle with the forefinger and thumb of his left hand. I get the meaning. Two "stinkin' thieves" laugh together.

Me and several of the crew are invited to visit inside a few Eskimo huts. They are hardly more than shacks of stone, sod, driftwood, and other debris. In each, there is a stench of urine, or of fish that must have died of old age, or of both. Much Eskimo clothing is of seal and other animal hides and [is] infested with lice. Before being fashioned into articles of clothing, skins must be cured, softened, or otherwise tenderized. As I recall from civilian life, salt is necessary in the process of curing hides. I feel sure the Danish government provides salt for whatever purpose needed, along with proper instructions on how to cure hides. We are told, however, that in some remote areas, Eskimos still cure hides in a primitive manner. They choose to use their own urine salts for curing purposes. One of the English-speaking natives explains how urine curing is done. As best we can understand, one urinates onto the skin and then chews on it until it becomes sufficiently pliable for clothing purposes.

Late in the evening, all but Cookie Clark have returned to the *Nanok*. Maggie is angry and will not allow anyone to go to fetch Clark. I stand late evening watch in the pilot house with the skipper. Every few moments he blasts the *Nanok*'s whistle to signal Clark to return. He constantly scans the beach with binoculars. Even without binoculars I can see, and faintly hear, female laughter.

September 4, Friday; Julianehåb.

Cookie got back on board very late last night. Don't know how because we left him no dory to use. He had to have returned via *umiak*. Several hitch hikers on board. Among them our friend Tiny. He brings along a heavy quilt to assure himself optimum comfort. He offers to pay crew members to carry his meager belongings on board. Even for a hundred [in] cash he would be hard pressed to find anyone to assist his laziness.

Many kayaks come out to the anchored *Nanok* to trade and to surround the *Nanok*. Trading is good. I acquire a four-inch-high hand-carved wooden Eskimo head and two leather match box covers. Most of the crew is allowed ashore for one last visit before we leave.

Eskimos love music. Most of theirs is made by beating a shallow drum with a thin stick. The drum resembles a tambourine without the small metal discs. The drum is struck in rhythm with their singing and their chanting. Eskimo dance motions mimic actions of legendary birds and beasts of prey. Chantings are of ancient days and deeds of old.

The villagers perform an impromptu dance in the *Nanok* crew's honor. In appreciation, Cookie and I do a half-assed version of a country-style barn dance. The Greenlanders went wild at our "do-si-do" gyrations. We become instantaneous matinee idols. Elders grinned in toothless delight. We bow and curtsy to flatter them. John Barrymore would envy Clark's flourishing gestures. An ancient gentleman was carried away by our performance. He forgot his age and shriveled muscles. He joined our dance and beat hell out of his thin drum like Gene Krupa might have. He ignored the fact that his drum had no skin cover. He beat his stick on the rim of the drum.

After we all had tired of the dance, we casually strolled through the area of mostly huts and the occasional brightly painted houses where the Danes lived. We wound our way up the gently sloping hillside on narrow paths that snaked their way between large boulders.

A large group of children followed, begging for goodies. My parka pockets were stuffed, but selfishly I hoped to use the goodies for trading, [as] they were not easy to come by. Too, I had to deprive myself the pleasure of eating them. I gave none away freely. Eventually, kids would get their share through their parent's trading. If goodies were more available, I would enjoy sharing with the kids. Their grubby faces and pleading eyes told me what their language could not. It was most difficult to ignore the little beggars.

We paused at the top of a hill at the extreme outer edge of the village. Being occupied with the magnificent view and shouts of the children, I was not aware that all of the crew had fallen away and were distantly returning to the beach. I was alone with at least fifteen jumping, yelling, hyper children. Their pleadings were no longer bearable. I decided to distribute some "chew gum" and sections of a few Tootsie Rolls. Hands reached toward me from all directions. It was impossible to pass out the candy as quickly as the children wanted me to. They began to tear at my parka. I shouted at them to be patient. They did not understand. Hands had accidentally clawed my face and I panicked. A pudgy finger poked my open eye. I was unable to move in the crowd. A little girl about hip-height had grasped the edge of my parka pocket and I cannot pry her little hand loose. She is a determined little tyke and her eyes shined with the frenzy of her desire. Finally the hand came away but it held a part of my pocket and several packets of "chew gum." She had won her phase of the battle and disappeared in the mass of struggling children.

Instead of scaring the kids with my shouting, I attracted many women who poked heads out of huts. My plight was seen. Women rushed to yank their children off me. Soon the children were gone. I was safe, but panting. No!! I am not safe! The women then were clawing at me for the goodies. I had no more left with which to appease the screaming females. Eskimo men looked on in amusement. Desperately I try to push the horde away. I break and run through them like a freshly castrated musk ox. A long line of women and children pursued me in a zigzag course. We must have resembled a conga chain in polka tempo. The tormentors were at my heels!

Buffalo Bill Hollingsworth and the others were at the base of the hill. They saw me in flight and my situation struck them as being hilariously funny. Bill and Oscar Dillon were taking snapshots of me and my pursuers.

I chose not to stop and chat, but dashed swiftly into a beached dory and shoved off. The beach was lined with panting, female demons! I will never play generous host again.

Back on board ship, Maggie assigns me to direct a group of Eskimos to load dories and sends me back ashore.

I am constantly amazed at how kids looking no more than five years old manage to master kayaks. They skitter about like water spiders that never seem to chew all of the flavor out of their everlasting "chew-gum." An entire family of Eskimos circle the *Nanok* at anchor. They come to say "good-bye" to their favorite ambassador of goodwill, Cookie Clark. He peers over the side and receives an ovation from them. I try to imagine how close they would be if they understood one-another's language.

We hoist hook and travel south and east. We heave-to and drift outside some unidentified fjord for the night.

September 5, Saturday; Unidentified fjord.

We enter the fjord in the a.m. just as heavy winds begin to rise. *Nanok* hurried into shelter of the fjord.

No white man is supposed to have ever been here before. We drop hook and a few kayaks come out to greet us. When the kayaks draw near, we hear a familiar word, *"nah-nook, nah-nook, nah-nook!"* How they learned the name of our vessel we can only guess. A second surprise, an adult male Eskimo is wearing a United States Army shirt with a sergeant's chevrons on the sleeves! It is at least a clue to how they know the *Nanok*'s name. Since the village is many miles from nowhere, the sergeant who originally owned the shirt must have been an excellent swimmer. Each of our crew has their own theory as to how the shirt got here.

We lay in the fjord and do a bit of trading. The guy in the sergeant's shirt is dubbed "Sarge." He is full of comical antics. I happen to have an ancient copy of *Life* magazine in my hand. Sarge wants to see it close-up. I hand it to him and allow him to keep it. He is fascinated. As he thumbs through it, one picture after another captures his delight. He points to a picture, then points southward and asks, "Ahmerika?"

I nod and say "yes."

He seems amazed that there are so many interesting-looking people in "Ahmerika." How he has even learned of America's existence is also a mystery. Someone suggested that Sarge is really Amerigo Vespucci.

Sarge soon comes across a full-page picture of a deeply tanned American beauty in a white, tight, and skimpy bathing suit. His heart must have stopped. He examines every fraction of the photo with caressing eyes. He gulps, points to the picture, then toward the south. He asks, incredulously, "Ahmerika!?"

"Yes," I laugh, "Ahmerika."

Without hesitation Sarge points first to himself, then southward.

"Ahmerika?"

Again I have to laugh. Obviously he wants to go to America with us. Our language barrier does not help me to disillusion him. I would like to tell him that if all American women looked like the magazine model every man on earth would head toward America.

For amusement, I promise him, "yes," with a nod, I would take him to America. He is elated to say the least. If I had any idea how serious the man was, I would not have made such a promise. He shoves off toward shore, swiftly!

Maggie and Dillon practice firing the three-inch twenty-three blunderbuss at white-capped mountains of stone nearby. Echoes of each shot seem to last five minutes. The sound ricochets from peak to peak and shock waves vibrate the surface of the water. Sound is like a giant steel ball bearing bouncing off one obstacle after another in a pin-ball machine. Both men also practice firing our 20mm anti-aircraft guns. Every fifth cartridge is called a "tracer." Each tracer slug is a ball of red flame whose flight can be followed with the naked eye. It is fascinating to see the red balls of fire pierce walls of ice and disappear within them.

In evening we get under way with scow in tow hundreds of feet astern of the *Nanok*.

Abe Brill is madder than hell at me. Someone told him I stole some of his chocolate bars but I have not. If I had known where he had them stashed, I may well have gobbled a few.

As we move slowly out of the fjord, I see Sarge paddling toward the *Nanok* as fast as a speedboat. He is shouting. I interpret his shouts to mean "Hey! Wait for me!" Maggie wonders what in hell is going on. I pretend not to know. Sarge has a large bundle on the front of his kayak. Odds are that it contains all of his earthly belongings. Several Eskimos in other kayaks paddle swiftly on either side of the Sarge. They keep trying to snatch things from Sarge's bundle. It may be the magazine they are after. Sarge is alternately shouting at me and slapping away the probing hands of his escorts. I feel guilty for aiding the Sarge's fantasy.

The *Nanok* picks up speed and heads toward the open sea. For a time Sarge keeps pace and screams himself hoarse. I wish I had jotted down the magazine's date and the model's name. It's a shame she will never know of her greatest admirer's existence. I must remember to inform *Life* magazine to begin a lucrative Greenland distribution center.

The Sarge's strength wanes. He is seeing his dream fade toward the horizon. *Nanok* runs at her maximum pace now. Perhaps Sarge will carry a torch for his dream-love forever. Could be he may join the French Foreign Legion to forget. I am a lousy cupid.

September 6, Sunday; Unidentified fjord.

We are anchored in an unidentified fjord. Captain Magnusson never ceases to amaze me with his uncanny sixth sense. Daylight is breaking. I half-doze, alone on watch in the pilot house. Suddenly there is commotion in the skipper's cabin. His hatch pops open and in flies the skipper! I think he has lost his sanity. He is barefoot and is wearing long, winter underwear and his visored cap, nothing else! His eyes are wild and he shouts: "What would you do if the ship was drifting!?"

I was startled full awake. "Why," I stammered, "I'd call you sir!"

"Well, call me then," he snarled, "because we *are* drifting!"

I opened an outer hatch and looked aft. Sure enough, the *Nanok*'s stern was no more than a hundred feet off a rock-strewn shore! No time to waken the deck crew. As I raised the anchor, Captain Maggie drove the *Nanok* forward and away from danger.

It took a bit of time to figure out how he knew the ship was drifting. It was quite simple really. As he lay in his bunk with the side of his face firmly down into his pillow, he could hear the anchor drag across the fjord's rocky bottom! We leave the sanctity of the fjord and proceed to sea once again. Days such as this, that have a bad beginning, seem to embrace bad things all day.

Tiny complains loudly and continuously about the heavy seas that pound the *Nanok*. Someone offers to calm the sea for ten bucks. Without thinking, Tiny reaches for his wallet.

Scow in tow is coming along fine. Damned waves . . . feeling sick in the stomach.

September 7, Monday; At sea.

As Maggie has often warned, trouble with ship equipment occurs during bad weather. We were to learn whether or not his teachings are of merit because the scow in tow has broken loose from its hawser! Ragged seas and monstrous waves dwarf the *Nanok*. Solid walls of black and gray-blue waters break over the deck. Heavy rain is driven by howling winds that gust over 100 miles per hour. Dark, fractured clouds appear to touch wave tops.

Maggie signals the engine room and the diesel is loping to a halt. The skipper sounds the emergency alarm: "All hands on deck!"

As men break topside, the scow has already been blown from sight. Sheets of rain and scattered icebergs hamper vision. Before the propeller stops turning, the slackened hawser becomes entangled in it. Several loops of the heavy manila rope are wound around the propeller's axle shaft. Some six hundred feet of it hangs straight down in the ocean. Captain Magnusson makes clear the importance of recovering the scow. It is extremely valuable mostly because of irreplaceable scientific equipment in its hold. Too, it is almost priceless in itself because it could take months to duplicate and to haul it from the States. There is an urgent need for the scow at Pikiutdleq where it is to be used as a floating dock.

Before attempting to locate the drifting scow, we must first retrieve the hawser. Robbins, Stan, and I alternate being lowered over the *Nanok*'s stern by rope. Objective is to secure the hawser with a light line so that men can lift a portion of it up so that it can be unwound one loop at a time.

Work is laborious, frustrating, wet, and extremely cold. To acquire a purchase on the hawser, we must work under water. Roll of the vessel and smashing waves add to the difficulty. Arms, legs, and fingers stiffen quickly. Thank heaven there are but two loops to remove. Both Stan and I are unsuccessful in our attempts. It is for Robbie to achieve the impossible. Eternity ends, the hawser is lifted and pulled free through use of a capstan on deck, but not before Stan nearly loses a few gloved fingers trapped in the many turns of [the] hawser around the turning capstan. No one is ever to wear gloves under these circumstances, Maggie growls at Stan.

There is time for warmth, a breather, cup of coffee, and a change into warm, dry clothing as the *Nanok* seeks its wayward tow. All hands are again summoned when the scow is again sighted. Seas are much too rough to pull alongside. Waves could easily toss at least a section of the scow onto the *Nanok* or vice versa. Maggie decides a dory must be put over the side with three men in it. They are to carry a line and secure it to the scow's chain bridle and row back to the *Nanok*.

Volunteers are requested. Chief Talledo, Connors, and I offer our services. A dory is lowered over the port side and twice the raging sea tosses it back atop the *Nanok*'s gunwale. The second time, it slides off the gunwale and lands atop several men. There are bruises and curses but no serious injuries.

By now the scow has again drifted from sight. We locate her again. Maggie positions the *Nanok* between wind and scow and stops the engine. Several barrels of oil are poured onto the sea. Oil film helps to level choppy waves. Portside is to leeward.

Again a dory is slid over the gunwale by hand and is allowed to fall into the sea. Oars had been lashed atop the dory's thwarts. My sheath knife has been wedged between strakes and ribs. We three wear thick, kapok-filled life jackets in case the dory should capsize.

The plan is for all three men to leap into the dory. Chief Talledo insists on being the oarsman. He is to pull my sheath knife loose, cut away the oar lashings, and row the dory away from the *Nanok*'s side as quickly as possible. Connors and I are to fend the dory away from the *Nanok*'s side to avoid capsizing and to give Talledo time to extend and use the oars.

Time has come, we scramble over the gunwale and are about to leap . . . but the dory is gone! On a receding wave it has plummeted downward and partially under the ship's belly, completely out of our sight! Suddenly, she rises atop another wave! Up it comes and over the side go Talledo and Connors. I jump but the dory is gone and I am left clinging to the outboard side of the ship's gunwale! Several men yank me back on board. I poise to leap when the dory appears once more.

Talledo has pulled my sheath knife loose but had no time to use it. Both hands of both men are required to fend the dory away from the *Nanok*'s side. All that is transpiring is swifter than my thoughts.

I see the dory rising again. Talledo is frantically trying to fend away, using his bare left hand and the knife in his right. Connors is just as busy. I have no time to think or act. Dory and men fly upward on a wave that raises their gunwale to the level of the *Nanok*'s! In his excitement as he comes upward, Talledo fends off by poking me in the chest several times with the knife! Its blade tip pierces my life jacket but does not reach my flesh. The situation, despite its serious and dangerous nature, has a Keystone Kops comedy aspect to it.

Down goes the dory!

Maggie must have realized his plan was doomed to failure. He shouts for us to bring Talledo and Connors back on board. When the dory rises and Talledo is abreast of me, I lunge partly over the gunwale and grasp the chief in a tight bear hug. Someone else has gotten hold of Connors. Both men are pulled on board and the dory then capsizes. It is of wood and does not sink. As the sea brings her back to gunwale height, she too is pulled on board.

The *Nanok* rolls heavily to port. A great wave spills over the gunwale and I fall beneath the water's weight. My right leg catches in something as I fall. Momentum of the wave carries me further inboard. My leg feels as if it has been wrung from its hip socket! Much confusion prevails. Several others have been knocked down by waves. Men are strewn across the deck and smash against the pilot house and boom cradle. I am helped to stand upright. My leg is numb and I can't do it alone. Great waves strike again and again. The deck pitches and heaves crazily. Most men retreat to safe shelter in the fo'c's'le.

The engine is restarted and the *Nanok's* bow is pointed directly at the scow several hundred yards away. We know the skipper too well to assume he will abandon the recovery effort. Another attempt will be made to board the scow. Maggie decided to approach the scow head-on. When we are close enough, he will reverse engine and three men will leap from the bow onto the scow. A light heaving line will be tossed to them. The leading end of the hawser will be attached to the trailing end of the heaving line. The three men then on the scow will pull it on board and secure hawser to the scow's bridle chain. It must all be done quickly for if we drift too far apart, too much heavy hawser will be payed out into the sea. Men on the scow may not have strength enough to cope with the weight.

Cookie Clark volunteers to take my place for I can barely walk. And if I were able, I would no longer volunteer for such madness.

We are close together. Engine is reversed. Scow rises on a wave as the *Nanok* descends on another. *Nanok's* bow smashes down upon a front corner of the scow. There is a loud cracking sound. A great hole is stove into the *Nanok's* bow. Sea water rushes in.

Connors and Clark leap, closely followed by Talledo. The first two men tumble across the scow's wet deck. Talledo, in mid-air, grasps the arch of a davit on the scow to break his fall. Grasping the davit causes him to swing like a pendulum and he loses his grip. He falls flat on his back and slides across the steel deck. I fear his back has been broken, but no! Old Grisly clambers back to his feet! Ship and scow are [again] drifting apart. We close on her once more. Bos'n Robbins tosses the heaving line on board the scow. Engine is stopped.

It grows dark quickly now, making it difficult to see clearly. Wind rises ever higher and shrieks through the rigging. Men on board the scow have pulled the entire heaving line on board and have reached the hawser's leading end.

My eyes do not believe what they see! Wind tears away Talledo's sou'wester hat. It shreds his foul weather jacket, and then his rubber bib trousers tear off and fly away! Clark and Connors fare the same. In semi-darkness, scow and ship drift apart. The scow can no longer be seen. Wind-carried rain makes it impossible to even look in the direction of the scow's last known location. Maggie is reluctant to start engine. There is no way for him to know whether or not the scow has been secured to the hawser. The hawser feeds downward into the sea from the *Nanok*'s stern. It could become entangled in the propeller once again. Maggie chances the use of a powerful searchlight but it is inadequate to penetrate both rain and darkness. We watch the hawser and after an eternity its limp form springs to life and stretches taut! The scow is secured!

Half of our prayers have been answered. We still don't know the fate of the three men on the scow. We can only hope the cabin latch of the motor-sailor on the scow is unlocked. If not, the men will have to break out a pane of the shutter glass to gain entry into the tiny cabin for refuge. If this should be necessary, water would spill into the cabin and the men could freeze to death, providing they have not already been swept overboard.

Radioman Carroll Jenner refuses to leave the stern of the *Nanok*. He watches the hawser throughout the night. As long as it remains taut, he knows the scow is still attached.

Maggie is concerned that either the *Nanok* or the scow could strike an iceberg for the night is completely black. He cannot chance even an occasional searchlight beam. One never knows if an enemy war vessel or submarine may be in the vicinity. A light would attract them. True, it might not be possible for the enemy to engage us during the night, but [it] could follow until the winds die and daylight comes. We proceed forward and hope for the best.

My leg aches so I lay below. I have no strength to remove my remaining wet clothing. As do others, I wrap into a blanket and drop into my sack. Over-tiredness keeps some awake. The fo'c's'le reverberates with noise from the onslaught of smashing waves. *Nanok* lurches and rolls crazily. At one point we roll suddenly to such a degree, I am rolled bodily out of my sack. I land upon the dining table's seat below and alongside my bunk. It is a day and night that will not easily be forgotten. From off somewhere I hear Tiny reading his Bible aloud and as swiftly as possible.

September 8, Tuesday; At sea.

Sometime during the night Morpheus arrived and I fell asleep. During sleep, weather has abated. All is silent in the fo'c's'le. Judging by gentle motion of the *Nanok* the sea is quite calm. As quickly as possible I change into dry clothes. My naked body resembles a prune. Climbing topside I find the sun so bright it hurts the eyes. Several of the crew are in the ship's stern. Behind us rides the scow as pretty as a kite. Her rust-resistant orange color flashes reflections from the sun. Wind is but a gentle breath. About a mile ahead is the entrance to a fjord surrounded by the usual giant, snow-capped peaks of multi-colored rock. Tiny the Detestable stands outside the fo'c's'le reading his Bible half-aloud. Surface of the sea has a slight ground swell and nothing more. A thin layer of vapor-like fog clings to the water. Captain Maggie stills the engine and many men pull at the hawser. Slowly, slowly comes the scow like a played-out whale. No one comments on the fact that there is no sign of life on board her. As she is brought close up, we are able to see completely through the tiny, glass-sided cabin of the motor-sailor on the scow's deck. All eyes turn toward the skipper. His eyes are sleepless, red and anxious. Long and repeated blasts of the *Nanok*'s whistle shatters the silence and their echoes return from shore.

Ho!!

The motor-sailor's pilot cabin's hatch opens! Cookie Clark tumbles out, stiff-legged. He puts a fist into each armpit, flaps his elbows up and down as wings. He loudly crows "cock-a-doodle-doo" like a rooster! Smiles break out on board the *Nanok*. Skipper pretends anger and disgust. Even though he cusses Clark's nonsense, he is obviously relieved of great tension and concern.

After Clark comes Talledo and Connors. All are safe! It is a great morning. Scow is pulled alongside and the three men come on board. They consume great mounds of bacon and eggs and several pitchers of hot coffee. The three had huddled in a corner of the motor-sailor's pilot house for warmth. Their only complaint was that cigarettes and matches had gotten wet. Maggie orders them to their sacks to sleep the clock around.

The day has a holiday spirit without festivity. There is much backslapping and congratulations. From this day on, no one will doubt the skipper's superior courage and determination. Many doubt his judgment.

Tiny falls asleep sitting up in a corner of the galley's deck. The Bible falls from his chubby fingers. I stuff it into his parka and throw a blanket over him. Perhaps his share of effort has been most important of all.

We pull near shore and a small spit of beach. Chips Delaney, the skipper, Talledo and McClay survey the hole in *Nanok*'s port bow. It proves to be more like a giant starburst fracture. Delaney feels he can mend the injury with a giant sheet of lead and other materials. With minimum assistance he does so. The *Nanok* is once again water tight. A truly masterful accomplishment.

September 9, Wednesday; At sea.

Sea fairly calm. Scow behaving beautifully, gliding through a field of icebergs as large as battleships.

Fireman John Petrenko complains he should have joined the army. The horrible stench of rotted fish cargo causes John to retch. Fish odor affords Cookie Clark a semi-vacation. Many feel as Petrenko does. It is impossible to eat when nauseated. Our lack of appetite amuses Clark until he too becomes nauseous. Tiny is able to eat voraciously.

September 10, Thursday; BE 2, Comanche Bay, Pikiutdleq.

Plowing through icebergs and guided by inaccurate hand-made charts, we arrive at Pikiutdleq in the afternoon with scow in tow.

This bay is nature's wind tunnel. Constant, frigid wind blows from the top of a glacier that is bordered on both sides by snow-capped rocky mountains. The glacier's valley funnels the frosty wind down into and across the bay and chases itself out onto the sea.

Entering the bay's mouth from a calm ocean, the *Nanok* is struck head on by gale force winds that rarely rest. We are advised by Morse code blinker light to anchor in mid-bay rather than attempt to tie up near shore. Thus the wind should be unable to blow us aground. The great depth of the bay is also a problem. We race into the bay and unleash the starboard anchor while still underway at substantial speed. As the hook plummets down into the depths, the *Nanok*'s course veers sharply to port. After some distance of travel, the port anchor is dropped simultaneously with the shutting down of the engine.

After both anchors touch bottom, adjustments are made so that the *Nanok* is tethered by both anchors, far apart and far forward of the *Nanok*'s prow, like a kite fastened to two kite strings.

When there is somewhat of a let-up in the wind, I row Dilly and Maggie ashore in a dory. The pitiful-looking settlement lies at the base of the skyscraping glacier, but out of its path of travel. It consists of one rather large clapboard building and several small outhouse-looking sheds. I count a population of six men and five sled dogs. The place is a weather observation base. There is scientific research going on as well, but we are advised not to inquire about details.

The commander is an army captain named Taylor. Supposedly, there are additional personnel stationed here, but [they] are away on some sort of Ice Cap duty. We are anxious to rid the *Nanok* of its cargo of fast ripening, frozen fish.

A closer look at this god-forsaken settlement is depressing. Much of the base personnel's food-stuff is buried deep in a horizontal tunnel dug into the glacier. It is a natural freezer. The base's larger building and living quarters is one large room filled with much radio parts and weather study equipment. Included are the personnel's personal belongings and stacked sleeping bunks. The place is a combination work shop and living quarters. The men take turns cooking and cleaning. After seeing this hell-hole up close, my heart goes out to the men who somehow manage to appear cheerful and in good spirits. The place makes the *Nanok* appear as a floating palace. I appreciate my lot much more.

September 11, Friday; Comanche Bay.

We offload the dog food from the *Nanok* to the scow and from the scow to shore. I run the winch but cannot escape the stench. Jonesy rows the old man ashore and does not return. I should have thought of that escape.

It begins to rain heavily. I swear each raindrop is the size of a golf ball and colder than billy-hell. Despite my parka hood, some of the stuff strikes my face, rolls down my neck, across my shoulders, down the center of my back and through the crack of my ass!

After knocking off at 1400, some of us go ashore. Elmer and I enjoy a hot cup of cocoa provided by a friendly army sergeant. I never cared for cocoa, but now it tastes as if it were delivered from heaven.

As the time passes, tempers of crew members are growing ever thinner. Most anger easily and at the slightest provocation. Much is caused by the loneliness Greenland's bleak and barren rocks and glaciers impart. Too, not knowing when, if ever, we will return stateside and see our loved ones is a strong factor. Heavy rain turns the world into a caldron of dismal sadness and discomfort. Homesickness is overabundant. Dreariness is Greenland and Greenland is dreariness. It is the world at end, the chill of ages, a tombstone for lost ships and men. It is a blanket of ice smoothed by unbelievable winds. The largest island on earth lying mostly inside the Arctic Circle. Approximately 840,000 square miles covered by some 710,000 square miles of ice. Oddly enough, the short summer in its south has a mean temperature of 48 degrees Fahrenheit. To me, the island's only beauty is its primitive vastness, its solar phenomena and its simple, unspoiled natives, "Greenlanders" if you will. We have seen so little of them thus far.

New rumor: we will return stateside in a month or so. . . . Aaaaaah, hope!

September 12, Saturday; Comanche Bay.

Towed scow ashore and ebb of tide leaves her high and dry. We offload much miscellaneous cargo from *Nanok*'s hold and grow tired to the point of despair. Our last job is the meanest. We must haul two very large motorized sleds. They are not only very long, but bulky and heavy as well. No one on board or ashore has ever seen one before. Something new for the Arctic and Antarctic. After getting them ashore, we must carry them up a steep hill of snow and rock. My legs sink in snow halfway to the knees and twist and slide on small sections of ice. It is a travel of several inches at a time.

An army lieutenant named Max H. Demorest follows our movements as though the sleds were priceless. I ask his interest and learn that he travels the Ice Cap often on skis or by dog sled. To him the motor sleds are a Godsend. He says there have never been any motorized sleds in Greenland before. As matter of fact, these are the only ones he has ever heard of. A new invention? [28]

We tell the lieutenant to treat the sleds well but under no circumstances return them to the *Nanok*. We have no desire to see the monsters again. Demorest laughs good-naturedly. He is a very likeable guy, tall, lean and bears a striking resemblance to John Carradine of the movies.

Army captain Taylor rewards our efforts with two double cases of canned beer. Maggie donates a large bottle of dry gin. Clark prepares a steak dinner for all. The day has some rewards. Guns Owens mixes his slug of gin into his beer. His normally pale blue eyes turn almost white after he downs the mixture.

September 13, Sunday; Comanche Bay.

A deluge of snow falls as we turn-to this a.m. Snowflakes the size of large maple leaves are coming down. I catch one after the other in my cold, gloved hand and study their beauty and structure as quickly as I can before they disintegrate and become water. There must be some designer high in the sky that specializes in filigree design.

Jonesy rows Maggie ashore in a dory and returns alone. Then he and I transport sixteen double cases of beer ashore, property of Captain Taylor.

We then place a small dory inside a larger one, tow both ashore with our outboard motor boat. We fill the inner dory with bucketfuls of glacier-falls water and pump it on board the *Nanok*.

Comer and I bum a cup of tea and a can of beer each, and then haul two Eskimo huskies back to the ship for delivery somewhere nearby. Snow becomes freezing rain. At midnight I stand watch atop the gun deck alongside the three-inch twenty-three cannon. I experience an overwhelming wave of melancholia. I am alone in onyx darkness. Aurora borealis, sensing my mood, presents a special performance for me. Mountainous globules of multi-colored paint pours down from the heavens in a straight line from horizon to horizon. Colors are exceptionally brilliant this night. They drip and sag as liquid pouring down an invisible pane of glass across the sky above me. The colors appear to be reachable by hand. Icebergs and sea reflect the colors above. It is a wondrous sight! Patterns and tones are ever-changing. Colors fade and are replaced by other phenomena I call "slow lightning." In the black sky, "slow lightning" does indeed resemble lightning in slow motion. It constantly changes direction at varied slow speeds. It hovers many seconds at a time, suspended in still, chill air. I have never heard it described before.

After enjoying the display for quite some time, I feel reconditioned enough to tolerate the presence of others. Perhaps too, others may once again bear my countenance.

As if on cue, Cookie Clark joins me to view the overhead panorama. His presence and conversation is most welcome. We talk about our favorite subject, food. Not our every day diet, but choice unavailable items such as oranges, barrel-cured dill pickles, corned beef on rye, filet mignon, green onions, and draft beer to name a few. Such shared inner thoughts bring us together in close friendship.

My watch ends and I hit the sack.

September 14, Monday; BE 1, Optimist, Angmagssalik.

Greenland keeps me in a constant chill here, high up on the east coast. I awakened during the night with a numbed face that has lain in contact with the frosty cold outer skin of the *Nanok*. The ship's skin is one side of my shelf-like bunk.

Ice has formed on the waters for I can hear it crack and crumble beneath the *Nanok*'s bow as we leave Comanche Bay at 0200. I lay on my back, trying vainly to return to slumberland. Noise of cracking ice is amplified in our undersized forecastle quarters. A large, wooden, overhead beam running from the port to starboard side of the ship splinters under severe pressure. We must have struck a large iceberg. There is a sharp, whip-cracking sound as the beam splits. It is as if a rifle has been fired. I am startled and leap from my bunk.

Another fractured bone for old dame *Nanok*. She is impervious to pain and continues along her waddling way.

As days grow ever colder and ice cakes thicken, there will surely be more fractures and leaking seams. It is fortunate the old girl has a hard head. The scow is neatly in tow as we near the entrance of Kong Oscar's Havn [King Oscar's Harbor]. There is a single, high mountain peak on the south shore near the harbor's entrance. The peak is quite pointed, somewhat like a pyramid. A small, dense cloud drifts into the peak and circles around it, slowly at first, then faster and faster. Finally, ever increasing momentum flings fractured sections of the cloud out and away from the peak. Another Greenland phenomenon.

Just inside the harbor on its south side is a small cluster of U.S. Army clapboard buildings. Beyond them, a bit further inland lays the small village of Angmagssalik. Despite its small size, it is possibly the largest on Greenland's east coast. The army buildings house a U.S. weather observation station.

The village was founded in 1894 and has probably remained unchanged since that time. On its downward slope toward the harbor, one can see a sprinkling of three- or four-room shiplap houses painted red and trimmed with green and vice-versa. There are also a variety of small, unpainted buildings used mostly for storage. All buildings are spread far apart from one another and joined together with a web of foot paths. The spread of buildings is for fire safety. There is no fire department. There are no roads or vehicles visible. The painted houses are occupied by the most socially prominent residents.

Most natives live in huts. The huts are usually one large room built in crevasses between large rocks. The rocks form two or three of the walls. Roofs and balance of the structures are made of driftwood, animal skins, chunks of moss, and such.

Late in the evening we have occasion to change *Nanok*'s place of anchorage. Fairbanks, Jones, Stan, Connors, and I work in semi-darkness. Talledo is in charge. Stan takes the opportunity to goad Fairbanks about the length of a shot of chain for the second time. I make the mistake of joining the fracas. I seek the truth from Talledo. He is in an exceptionally bad mood and has been literally shouting orders. I should have gone elsewhere for an answer. Instead of an answer to my question, he displays his fierce Indian temper and informs me in an irritable, raspy voice that I should have learned long ago that a shot of chain measures ninety feet. He then added that if it had been his decision, I never would have been made seaman 1/c. For an instant, anger suppressed good judgment and I told him that if it had been my decision, he never would have become a boatswain's mate!

The anchorage was secure with the scow tied alongside. I turned to leave the gun deck and came face to face with the chief. He had removed his hat which bore the Coast Guard symbol of authority. This act permitted him to challenge me physically. He planted his feet wide apart and demanded satisfaction for my insult toward him. My feelings were strange, never experienced before. I inform Talledo that he too has insulted me, and he was the first to insult. The man was more than twice my age. A foot shorter in height and plagued with many illnesses, but did not lack for guts. It was not too dark to see his flashing eyes and upraised fists. He crouched somewhat and came at me. My first reaction was to laugh, but I did not. I had no desire to fight the old man. I did not dislike him that much. I tried to say, "I don't want to fight you, Chief," but the words never left my mouth. His overhand right fist missed my retreating chin. So did a ridiculously slow left hook.

I did not raise my fists. "I don't want to fight you, Chief!" I finally managed to say. I could not force myself to strike back. He cocked his arm several more times, then dropped it to his side. He turned, picked up his hat from the deck, and scrambled down the fo'c's'le ladder without a word.

A vision of the Russian Pole at the Brunswick bar came to mind. I could visualize his fiendish, sarcastic smile, and almost hear his laugh. Had he been right? Was I an American coward who refuses to fight for lack of guts? The thought was disturbing. Wind is gone from my sail, my spirit ebbs. I slink off to bed.

September 15, Tuesday; Angmagssalik.

Of the three names that identify this place, Angmagssalik is the most often used, so I use it also. None of the crew that witnessed last night's fiasco chooses to speak to me about it. I am grateful.

Weather is fine. I practice typing with Rollston but my heart isn't in it. I can't get over last night's altercation. I visit Chief McClay, looking for some understanding, I suppose. I told him all about last night's incident. He listened intently, closed his eyes, and nodded his head slowly.

"You heard about it?" I asked.

Another nod.

"Jesus Christ, McClay, what have I done!?"

He gave me a sympathetic look. I then felt ever more sorry for myself.

"I really did not want to fight him, Mac."

He softly said, "I know. This might be the best time to tell you this, 'ski. Sit down.

I sat.

"Not everyone knows this, 'ski, but Talledo has a severe hearing loss. Whenever possible, he reads lips. In darkness he has one hell of a time hearing. Since he doesn't hear well, he doesn't realize how loud his voice is, how offensive he sounds to many of us. As for his sour looks, that is his natural appearance. I've learned that inside he is one hell of a nice guy. When we first met, I thought him to be a loud-mouthed scowling bastard. Later, I learned from his previous commander and some of his old crew, a number of his guys actually shed tears when he was transferred to the *Nanok*."

I felt worse by the minute.

McClay continued. "Talledo was given a really raw deal that may contribute toward his temperament. Just before his retirement date, war was declared and all retirements were cancelled until the war's end. I'm sure he could have obtained a medical exception, but he's not the kind to ask for special consideration. So here he is, in poor physical condition, but overloaded with dogged determination."

All McClay's information added to my poor feelings. With hindsight I could now understand many of the unpleasant things Talledo had said to anger me. Before I left McClay, I had a brand new opinion of Talledo.

As soon as I knew Talledo to be alone, I went to him. Obviously he was surprised to see me.

"What the hell do you want," he barked.

Without being asked, I sat down. I looked at the old man and said, "Chief, I don't know how to begin."

He looked at me even more surprised, and, doubtlessly, confused. I told him in detail all that McClay had told me. He sat down, silently staring at his hands on his knees. He silently nodded as he spoke. I felt so badly I could not continue. He stood up and without looking down at me, he grasped my shoulder with one hand and squeezed. It was all I needed to know that he understood. His face remained placid, but his voice was very gruff and loud, as usual.

"'ski, you're a good kid. Maybe you don't know it, but I see how hard you try and how good you do your work. You're gonna be a damn good sailor, not like some of the braggart ones. I wondered why you always had a hard nose toward me. Now I know. Things should now get better. I'm sorry for last night's business too, but I just couldn't stand you any longer. Now we both understand each other . . . right?" he said, holding out his right hand to me.

"Right!" I smiled, took his hand and we pumped them together. I didn't want him to notice how badly his grip was crushing my hand. He actually gave me a hug and I hugged back. I walked on air to my quarters forward. Sleep would come easy. All I had left to do was to sign some papers for Elmer to cancel Lucille's allotment and begin her new one at an increase to sixty dollars per month.

September 16, Wednesday; Angmagssalik.

Talledo shouts instructions at me, but there is a softer look in his eyes. He shows me several tricks of seamanship and how to tie a monkey-fist knot. He winks at me as I duplicate the feat. He even smiles, one of his rare ones. I suspect I may have a new friend. I know I have become one. He has motivated me. I practice, and in surprisingly short time learn to tie a masthead as well as a Flemish eye knot.

Some cargo remains in the scow and we offload it. There are also seventy-five double cases of canned beer. We eye the brew mischievously, but we are being eyed officially. None of the cases become lost or missing.

The army weather observation buildings are high on a hill. Personnel consists of some twenty weather men and a few army maintenance men. Much of the remaining cargo, including the beer, goes to them.

The large U.S.C.G. cutter *North Star* is at anchor here. We tie to her and visit on board. The cutter *Northland* is here also, as well as the U.S.C.G. trawlers *Aklak* and *Natsek*. [29] We exchange visits with them also. The trawler crews are a nice bunch of swab-jockeys [and] about as homesick as we are. They don't cry aloud as we of the *Nanok* relieve them of much of their cash via poker games, craps, and acey-deucey.

Word comes that the U.S. aircraft carrier *Wasp* has been torpedoed and sunk in the Battle of Guadalcanal.

September 17, Thursday; Angmagssalik.

During the night we are forced to move away from the *North Star* as we were threatened by large icebergs drifting into us. The deck crew on watch found it possible to fend off smaller bergs by pushing them aside with pike poles and boat hooks. However, a large berg can become wedged between both vessels and create an exasperating problem.

The twenty-some-foot motor-sailor is removed from its cradle on the scow by using the boom of a large freighter. The vessel is to remain in this area in custody of Mister Hollingsworth. The scow remains tied to the *Nanok* for the time being. It seems as though we have towed the blasted thing half way around the world and for at least eighteen years. Actually we've had her in tow (on and off) since September 2, only sixteen days.

We leave Angmagssalik in the a.m. and move to a very small army base and Eskimo village called Simiutaq, part two of BE 1. It is here we kiss the scow goodbye (forever, we hope), and scoot back to Angmagssalik. There is still a long day ahead so we sit in dories and slap paint on *Nanok*'s hips. Colliding ice cakes and small bergs have scraped off most of the *Nanok*'s makeup. Hands are so cold it is difficult to release the paint brush.

I wonder how long cold paint will adhere? I always thought one should not paint in less than 65 or 70 degrees. [In any case], our efforts seem worthwhile. The lady was near naked. Painted, she looks proud, proper and dignified, even with the small amount of paint we were able to apply today.

Seven Eskimo husky dogs are brought on board and lashed with very short lines. They are spaced no more than six feet apart, and are tied to the gunwale. The short lashings allow them only to lie down or stand close enough to merely touch noses together. No sooner are the dogs tied, they begin to cover the deck with their droppings! Each beast has generated a mound of excreta half the size of the beast itself! [As if] this is not bad enough, they roll and slide in it! The odor is terrible! Robbins walks by and as usual retches. I have renamed him "Retching Robin." Naturally I do not tell him this. Robbie spits forth unrepeatable words at the animals.

In return, the dogs wag their tales affectionately. Robby does not share their happiness.

Fairbanks is particularly angry about the situation. He has had to scrub hardened animal droppings from the deck before. He creeps up to one of the animals that has its stern section exposed and is about to reward the dog for its rotten housekeeping habits. Fairbanks lets fly an army-booted foot at the dog's transom. At that very moment the dog has heard its stalker and wheels about. Result, the shoe does not land exactly on target. The poor animal is nearly castrated, and an army shoe is covered with dog droppings. Fairbanks has heard Robbie's special cuss words and repeats them loudly at several members of the crew who are witnessing his demise with much laughter.

Buffalo Bill Hollingsworth comes on board and we have a gab fest. He shows us many pictures of his family and thereby manages to make Brill, Petrenko, Clark, Jonesy, and Dexter homesick. Bill smoothes things with a donation of two cartons of candy bars. Nice guy.

Clark crawls into his sack and with tear-filled eyes studies his pin-up picture of movie actress Paulette Goddard. She is mounted upside-down on the overhead above where he lay.

September 18, Friday; Angmagssalik.

Late last p.m. we take on board thirteen more dogs. Talk about howling! All night long like a pack of wolves. Their trainer and dog sled driver Johann Johanson comes on board with them. The dogs fear Johanson even though he is mild looking and less than average size. Whenever he appears on deck, the howling ceases as though a switch has been thrown. Despite the fact that howling ceases, Johann swats each animal a resounding crack across the snout with a heavy club. He says he must retain respect and control and this is the only way he knows how to do it. Should there be an Animal Humane Society in Greenland, Johanson would be in dire straits and probably sliding about in his own excrement.

The day is a lazy one. Very few chores to do. A small dory pulls alongside. I help to unload it and get four cans of beer for the effort.

Oscar Dillon speculates we will remain in Greenland for about six more weeks at the most. He must have a crystal ball or balls.

The *Northstar* and *Natsek* leave.

Members of the crew autographed my phony-baloney certificate I received for crossing the Arctic Circle for the first time. I had each of them include an address they felt might remain more or less permanent and they did so.

Chief Motor Machinist Mate Nelson McClay tempered the blade of my sheath knife. In return, I sew him a nice but small ditty bag he wanted.

September 19, Saturday; Comanche Bay.

We take on board two army weather observation sergeants. One is Warren Morris who brings along his own Eskimo husky puppy named Rusty. Rust is the pup's color. I don't learn the other sergeant's name.

It is said Warren is "going native." He wears an Eskimo jumper and boots and has several Eskimo women pregnant. Maggie says that if any serviceman impregnates a native woman he must pay the Danish government the sum of five hundred dollars to provide medical attention at the child's birth and thereafter. Some tease Warren about his fifteen hundred dollar medical bill. He just grins and denies all guilt.

We leave Angmagssalik in the a.m. and arrive at Comanche Bay in early p.m. The hook is dropped. The *Natsek* is at anchor nearby. She has not yet [been] blessed to go stateside.

We borrow *Natsek*'s clinker-built outboard motorboat. Jones and I use it to haul Johann Johanson and his sled dogs ashore. The dogs promptly cover the boat bottom with excrement. There is no doubt, they eat less than they excrete. Jones says we can go into business if we get the dogs to eat a small amount of cement.

"They will then crap bricks and we can sell them" he said.

I said: "Fine, but who is going to mold the stuff from cigar shapes to brick shapes?"

We immediately went out of business.

What a job getting the animals ashore! When we do, two of them drag me around on my stomach! I dare not release the hold on their leashes. They are too valuable to lose in the snow or on the glacier. My body receives many bruises. Perhaps I can learn to tolerate seeing the dogs beaten by Johanson if they continue thus.

Both army sergeants and Rusty are also hauled ashore.

It grows very cold. Rain falls and freezes. Ice cakes are being blown out to sea by a vicious wind.

September 20, Sunday; Comanche Bay.

Ice is melting. Dog droppings are scraped and washed away but stench remains imbedded in the wooden deck. Rest of cargo is hauled ashore, including Johann's dog sleds, tarpaulins, food, lumber, wire, etc.

As often, Maggie worked along with us. He seemed delighted with my demonstration of seamanship. So was I until I fouled-up in securing a holding hitch around an oil drum. Maggie muttered a few uncomplimentary words about my efforts and I'm afraid I mildly sassed him back. My elevation to coxswain had to have slipped a bit. One does not sass one's skipper. In truth, I felt as if I were sassing myself for being stupid.

Cookie Clark never ceases to amaze me with his culinary artistry. We had hot turkey with stuffing, hot biscuits, cranberries, corn, mashed potatoes with gravy, and a slice of pineapple in jello for dinner. In the worst of seas Clark cooks and if any swabby that can hold food down makes an appearance at the table, Clark will have cooked food for him. Many of the other trawler's so-called cooks secure their respective galleys whenever the anchor is upped. They force their crew to shift for themselves. The crew must eat whatever they can find in the cupboard or refrigerator. I've seen Clark cook in weather so bad the *Nanok* would alternately stand on her tail, then on her head. He has fitted thick, wide, and long steel straps that crisscross his extra large galley cook stove. The straps hold pots in place so they cannot slide about. However, Clark has never found a way to keep himself from sliding about and ricocheting off bulkheads, cupboards, and stove.

It was that way once when Clark not only had the pots anchored to the stove, but also a large garbage can onto the deck. He was trying to make stew. He began with a giant-sized pot nearly full, and finished with one sixth of the pot full. With the heavy roll of the ship, he would slide on stew that had splashed onto the deck. Whenever able, he would stir the stew to keep it from burning. Occasionally he would vomit into the garbage can. Someone told Abe Brill that Clark was not always able to reach the garbage can. And Brill never ate stew again.

September 21, Monday; Comanche Bay.

Maggie declares a holiday. Thank God!

It is a day of heavy rain alternating with snow. In afternoon, Oscar Dillon decides to give me a nautical IQ test. Most of his stupid questions pertain to sailing vessels for crissake!

"What does fore, main, and mizzen pertain to?"

"Masts," I reply, and—to myself—I add "dummy!"

What in hell will I ever have to do with a sailing vessel!? It begins to blow and I am thrilled because the ridiculous session comes to an end.

The anchor begins to drag so we drop a second hook. It somehow wraps its cable around the other anchor's cable. Who in hell knows how! But it did! Had to have happened as it plummeted toward sea bottom. We up both anchors as high as possible. They are not very large. They are Baldt-type and weigh only 500 pounds each. We hold them suspended just above the water and the *Nanok* drifts gently with the wind. Sully Jones is tied about the waist and lowered over the bow to try to unwrap the one turn of the cable. He stands precariously on the lower one and tries to push the other which hangs somewhat higher. Waves cause them to swing rather slowly, but they bang against *Nanok*'s bow again and again. A ticklish job and trying moments for Jones. Everyone is excited but Jones. I never hope to see so fine but dangerous [an] exhibition of seamanship. How he avoided being cast into the sea, or losing a few fingers or legs I will never know.

Voila!! Jones is a hero!

As the anchors swung, he guided and pushed the top one across the lower one, almost knocking himself into the sea. He lost his footing but dangled on an anchor chain with one hand as the two anchors separate from one another. He then managed to grasp the chain with both hands, twist his lower body upwards and wrap both legs around an anchor flute. We then wrestled him on board and pull both anchors chock-a-block.

Wind gusts begin to blow beyond one hundred miles per hour. It is of no use to drop the hooks again. They would never hold bottom. Skipper decides it is safer to ride out the blow throughout the night and we do so. The sudden wind must have come from hell! It is as cold as coveralls filled with crushed ice.

September 22, Tuesday; Angmagssalik.

I awaken with a severely sore throat.

In the a.m. we secure for sea as best we can in high wind and roller-coaster waves. As we put about, wind and sea lays the ship on her side. Madam *Nanok* runs as if a rapist pursues her. The moment we reach open seas, the wind runs off to harass some other vessel somewhere else.

I am forever awed by the mountainous glaciers that come to an end at the sea and bottomless fjords. I thrill when they fracture and break apart with roars that tremble the sea and disturb my ear-drums. Every roar heralds the birth of a floating iceberg. These giant chunks of emerald and diamond plunge into the sea depths and are gone from sight. An eternity later the chunks reappear. They rise slowly, majestically, to ride proud and high in the blue-black sea. These monstrous giants bob in very slow motion as they begin their voyage southward to eternity. They move by will of wind and current. Eventually they are consumed by warmer water and brine of the sea. They are beautiful but fearful to those who sail their playgrounds.

En route to Angmagssalik we receive message that the freighter *Alcoa Pilot* has been blown onto the rocks there, and we are needed to assist pulling her off. Before we arrive, she has freed herself. Saves us much hard work.

In a.m. yesterday, Talledo and Maggie brought back the puppy Rusty as well as a totally black Labrador retriever named Quick. We are to hold Rusty until his master Warren Morris returns. Looks like Maggie has adopted Quick. Today both animals scatter feces throughout the main deck forecastle and the shower room. Thank heaven the dogs can't crawl down the ladder into the crew quarters. I make myself scarce until Fairbanks has cleaned up the mess.

Arriving at Angmagssalik, we drop a hook in the harbor as usual. Sea is calm, only a gentle ground swell. In evening, Mister Dillon and I have a bull session about what a seaman 1/c like myself should know. His questions still pertain mostly to sailing vessels. I suspect that he must own one. [30]

September 23, Wednesday; Angmagssalik.

During 4 to 8 a.m. watch I took the opportunity to make coffee for Chief Talledo. He looked happy as a grinning coon dog.

Scrubbed out two dories with intention of using them as containers for hauling fresh water. Only thing on today's agenda is to dash over to nearby Simiutaq, pick up our old scow, and tow her back here to the vessel *Alcoa Pilot*. Maggie watches as I perform a few minor feats of seamanship but makes no comment. No matter, just so he watches. Chief Talledo is working close with me. I [now] find myself at ease with him.

Evening comes. Chips Delaney, Clark, and I have a singing session. Staneczak lies in his bunk and is reading a book. We sing purposely louder and louder so as to aggravate Stan. We cease when we can no longer bear the din ourselves. Stan continues to read unperturbed. He has lost himself in a world of novels and western magazines. His ability to concentrate despite our raucous singing is amazing. I walk over to make sure Stan is alive. He lies on his back, holding the open book before his eyes, and he is sound asleep!

All in all a good day. Wonder what Lucille is doing at the moment. I sure miss her. Don't dare to dwell on the thought, as it gets too heavy.

September 24, Thursday; Angmagssalik.

Sullivan Jones, Elmer Comer, and the old man plod about the area trying to find a new source of fresh water. Ended up getting it from the same place everyone does, from a small stream running through the village. For some reason Maggie is reluctant to take water from this stream. He must fear pollution from the villagers.

Two-gun Dexter and Balboa stand near shore in rubber juke suits, fending the water-container dories off the rocks while water is being put into them. They stand waist deep in snow and slush. Both clown around and float on their backs in the buoyant rubber suits. Dexter makes the sound of a ship's whistle but it is a tenor whistle. Balboa sounds as deep as a Mississippi riverboat. Using a small, portable gasoline-powered pump, we fill and transport three dories, twice, to the *Nanok*.

Heavy winds late in evening. Our three dories are tied to one another alongside the *Nanok*. The plan is to use them for hauling water again tomorrow. Because of the wind, we think it best to lift the dories back on board. In my haste to separate them to hoist them individually, I accidentally cut the bow line of the only one actually fastened to the *Nanok*. Very quickly, Fairbanks tosses me the end of another line. Several of the crew manage to pull me and the three dories back to the *Nanok*. Very fortunate because I would have been blown quickly out to sea without motor or oars. There was no other small vessel on board the ship, so the *Nanok's* anchor would have to be raised before rescue could even begin. In that long lapse of time, the choppy seas would have capsized all three dories. I am indebted to Fairbanks.

As I and the three dories are being pulled back to the ship, I lose my balance and tumble half out of the dory I am in. A very close call, and a very stupid piece of seamanship. Lucky in a way because neither Talledo, Maggie, nor Dillon was around to witness my faux pas.

September 25, Friday; Angmagssalik.

I chip and scrape away flaking paint from the poop deck and make up a new four inch mooring line by splicing a large loop in one end and back splicing the other so it cannot unravel.

Wind blowing like the devil all day. Freighter *Alcoa Pilot* runs in and out of harbor three times. She is finding it difficult to get into proper position to drop a hook.

Feeling fine but very tired. *Nanok* will rock me to sleep.

September 26, Saturday; Angmagssalik.

Did some red-leading.

Stan, skipper, Jones, and Dreams go ashore to get fresh water from a waterfall Maggie and I located earlier in the day. Jones and Connors left the water-laden dories to go aground and Maggie popped his cork in anger. He threatened to leave them "freezing your asses off throughout dinner." Happily, he changed his mind. Between boatloads of water, Jonesy, the curious one, clambers about and locates two small ponds that feed the waterfall.

September 27, Sunday; At sea.

Up anchor and leave Angmagssalik with another army sergeant and a welding outfit for Captain Taylor. As soon as we enter Comanche Bay, we are struck by a hurricane-type beast of a wind. At the same time, giant waves leap over the bow and smash me to my knees. I had anticipated Comanche Bay's behavior and had tied myself to the three-inch gun before our entrance. I did not want to take the chance of being washed overboard. Talledo had urged me to carry a fifteen foot length of twenty-one thread line at all times in the pocket of my "Mae West" life jacket; one hell of a good habit I have learned.

The *Nanok* did an about face and beat it back out to sea. Hell waited there for us also. I have no idea where they came from, but we were greeted by what seemed like a million icebergs! Boy! What a job zigzagging through them to open water! The instant we are free, the wind disappeared. Just like that!

Very late in the evening's calm, the old man had Guns Owens fire the portside K gun just for the hell of it, to see if it would have any effect on the icebergs nearby. Most of the crew were either resting or sleeping in their sacks and did not know the tremendous blast was a practice shot. A big bunch of wild-eyed sailors suddenly hit the topside deck in long-john underwear with Mae West jackets tucked underarm. No one thinks the exercise is funny except Maggie (as usual) and dumb-ass Guns.

Fracto-nimbus clouds hang from the sky. Their very dark, fractured strands reach down toward the *Nanok*. Heavy rains are on the way! Everyone tries to duck inside the fo'c's'le hatch at the same time!

September 28, Monday; Angmagssalik.

Voila!

Banshees are asleep as we tiptoe into the harbor after spending the night outside, amongst the bergs. The hook is dropped and the sergeant and welding outfit are ferried ashore. In return, five soldiers [come on board], including Warren Morris, dog Rusty's master. We leave the hell hole immediately for Angmagssalik through the field of icebergs.

The wind has found us! *Nanok* keeps nodding like a parrot atop monumental waves. Clark performs his high-seas magic but there are very few takers. Clark bristles in anger as Petrenko tells him the stew came out of the head. Clark would never do such an awful thing, I am sure. I think.

The hook is dropped in Ang. Harbor. It is too rough to ferry our passengers ashore so they are to stay the night. They sleep on galley benches and in empty sacks of men on watch.

Despite the rough sea, Bos'n Robbins practices blinker light and semaphore with me. Lord knows I need the practice.

September 29, Tuesday; Angmagssalik.

Not much work on agenda. Rain and heavy snow all day. The passengers are ferried ashore. We fetch some old scow from the *Alcoa Pilot* and tow her to shore also. I practice more blinker light with Robbie.

Oscar the Dilly raises my ire. Still insists I memorize various parts of sailing vessels! What in hell is he thinking of!? Are we at war with *H.M.S. Bounty*? When will we graduate to the *Merrimac* and the *Monitor*?! What in heaven's name do I care about a sprit or spanker!? I wonder if the army has to learn about muzzle-loaders, Gatling guns, and the curing of buffalo hides?

Maggie blesses me with a can of beer and some potato chips. I look at him and wonder if he knows that an oar has a tip, blade, loom, leather, and a handle and has committed this extremely valuable information to memory.

Sergeant Warren Morris left his dog Rusty on board and promised to pick the beastie up as soon as possible. He is anxious to get ashore to see if his kayak has been built as his Eskimo friend had promised it would be. This guy would like to become an Eskimo, I'm thinkin'. In gratitude for letting him stay on board, dog Rusty has gifted us with a variety of small volcanoes across the shower room deck. I swore never to scoop poop again and I will not. Believe it or not, the super-sensitive Robbins does the job to rid the place of the odor, and to be able to cease retching.

Afterthought, where in tarnation did Maggie get fresh potato chips hereabouts? There isn't even a PX in Angmagssalik.

I ask Maggie again about my coxswain's rating and he again says: "we'll see what we can do."

September 30, Wednesday; Angmagssalik.

Had 4 to 8 watch.

We were supposed to tow a small scow to a nearby village but the winds are too heavy. The *Nanok* tugs at her anchor chain much like an angry dog. Morale worsens. Men grow angry at slightest provocation. Petrenko is furious with Delaney who beat him out of several packs of cigarettes in a card game last night. Pete is one hell of a lousy loser.

Compared to Pete, Delaney is much shorter and very slender. Pete is the rawboned giant whose teeth are almost always bared. Delaney is as feisty as a bantam rooster. Face to chest, he tells Pete to look into a mirror and scare himself. Pete says Delaney is a termite, not a carpenter.

Many other things gnaw at morale. Small luxuries are growing ever more difficult to come by. The smell of a chocolate bar is a treat in itself. Chips finishes up his turn as mess punk and Elmer Comer gets his turn. Fairbanks was to take over but he somehow managed to avoid the chore.

U.S.C.G. cutter *Comanche* was to escort two vessels into the harbor today, but there is no sign of her.

Did some typing and splicing. Thinking too much about not getting promoted and manage to anger myself. I think of Dillon's dumb questions and say aloud to no one: "how am I ever going to learn when and how to hoist the topgallant sails or splice a new mizzen mast?"

October

Ice bergs and thick cake ice fields stretch to the horizon. Nanok *has a narrow escape. As we push aside a very large berg, it decides it does not want to be pushed aside. Pressure from the starboard side of the* Nanok's *bow causes the berg to roll over onto its back. After a great amount of pushing, the berg decides to turn right side up, then down onto the* Nanok's *bow. The berg's weight pushes the bow deep under water.*

October 1, Thursday; Angmagssalik.

Homesickness prevails. Most show it at least in little ways, but no one speaks of it aloud. All I had to say was: "Gee I wish Lucille were here," and a couple of giant tears roll down Robbie's cheeks. I thought homesickness was only a female weakness.

Elmer says I have a loss of memory because I was struck in the head with a blivet which is supposed to be two pounds of shit in a one pound sack. Mr. Dillon chimes in to teach me things beyond the call of duty. I am taught that a lounge lizard is a sailor who has teeth up his rectum and goes around biting the buttons off sofa seats. I doubt I could ever learn to be a coxswain without his help.

October 2, Friday; Angmagssalik.

Sullivan Jones and I have the 4 to 8 watch. We move to and anchor at a new position in the harbor. After off-loading a few things, we head for the open sea. From there we escort the civilian freighter *Hilton* and the U.S.C.G. trawler *Aklak* into anchor area. *Aklak* has much mail for the *Nanok*. Hot dog! I receive 17 letters!

Elmer Comer, whose responsibility it is, manages to purchase a large supply of pogey bait for the crew. I receive eight chocolate bars. Talledo gives each of us two cans of beer. I trade mine for Petrenko's chocolate.

Playing black jack and acey-deucey I win a carton of Lucky Strike cigs from Pete. As usual he bares and grinds his teeth.

Not much heavy work to do so Dillon, Clark, Sully Jones, and I have a bull session. I try my damndest to avoid discussing sailing vessels. Most of the crew go ashore to see a movie. Abe Brill makes a rare visit to the forecastle. His skin has become powder white. He will never become accustomed to sailing. I think he may die before we see Boston again. He is losing much weight. Nick Vacar and his boss McClay visit forward quarters too. Must be old home week. Conversations are mostly about the States and home, families, etc. All voices have a tint of loneliness.

October 3, Saturday; Angmagssalik.

I begin to fashion three manila rope fenders but Robbins and Dillon ask for my assistance. We on-load twenty drums of oil and a few stores from the *Alcoa Pilot* via the *Aklak*. I wonder where Talledo is at and why he is not in charge. In evening Dilly begins to teach me basic astronomy. I don't enjoy it but I study.

Maggie says it will now be the responsibility of the *Nanok* to advise headquarters and area vessels of ice conditions and when ships are to head southward. All will depend on location and density of ice fields and bergs. Conditions grow worse daily.

Eskimo children enjoy following Oscar Dillon around. Oscar's complexion being similar to that of the Eskimos, plus his round and plump face, leads the kids to believe he is one of their kind. While Oscar is annoyed at the ever-present children, the crew is secretly amused.

As during a number of other occasions, I stand wheel watch with only Oscar doing the 4 to 8 with me. The pilot house interior is blacked-out except for the tiny white light illuminating the forward-most area of the compass card. The ship's diesel engine below our deck throbs loudly. Deck beneath our feet pulsates in tempo with the engine. Oscar begins humming, quietly at the beginning. The left side of his back is turned toward me. I am sure he is unaware that I hear him. He hums but one note. It grows louder and louder. The pulsating deck breaks Oscar's hum into a staccato. I find the sound to be rather pleasant as I steer the ship with the aid of the tiny compass light. The sound lulls me and I begin to doze. Suddenly I lose my balance and nearly fall. I come awake with a start. The hair on the back of my neck bristles. I am 15 degrees off course!! I have to nurse the *Nanok* back onto course without Dillon becoming aware. If he was to learn what I had done, it would doubtlessly set my advancement back a knot or two. He would never believe his hum lullaby contributed toward my behavior. Luckily, in near total darkness, he was unable to see or feel the correcting of *Nanok*'s course.

Back on course again, I wished Oscar would shut up. Mental telepathy . . . he shuts up! Suddenly it is much too quiet in the pilot house. I begin to doze.

October 4, Sunday; Angmagssalik.

On-loaded more drums of oil and two oil-burning heating stoves. Robbins assumes deck leadership. Talledo failed to appear. Robbie was in his own private glory world. Robbins once had the rating of "surfman," a petty officer that excels in the operation and maintenance of small boats, particularly surfboats used mostly for coastal rescue work. He had been located at a surf station on the Atlantic Coast in the Boston area. For more than fifteen years, his main duty was to rescue small vessels and crews in distress.

About the same time that World War II came along, the Coast Guard abolished all surfman ratings and reidentified them as boatswain's mates. Robbie knew surfman duties well, but was not skilled in the functions and duties of large vessels for he had never served on board any. Maggie never lets Robbie forget his shortcomings. Robbins is never treated as a boatswain's mate 1/c on the *Nanok*, but rather as another deck force crew member. (But then the captain considered all ratings to be nonsense and said so a number of times.) He considered ratings to be only pay-level differences, nothing more. I wondered in what category he placed himself.

Robbins was always over-anxious to prove he was a capable boatswain. In doing so, many secretly laughed at his efforts. I feel very sorry for him and his circumstance. He is one of my best buddies. Despite our friendship, he and I tie into it a bit on occasion. In his zeal he sometimes snarls at me without good reason. Perhaps because I rarely snarl back. Today, he and Clark get into it. Who really knows why. Perhaps just to let off steam.

Some of the guys get into discussing stag and smoker parties. This is not good for lonely men. It makes a guy . . .

October 5, Monday; Angmagssalik.

Quarters on board the *Nanok* are almost as crowded as that of a submarine. Our close, constant proximity to one another is irritating at best. Time and boredom is no helpmate either, it wears the skin off raw tempers.

Clark terminates an argument at the dining table by smashing a giant chunk of raw meat on the great-board between the arguers. Snarling ceases as Clark shouts, "fight like dogs, eat like dogs!"

Nanok rests moored in the distance while her sailors in "juke suits" gather Greenland ice for freshwater. (Photo courtesy of Bernard Delaney, private collection.)

Up anchor, move to new location closer to shore and drop hook. It is already time to obtain a supply of fresh water. Skipper decides it should be gotten from the waterfall nearby. Waterfalls are easy to locate. Just look for a giant icicle that begins at the top of an escarpment and ends down in the fjord. Chances are the icicle contains a core of down-falling water.

We climb perhaps fifty feet up the face of the cliff alongside the icicle. This is about as far up as is safe to climb the sometimes loose, rocky face of the escarpment. We chop a large, horizontal wedge out of the icicle with a fire axe. As we near the core, there is indeed a waterfall core enclosed. A large, clean, garbage can is inserted into the icicle just far enough to catch the edge of the swiftly-falling water.

Welded to the side of the can, near its bottom, is a pipe-nipple outlet, threaded to accept the threaded fitting at the leading end of a long fire hose. The fitting is fastened to the nipple and the hose is led down the escarpment's side and into the dory. As water fills the garbage can, a pressure is developed and forces water into the hose and swiftly down into the dory. It is an arduous task because it requires many dory-fuls to fill the

Nanok's tanks. Our usual compensation for hauling fresh water is an enjoyable shower and laundry. I never dreamt fresh water could become a luxury.

Today my job is to stand amongst the shore rocks and fend the dories off of them. I wear a hooded, coverall design rubber juke suit. A small, clean dory has been set inside a larger dory. In tow, this arrangement, supposedly, will prevent the occasional splash of sea water from entering the inner, freshwater dory. It is similar to placing a small cup inside of a large bowl. The larger container will catch the salt water, not the inner container.

I hold the hose-end inside the small dory and soon fill it. Chips, Connors, Talledo, and I haul the first load to the *Nanok* at anchor. Dexter chooses to remain ashore and wait for our return. Part way to the *Nanok*, our tow begins to yaw. The outer dory takes on much sea water and finally submerges. All is lost. Since both dories are of wood, they still float. At the *Nanok*, we hoist both on board, empty them, insert the smaller into the larger and return to the waterfall.

After Dexter filled the small dory, I straddle the narrow stern of the outer dory, still in my juke suit. With an oar I am to steer and keep the boats from yawing. Talledo, Chips, Connors, and Dexter are in the outboard motor boat, towing me and the dories some distance behind them. It grows dark quickly now. Perhaps Talledo is over-anxious to reach the *Nanok* while daylight still remains. At any rate, we move too fast. All my strength is not enough to keep the dories from yawing somewhat. I notice small quantities of salt water splash again and again into the outer dory. I did not consider the amount to be of any consequence. Besides, the gloom-shrouded *Nanok* is near.

Quite suddenly I find myself in water up to my neck! One splash too many has entered the outer dory and it has submerged! My juke suit keeps me afloat, but I lost hold of the steering oar.

Men in the motorboat are intent upon reaching the *Nanok*. None are looking back to see how I am faring! The hood of my juke suit is up over my head, but it is not secured tightly about my face or neck. I yell loudly as possible but I am unheard above noise of the outboard motor! Finally, just before they were to disappear in the growing darkness, one of the men happened to look back and saw my plight. The motorboat came to a halt. I reached for the stern of the sunken dory but missed. It was beyond my reach.

Those in the motorboat concentrated on saving the fresh water–filled dory whose gunwale still protruded perhaps an inch above fjord level.

Seawater trickled slowly into my juke suit from around my neck. I was trapped inside my water-filling suit! The oar floated nearby but it also was beyond my reach.

"Help!" I yelled, "I'm sinking!"

By now the water level inside my juke suit was at knee level! I [was] thrashing about, trying to swim toward the submerged but still-floating dories.

"You bastards!" I screamed, "I'm sinking!"

When enough water had entered my suit I began to sink like a fishing lure. The men in the motorboat were busy as hell trying to steady the small dory filled with fresh water. Chips Delaney wheeled about, reached out as far as he possibly could without falling out of the boat and grabbed the head-top of my suit. Several others joined in and pulled me into their boat. I cursed the men all the way to the *Nanok*. Some of them were laughing. Disregarding the fact that one of the men was Talledo, I swore at all of them. Fear and numbing cold shivered me. I didn't give a good damn what I said.

Wind has risen some and so have the waves. The night is clear but cold. I've had my very hot shower. When my body stopped steaming, I dressed heavily and paced the deck. I must count my blessings. I also wondered how Lucille would react if told I drowned in a juke suit.

October 6, Tuesday; Angmagssalik.

Warren Morris is dead!

Drowned last night.

He had spoken about his great desire to master the kayak but we pooh-poohed the idea. Warren enjoyed all native things, especially clothing.

Supposedly, Warren was coming out to the *Nanok* to get his dog Rusty. I can't imagine how he intended to carry the one-third-sized Eskimo husky on his kayak. He must have drowned about the time I was taking my shower. They assumed he was tightly secured about the waist as necessary to keep water from seeping into the low-lying kayak cockpit. The rising wind and short, choppy waves might have caused him to capsize. The craft is narrow and Warren was not skilled enough to untie his waist and wriggle out of the craft. We are told he was found near the shore floating upside down. What a waste! He was a very nice young man and will be missed. They have his body in the army storage shed to protect it from animals.

Impossible to boat more water today, too much ice along the shore. It is too thick to break through with the motor boat, and too dangerous for the *Nanok* to try. Loaded yet more supplies for Comanche Bay.

We are tied to the *Aklak* to combine resistance against the wind. If our anchor fails to hold, maybe hers will. I wonder if anyone has considered what would happen if both vessels lost anchorage at the same time? Tangled anchors? Worse?

In evening winds die. We go to see a movie in the small army base mess hall. The local governor and his wife are with us. Movie is called *Unfinished Business*. A very nice name for the dumb picture. Don't know why we want to see a movie at this time of tragedy anyway. There is no spirit in the soldiers who are present. Morris' death hangs a pall over the entire village. Another movie, *The Bugle Sounds*, was about to be shown, but Elmer Comer and I have no heart to watch it. Besides, we have seen it before.

Back to the *Nanok* we go along with others. Macon Leroy Roach is already on board and has hot coffee waiting. We drink and discuss Morris' fate. A pity.

October 7, Wednesday; Comanche Bay.

Was routed out of my sack at 4 a.m. to get underway. Our mooring lines are frozen stiff and some come apart when wrapped around our powerful winch's drum.

The *Aklak* gets herself blown ashore but manages to free herself.

Arriving at Comanche Bay we drop both hooks. As usual, winds near seventy-five miles per hour plague the *Nanok*. The hooks hold, but for how long? *Nanok* is covered with a four to six inch-thick blanket of ice.

Skipper says we must remain in this hell hole's wind tunnel until we unload, but it is too rough to attempt any landing.

I stand the pilot house watch in the evening. Former Lt. Crockett of the U.S. Navy keeps me company. He is now a U.S. Army major. As a Navy man, he was with Admiral Richard E. Byrd. He is a class gentleman and a fascinating storyteller.

October 8, Thursday; Comanche Bay.

Wind is hiding out there somewhere, ready to pounce upon us at any time. We have much work to do and begin to do it. Captain Mag is not snarling at me as often as he had a few days ago. He actually smiled at me several times within a few minutes. This is a mistake on his part. I now know that he must be human. He tells me several unfunny jokes and I laugh like hell.

God-a-mighty-damn-boy! What a job!

Dilly, Talledo, Connors, and I work our asses tight off-loading. Again we have to break ice off our lines in order to flex them and raise the boom.

We are relieved in the afternoon. To rest? Hell no!! We are sent ashore to work. Spent rest of day pulling drums of fuel oil up hill. The morning was tough, but this is medieval torture.

October 9, Friday; Comanche Bay.

Waited for Captain Taylor and Major Crockett to come on board. We leave the bay hopefully for the last time this year, but I've hoped that before.

It got colder and rougher than hell in the afternoon and I took sick. A combination of flu and seasickness methinks. Good buddy Jones relieves me of the last hour of my wheel watch. I go below and heave all the salmon I had eaten earlier.

Robby, Clark, Roach, and several others are singing one of our favorite, unnamed songs:

Eyes right! Foreskins tight!
Assholes to the rear!
We're the boys who make no noise
We've all got gonorrhea.
We're the heroes of the night,
We would rather fuck than fight,
We're the heroes of
The "skinback fusiliers."

Hot damn! I've never laughed and vomited at the same time before!

October 10, Saturday; Angmagssalik.

Unable to stand a.m. watch. Have high fever and no strength and in a constant chill. As the day progresses I feel better and conclude that what I have is a common cold.

We pull into Angmagssalik Harbor and tie alongside the U.S.C.G. cutter *Northland*. Our two passengers go ashore. Many of us go on board the *Northland* and buy as much pogey bait as they allow us to. We then get to see a movie called *Riders of the Purple Sage*. Talk about an oldie!!! It must have been Thomas Alva Edison's first movie!

Fish chowder in the evening. I have no appetite even for the chocolate bars I purchased. My legs wobble with weakness and I have difficulty breathing. Too bad we don't have a hospital-full of nurses.

Our swabbies played touch-tackle football with the army and the Coasties won! Captain Maggie must have been the referee.

Northland has several Eskimo women on board who were wounded supposedly in or near Iceland. No other details.

October 11, Sunday; Kap Dan.

A group from the *Nanok* go ashore to attend the funeral of Warren Morris. I go also. It was suggested that Captain Magnusson bury Warren at sea because there is only a shallow depth of earth or silt in which to bury a coffin. There is fear that a shallow grave could be easily desecrated by animals. Our skipper wisely refuses to even participate. He feels that one day Morris' family would question why their soldier son was not buried ashore. He doubted that they would accept the excuse of "lack of earth-depth."

Because of animals, it is decided that Warren should be buried as close as possible to the army barracks. Since there are no genuine coffins available, a wide, flat, wooden packing crate was used. What a difficult job carrying even the packing-crate coffin around the rock-strewn hillside. Many Eskimos, particularly women, sit atop large rocks nearby to watch the proceedings. There is much weeping and cries of grief coming from them. Perhaps there is merit to the rumor the handsome sergeant is the father of several local children.

The packing crate coffin is lowered into the shallow silt. Honor guards from army, navy, and coast guard stand at attention. The squad I am in face one side of the grave and the rest of the guard are on the opposite side, and some at the coffin's foot.

The *Northland's* skipper stands at the foot of the coffin. There are gaping openings between crate boards. The *Northland's* skipper reads a short, simple eulogy and tosses a symbolic handful of soil onto the crate.

"Ashes to ashes, dust to dust . . ."

Solemnity embraces everyone. I see thin lines of Warren's body through the spaces between boards. As soil lands on the coffin, much of it falls through the cracks onto Morris. As I watch, my mind wanders. I think of Warren's parents so far away, unknowing at the moment that their son is being buried. I stupidly think of what it would have been like to visualize at his birth that one day he would drown himself in, of all things, a kayak, in Greenland, and then be buried in a packing crate near the Arctic Circle.

At funeral's end, I met the old Greenlandic gentleman that built the kayak for Morris. My first reaction was to shout profanities at the guy, but he was so genuinely remorseful, I just smiled and patted his shoulder.

After services, we return to the *Nanok*, up the anchor and head for some small army base known as Kap Dan. Roach, Rollston, and Connors are left visiting on board the *Northland*. Our skipper doesn't seem to be worried about them; what a guy!

If the *Northland* receives orders to leave for some distant place, what will become of our men?

At Kap Dan we off-load many barrels of fuel oil and bagged food of some sort, flour, sugar, rice, etc. Eskimo women assist to swiftly off-load three small cargo boats onto shore. An extremely overweight woman rolls her eyes at Talledo. He surprises me. He is embarrassed and flustered! I wonder if the lady knows about such things as diets.

Eskimo women are much like many other women I know. They prize attractive, colorful clothing, their children, and their man. If they resent the meagerness of their belongings or their social status, it is not visible.

Eskimo women carry their babies in a leather pouch slung across their back like an Indian papoose . . . somewhat like arrows in a quiver. One mom carries a large basket of coal atop her head while baby is free to watch over mother's shoulder. Mom stumbles under the load she carries and almost falls to her knees. Father, sitting atop a boulder nearby, casually watching the proceedings, removes the pipe from his mouth and with a somewhat impatient voice reprimands mom for her clumsiness. Mom scrambles to her feet without a word of protest and hurries up the hill with her load.

All is not work for mothers. Occasionally, one of the menfolk will take six or eight women for a pleasure ride in an *umiak*, a long, wide, and deep, sealskin-covered woman's boat. The man will sit in the stern with a steering paddle. Each woman must pull an oar. Length of the pleasure trip seems to be limited only by the woman's energy.

Hair stylists would envy the elaborate hairdos of Eskimo women. The hair is usually long and very dark. It is rolled and fashioned into magnificent loops, swirls, rolls, pleats, and braids. It shines as if varnished. The varnish is really whale, seal, or musk oxen oil. It has an unpleasant odor but the artistic results justify the odor.

October 12, Monday; Angmagssalik.

Up anchor, leave Kap Dan early in a.m. and arrive at another tiny village in a couple of hours. Maggie does not mention the name of the place.

The villagers perform a drum dance for our entertainment. It varies somewhat from the dance performed at Julianehåb on September fourth. As before, Clark and I do our appreciation dance. Talledo says Clark and I resemble chickens that just had their heads cut off, but not as pretty. Dillon photographs our terpsichorean efforts and promises that after war's end each crew member will receive copies of all photos he has taken of us.

We leave the village and arrive at Angmagssalik. Since the *Northland* is here, I ask Maggie's permission to go fetch our three crewmen. Maggie refuses . . . must have some crotchety bug up his ass, telling me he must punish the guys for staying on board the *Northland*. Late in p.m., a small boat from the *Northland* brings the guys home.

October 13, Tuesday; Angmagssalik.

I purchase a new mattress cover, pillow case, and a dozen handkerchiefs from *Northland*'s small stores.

Lately, Robbie keeps picking on me for ridiculous little things, such as the fact I use too much salt, or I fail to fully throw the security dog on the forecastle hatch, or my shoes were left lying on the deck and in his path, etc. I am finally provoked into telling him to: "go piss up a rope!"

He tells me never to speak to him again, for crissake!! He is sure growing moody lately! Dillon says he is at a loss for something to do to bring Robbie back to earth.

Busy day of paint chipping. Learned some Eskimo language from Lars Ebersson. He has me repeating a very interesting sounding phrase but will not tell me what it means. He just smiles when I ask. I fear it is very bad so I never repeat it.

Skipper is ashore all day. Two giant, gasoline-powered electric generators come on board from the *Northland*. They are almost too heavy to lift with boom and rope falls. We carry and transfer them onto a small shoreside scow. They are a gift from heaven because Angmagssalik has never had electricity before. One unit will surely go to the army base.

Petrenko has repaired my harmonica so in gratitude I punish him by playing a few tunes.

Passengers come on board. They are named Brennan, Ki, Lars and Major Crockett. Abe Brill comes to complain that Robbie is picking on him. Brill has tears in his eyes. I believe Robbie dwells too much about returning home.

October 14, Wednesday; Angmagssalik.

Left in a.m. and arrived at another small, remote Eskimo village a short way up one of the many fjords hereabouts. All passengers and the skipper go ashore and later return with two dead seals that I load on board.

Back at anchor at Ang. An iceberg twice the size of the *Nanok* rammed into the anchored freighter *Hilton*. I signaled the *Hilton* with blinker light to warn her of the danger, but being at anchor, there wasn't much they could do but to accept the ram. Same thing happened to the *Northland* today.

October 15, Thursday; Unidentified village.

Northland wants the *Nanok* to tow a scow somewhere. Maggie says: "bull-shit!" He tells them we must leave and have no time to wait until the scow is ready. Away we fly toward some other village. Part way there, we come across a Danish nurse in an *umiak* being towed by a putt-putt. A putt-putt is a double prow boat made of thick, curved, wooden timbers. The boat has no ribs and requires none. It is about sixteen feet long, eight feet wide, and four feet deep. It has a miniature cabin amidships which houses a one cylinder, kerosene-powered engine.

The vessel resembles a toy tug boat. The engine fires once per second with an ear-splitting "pow!" Sound that echoes back from icebergs and distant mountains. Each "pow!" sends a giant, doughnut-shaped smoke ring out of the short, fat smokestack. Continual "Pow! Pow! Pow! Pow! Pow!" is enough to send one's brain running for cover from side to side in one's head.

The two vessels are escorted by two kayaks. We learn the nurse makes a round of each village periodically to tend to the sick and lame. No over-abundance of medical attention here. We take the passengers, *umiak*, and kayaks on board and tow the putt-putt to the village. All passengers are put ashore and Maggie goes with them while we boat fresh water.

Robbins and Delaney paw the dirt, bare their teeth and snarl at one another. A grave offense was committed. Delaney sat where Robbie was thinking of sitting. Chips has guts but no surplus of brains. He's about two-thirds the size of mean-ass Robbie. No blows are struck, but almost. I suppose we could have buried Chips at sea. His wife Catherine would be proud of her courageous hero. The two end their fracas by shouting dirty names at one another.

Skipper returns and distributes two cans of beer to each crew member. I trade mine for loud-mouth Stan's four candy bars. He sucks up beer like wolves suck-up water.

Lars invited me to visit his home but I am too tired to go. Guess I hurt his feelings.

It grows late but Robbie and Chips have not finished hissing. Tempers are thin as a thread of gossamer silk; everyone's are thin these days.

October 16, Friday; Angmagssalik.

While leaving the village, the *Nanok's* bow is pointed toward Ang. En route, Sullivan Jones is operating the boom's lift lines, trying to remove shrink twists that have developed. As the large block is being raised, I grasp its steel hook for the fun of it and am lifted from the deck. It is horseplay and I expect Sully will lower me to the deck after lifting me a few feet. Up, up, up I go, about eight feet high. If I let go the hook I could be injured in the fall.

"Down! You dog!" I shout at Jonesy. He is laughing and so am I. Up, up, up I go!

"Hey! Dammit!" I yell good-naturedly, "put me down you jackass!"

Sully wears a fiendish grin now. He secures the lift line to a cleat and tugs at the lines that swing the boom from side to side. Soon he swings the boom outboard. Maggie hangs partly out of the pilot house shutter opening, grinning from ear to ear. I expect him to order Jonesy to set me down but he does not!

Outboard I go, legs flailing in the air. This is madness! The *Nanok* is traveling at top speed and I am clothed heavily. If I should lose my grip on the hook, I'd drown for sure!

"Hot dammit!" I scream, "pull me in!!" I am no longer laughing, I'm scared as hell! Maggie does not intercede! Jonesy is guffawing hilariously as he begins to lower me down toward the sea. I fold up my legs to keep them out of the water. Jones shows no mercy and lowers me even more!

"Help!!" I yell in desperation. I can no longer hold my legs up so I drop them into the water. Rushing water tugs at my body and my arms are growing weak.

"Help! Help!" I scream. "God damn it, captain!" I yell. Still no response from him.

Finally Jones lifts me and swings me inboard. He lowers me partway down, then suddenly releases the lift line. I tumble onto the deck like a wet mop. I curse Jonesy with every dirty word I know. As quickly as I can regain my leg strength and breath, I go after him. It is my intention to literally toss him overboard without caring about consequence. I froth at the mouth. Jones is gone. Where in hell could he hide on a vessel this small?

After more than an hour, complete fatigue overtakes me and I quit searching. Much later Jones appears from somewhere, nonchalantly eating a candy bar. I throw a heavy army shoe and narrowly miss a nimble target. Had I drowned, what story would Jones and the skipper give to a board of inquiry?

In evening Clark teaches me to make oatmeal cookies, which the crew enjoy. Next, he is to teach me to make pies.

October 17, Saturday; Angmagssalik.

Boated one dory of fresh water.

Chips and I go to army base and haul back a load of food-stuffs *gratis*. Armed services will never organize a smooth-running logistics program. This handful of army weathermen have received enough sugar to feed the world for 200 years, several tons!

We leave Ang. and arrive at "Curio" or, as the Greenlanders call it, "Simiutaq." An army yardbird beats at a piano while a few of us Carusos sing a few screechy songs. Clark and I also play some ping-pong.

Back on board the *Nanok*, Clark guides and helps me create seven pies and a large batch of biscuits. Rumor number 30,000: the *Nanok* may stay northeast for quite a while. *Bull puckey*!! Supposedly there is much more work for us to do in this area. . . . What!! Back to Ang.

October 18, Sunday; Angmagssalik.

Moving south, high winds join us. In spurts, near the hundred mile per hour range. They tear at the *Nanok*. Wave tops become airborne and are carried into the smoke stack. The diesel falters but does not stop. There is fear that if the engine stops and the *Nanok* wallows, the ship could easily capsize.

I am seasick. Retching and vomiting have emptied my stomach and bowels, all the way to my rectum. I begin to vomit small shreds of blood. When the skipper notices this he orders me to leave the wheel and lay below. He personally takes over the wheel.

I clamber cautiously down the outside ladder and stumble forward across the crazily-pitching deck to the forecastle, down the ladder, and into my sack, soaking wet. Connors tells me that the heavy, wooden grating in the stern of the ship, on which hawsers are coiled for drying, has been torn loose and has drifted away. *Nanok* is below water more than it is atop it. She pitches and lurches. Twice I am tumbled from my sack. Connors says that the drums of diesel fuel oil lashed with cable on deck have also been torn away and are gone! Some life-boats have been damaged.

The forecastle ships much water. The patch over the hole in the bow is leaking profusely. It pours down the forecastle ladder and into the crew quarters. Mercifully, not into the bunks.

Warren Morris' dog Rusty and Labrador retriever Quick, howl and vomit and slide around in an aggregate of vomit, excrement, and salt water. Roll of the vessel hurls them helter-skelter into lockers and bulkheads. They do not allow themselves to be held or tied down in any way. Both are covered with yuk and haven't the sense to lie down in some narrow niche even though there are many places available to them.

October 19, Monday; Angmagssalik.

The sea and I are at peace today. I feel a bit better and manage to eat and retain a few dry soda crackers. Should anyone pass this way again, I hope they will find my stomach and intestines and return them to me.

Shortly after leaving our anchorage we receive radio instructions to return to Ang. So we do an about-face. I stand my watch on the bow. It will be too dark and treacherous to enter Ang. Harbor so the *Nanok* will have to heave-to and ride the waves all night outside. Hope this old wooden shoe holds together. She creaks and wails. I believe she is seasick also.

Loneliness is easy to come by, especially at sea and at night when all is blacked out. It is like late autumn ashore, when trees have been stripped bare of all leaves and shiver naked, facing the onslaught of the first freezing rain, after all four-legged creatures have found places to hide.

During wartime no lights are permitted on deck. Whenever a hatch is being opened, indoor lights switch off automatically and are replaced by very dim blue lights. When the hatch is closed again, off go the blue lights and on come the bright whites. Not even a match or cigarette flame is permitted to show on deck. It is a fact that the flame of a match can be seen from many miles away. Excellent assistance for an enemy.

This night is without moon, only faint shadows for the straining eye to see. Tilting decks cause a loss of equilibrium. I move along the deck more by sense of feel and memory rather than by sight. There loom black shadows of an air scoop, winch, booms and life-boats. It is not unlike being alone on an alien planet. There is a faint feeling of fear rather than cold.

When I was quite young, a number of us boys on a dare entered a cemetery on a cold winter night. Because I was the youngest, I found myself suddenly deserted by the older boys. They hid behind tombstones and as I ran in panic, they shouted weird sounds at me. It seems as though I can hear the same sounds coming at me from behind every shadow on deck.

I grope my way up the ladder and onto the gun deck to substitute-stand an 8:30 to 10:30 watch, after just completing my 4 to 8 stint. In the almost total darkness I cannot see or anticipate the oncoming smash of large waves. I can, however, feel that the vessel is rising swiftly up the peak of a monstrous wave and know I am about to plummet down into a valley between waves.

On the gun deck I stagger as a drunkard, groping for the three-inch cannon I know to be nearby. It is always a relief to reach the cannon without losing balance and tumbling into the sea.

As Talledo had taught me, I carry in my parka jacket's pocket that short length of 21-thread manila line. Sitting on the deck beneath the breach of the gun my legs are wrapped around its base. I use the line to lash myself to the gun. Thus the cannon partly shelters me from the onslaught of flying waves.

Rules are that a man must stand bow watch whenever the ship is underway, regardless of weather conditions. What purpose I serve on this totally black night is beyond my comprehension. If there were a giant iceberg out there, or a shoreline in our path, it would be impossible for me to see either of them. I now barely see the cannon I cling to. I curse myself for volunteering to substitute for an ailing crew member. My back aches and tires under continuous pounding of heavy, solid waves that manage to fall upon me. The two hour watch renders me physically exhausted.

Sometimes when I stand a watch such as this, I find myself intermittently dozing in a fitful stupor of dreams, not necessarily caused by homesickness, though it must be a contributing factor. Dreams offer relief from reality. They pacify my hunger for the feel of earth beneath my feet, for sounds of happy, familiar voices, good music, laughter, ethnic food, warmth, and clothing that is neither damp nor frosted. I dream too of picnics and car rides and walks along a sunny country road in summertime. How can I dream these things with ice water dripping off my face and drenching the inside of the collar of my parka?!

I think of civilization as something unreal, something I'd only read about. I often find solace in silent prayer that I fear would embarrass me if others could hear. During prayer I often experience a disturbing vision. After surviving several years of wartime privation and discomfort, I die just before war's end.

I am hating the confining closeness of the *Nanok* and blame her for most of my gloomy feelings.

October 20, Tuesday; Angmagssalik.

We remain hove-to until midday as the elements flail the *Nanok*. I think she too feels abandoned, lonely, and alone.

Raging weather pauses to catch its breath and Madam *Nanok* gently lifts her skirt and grasps the momentary opportunity to lope into harbor, literally sideways. We drop hook. Ki, Jensen and others come on board.

Word comes that the Russians repulse a German mass attack on Stalingrad yesterday. Thousands are killed and some forty-five army tanks are destroyed.

October 21, Wednesday; Angmagssalik.

We leave the harbor and await in the open sea for the arrival of several vessels that we are to guide into harbor. Radio informs us they feared bad weather and high-tailed it back to the safety of BW 1.

Some board the *Northland* for movies.

Guns and I wanted to whip-up some snow cream but Cookie would not allow us to do so. No reason except that he is irritated and has his porcupine quills cocked in readiness to fire. Snow cream is not too bad when you are in dire need for goody that is not too bad. Recipe: pack a cake pan full of clean snow, mix powdered egg yolks with powdered milk and water, sugar, splashes of vanilla or lemon extract and pour the goop over the snow. Mix, then demonstrate your gluttony.

During evening card game, Petrenko has again raised the ire of little Elmer Comer. The four-eyed bantam rooster challenges Goliath to a duel of fisticuffs. Everyone takes several steps backward, clearing the area for the slaughter about to take place. Happily, Goliath does not accept the challenge. There is a great, unison sigh of relief. It is certain that the courageous but foolish Elmer, with his spurs bristling, would surely have died on the spot he stood on.

I once witnessed a building being razed. A huge crane swung an eight-ton iron ball like a pendulum. The ball struck the doomed building one blow in its solar plexus and four stories collapsed. Petrenko's fist was reminiscent of that ball. His clenched fist is a mace. His knuckles are warts of steel. The two-thirds of his head-hair that is missing probably left in fear.

October 22, Thursday; Angmagssalik.

We wave "goodbye" to the cutter *Northland* and freighter *Hilton* as we clear a path for them through a dense field of small icebergs that glut the harbor's entrance. The freighter *Belle Isle* is waiting outside the harbor for us to guide her in and we do so. The name *Belle Isle* brings home closer to me. I am from Detroit, Michigan, which is on the western shore of the Detroit River. The river separates Detroit from Windsor, Canada. The river's south end empties into Lake Erie. Its north end is the funnel mouth for Lake St. Clair. In the river, between Detroit and Windsor, lies the "most beautiful island park in the world." It is some seven miles long and about one forth as wide. It is where young men take their dates to park, spark, and study the moon on warm summer evenings.

Robbie, Cookie, and I rip off a few songs that will never sound good again. Maggie and I have coffee together in the crew's quarters. He is in a very pleasant mood. We have a long, casual, enjoyable conversation at the galley's table. I try to steer conversation toward my desire for a promotion. Maggie ends our talk abruptly and excuses himself. Apparently I have not changed his mind about me . . . yet. Perhaps I should attend radio school or strike for a signalman's rating. But what the hell! I enjoy being in the deck force.

Hope we don't freeze solid in this hole for the entire winter. More and more icebergs, larger and larger.

October 23, Friday; Angmagssalik.

We pull alongside the *Belle Isle* in the a.m. and she loads us with much mail for BE 2. There is also a pile of valises, duffel bags, sleep sacks, footlockers, skis, snowshoes, soldiers and civilians. We do the *Belle Isle's* hauling because the *Nanok* stands a better chance of penetrating the iceberg field. The larger vessel with less maneuverability could easily become trapped and freeze-in solid. If the *Nanok* should freeze-in for the winter, she would not be as great a loss.

There is much mail for the *Nanok* as well. Packages of goodies too. It is customary to share whatever goodies we receive from home, with members of the crew. Elmer is most fortunate for he receives the largest, heaviest parcel of all. Elmer is very unselfish. Therefore he surprises me by fleeing aft in a peculiar, furtive fashion with his unopened parcel. He arouses curiosity so several of us follow stealthily behind him. He opened the parcel in what he thought to be [the] privacy of his miniature quarters. Amongst other tidbits he unpacked one quart of extra large, green olives. Almost immediately my mouth watered and jowls pinched at thought of savoring the briny flavor. It is near-miraculous that the glass jar arrived unbroken even though it was heavily protected with packing. Judging by the manner which Elmer caresses his windfall, I know that none but he will ever taste the pickled fruit. After sampling the olives, he hid the balance of them behind a drawer of his desk-like cabinet.

We retreat to the forecastle and Elmer arrives shortly thereafter and shares his other goodies, but no olives. Someone casually mentions that "it sure would be nice if someone were to receive a batch of olives for a change." Elmer is startled and studies face after face but sees no indication that anyone knows his secret. We are amused.

Elmer was called to the bridge to do some work for the skipper. Several of us took the opportunity to get at Elmer's olives. Each took a handful, leaving but a handful in the jar. Then, to confuse Elmer even more, we hid the jar behind some books where he was sure to find them and wonder how they had gotten there.

Note: We were never to hear another word about the olives.

We batter much ice to get to Simiutaq. After off-loading both cargo and personnel, as reward we are allowed to go ashore, mooch some pogey bait, play ping-pong, and listen to a half-crocked piano player play a half-cracked piano.

Several of my letters are from Lucille. The inside of one of the envelopes smells of cosmetics. I curl up in my sack and sniff the envelope far into the night.

Talledo and I are getting along great.

October 24, Saturday; Simiutaq.

Good lord what a guy will not do for entertainment!

Right after breakfast several of us go ashore to the recreation hall where they hold a command performance for the *Nanok* crew. A movie called *Ex-champ*. A good movie but older than the Ten Commandments.

Everything has gone awry today. We demonstrate seamanship equivalent to the activities of Keystone Kops. Our stupid seamanship inspires Chips Delaney to come roaring down the ladder shouting: "where are the seamen?! We had some when we left Boston!"

Chips did not know Maggie was having coffee with us at the time. Maggie explodes at Chips, calling him a "piss to the windward" sailor.

The *Nanok* hurries back to Angmagssalik.

October 25, Sunday; Angmagssalik.

Wow!! Corn on the cob up here near the Arctic Circle! I have one and one-half cobs and Guns gives me another. I guess the Old Tar Heel has eaten too much of it in his youth. I wonder where the cobs came from. Fairbanks said it was delivered through a secret tunnel that runs from Iowa to Angmagssalik.

Were supposed to see a movie ashore this p.m., but heavy winds caused Maggie to kill the idea. He is reluctant to leave the *Nanok* with only a skeleton crew on board. We are scheduled to meet and escort-in some vessel tomorrow. If she arrives early enough, we'll get to see a movie later.

October 26, Monday; Angmagssalik.

Worked fabricating a large rope fender. Been assigned "Captain of the Head" and "mess punk" duties for next week. At the evening movie the special light bulb inside the projector burned out. Sorry, no replacement. Some of the crew remain sitting in darkness, listening to the sound track of a Kay Kyser movie called, *That's Right, You're Wrong*. My imagination is not good enough to imagine an entire movie . . .

Back to the *Nanok* and my sack.

October 27, Tuesday; Angmagssalik.

Radioman Dexter has a scoop! Says he decoded a radio message stating the Nazis captured the United States and took it with them to Germany!

Petrenko looks serious and as if he is about to cry.

"Honest to God!?" he asks.

Dexter is not sure if Petrenko really means what he has said. Neither am I.

"Yes, it's true alright," says Two-Gun Dexter, "but they promise to return it after the war."

"Oh!" says Pete, obviously relieved.

I am beginning to think we all have some of our screws loose.

Later, Radioman Jenner receives a radio message that a soldier at Comanche Bay has broken a leg and the *Nanok* is requested to go fetch him. Since Maggie has agreed to go, it is suggested that we might as well take along a few additional supplies and mail. Instead of just a few supplies, it turns out to be a number of tons!

The stuff is onloaded and we dash over to C.B. As usual, it is a wind tunnel gone mad. Only good thing is that the winds have cleared most of the icebergs out of the bay and its entrance. The outboard putt-putt refuses to start so the dory, laden with supplies and mail, has to be rowed back and forth in terrible seas and wind. It is essential that we do not wait for better conditions. The man with the broken leg cannot wait to be treated.

Son of a bitch! Maggie learns the broken leg is a hoax! He is as mad as a bigamist supporting three mothers-in-law! The base pulled the hoax just to receive more mail. Can't blame them. They will be frozen-in here all winter. Maggie's orders are to plunk the bulk of the cargo on the beach at the water's edge. We then beat it back to Ang.

We heave-to outside the harbor all night to await the arrival of the freighter *Margaret Lykes* that should have arrived yesterday.

October 28, Wednesday; Angmagssalik.

Radio message indicates the *Margaret Lykes* will be here early this p.m., so we enter harbor and drop hook.

Late afternoon we slip out of harbor to greet the *Lykes* but she does not show. Instead she radios her arrival is changed until tomorrow. Is she a maiden that cannot make up her mind!?

Back into harbor to drop hook. Davey Jones has the watch so I lay below for a snooze.

October 29, Thursday; Angmagssalik.

At 0430 we again heave-to outside Ang. Harbor. In and out, out and in, in and out like a jack-in-the-box! Late in the p.m. her majesty *Margaret Lykes* announces her arrival. We escort her to anchor area.

Some go ashore for a movie. Dilly, Dreams, Vacar, Rollston, Two-gun Dexter, and I remain to stand watch.

I make a batch of snow cream, and Dilly breaks out a bottle of coke for each of us. Enjoyed mine with a piece of apple pie. Dilly speaks encouragingly about my rating possibility.

October 30, Friday; Angmagssalik.

During my watch, Maggie has me hoist anchor. Before it is fully aweigh, he pushes the annunciator to "Full Speed Ahead!" Like the rest of the crew, he too could use a long rest. He demonstrates unreasonable impatience quite often, too often lately.

Icebergs and thick cake ice fields stretch to the horizon. *Nanok* has a narrow escape. As we push aside a very large berg, it decides it does not want to be pushed aside. Pressure from the starboard side of the *Nanok*'s bow causes the berg to roll over onto its back. After a great amount of pushing, the berg decides to turn right side up, then down onto the *Nanok*'s bow. The berg's weight pushes the bow deep under water. We slide to port and away from the berg. The action causes both berg and *Nanok* to bob up and down, up and down, but not in unison.

We later rendezvous with the U.S.C.G. cutter *Ingham* and the freighter *Ozark*. The *Ingham* was the *Ozark*'s escort and therefore chose not to enter

Angmagssalik's ice-choked harbor. Instead she headed back to Iceland. The *Ozark* followed us in to a safe anchorage. [31]

October 31, Saturday; Angmagssalik.

Awakened at 0200. Four small scows have broken loose from the *Ozark*'s side with the help of several large, drifting icebergs. Talledo, Stan, and I recover and tow them back to the *Ozark*. Talledo is happy with my seamanship. He depends on me more often nowadays. I'm grateful and will not let him down.

Maggie is expecting the cutter *Northland* with Admiral "Iceberg" Smith on the 'morrow. Mr. Brennan the civilian contractor sent us a free, stuffed turkey from the *Ozark*. It was kind and thoughtful of him and much appreciated by the *Nanok*'s crew.

November

I decide to have some fun with the crew. I hurry down the ladder to the forward crew's quarters and shout: "Attention men, the Admiral has arrived!" I expected everyone to snap to attention and salute. I was to laugh fiendishly and inform them that I am joking.

The joke is on me!

The Admiral, several of his staff, and Maggie, were having coffee at the crew's mess table!! The Admiral looked at me as if I were demented. I believe I am also. My face must have resembled a red, portside running light. Being totally flustered, I salute awkwardly, poking my thumb into my eye, do an about-face, fly up the ladder, and fade away.

November 1, Sunday; Angmagssalik.

Not much to do except to haul a large scow from shore to the *Ozark*. Clark tosses out turkey and trimmings, cranberries, peas, corn on the cob, white potatoes, yams, apple pie, and ice cream. I wonder what the civilians are eating stateside with rationing in force.

My decision was to join the Coast Guard before they could draft me into the army infantry. Mud-filled trenches did not appeal to me. I figured that on board a ship, I would always have a clean place to sleep and some sort of warm food as long as I could stay alive. My decision was a good one. If it were not for petty haggling among *Nanok* crew members, things could be even more tolerable. Today's mouth-fights are between Fairbanks and Connors, then Fairbanks and Guns Owens, then Guns versus Clark, then Clark and Stan and I versus Davey Jones.

Now that it is November and the ice fields are choking the *Nanok*, we must be awful close to going stateside. Otherwise, we're gonna wake up one morning to find the *Nanok* frozen-in for the winter.

Admiral Smith does not appear as rumored. Why should he choose to visit on board a rag-tag lump such as the *Nanok*?

November 2, Monday; Angmagssalik.

We cleaned more than twelve inches of snow from the deck. The *Northland* is temporarily frozen-in outside the harbor. We tied up to a scow that was tied alongside the *Ozark*. Quick, Maggie's Labrador retriever somehow fell overboard. I heard a splash, looked over the side, and there she was, hopelessly trying to scramble onto the scow. I jumped over the side and down onto the scow. Quick was about to disappear as I reached under water and caught her by her upper lip. Pulling her on board was something else. She was heavy, cold, and wet. Worse, her legs flailed and scratched at my face as I pulled her on board. Her eyes bulged like inflated balloons! Clark rescued her in identical fashion once before.

Had coffee on board the *Ozark* late in the evening and visited her engine room.

We are about out of fresh water. The plan is to boat some tomorrow.

November 3, Tuesday; Angmagssalik.

Many in crew are assigned to boating fresh water. Skipper orders me to stay on board in the wheel house. He wanted just to chat. Asked me many things about my civilian life. I told him I left my production line job at the Dodge Brothers auto assembly plant to join the Coast Guard. He tells me much about his private life. A fascinating storyteller. I slowly guide the conversation toward my desire for a rating. He surprises and encourages me by saying, we'll see what we can do.

The harbor is still navigable despite all the ice, but barely so. The *Northland* is still frozen-in outside harbor. If she remains frozen-in how in hell will we be able to exit?!

I believe Maggie is just joking when he says negative things about the possibility of our returning stateside. He has mentioned more than once that he spends all of his Christmases at home and has no intention of doing otherwise.

November 4, Wednesday; Angmagssalik.

Nanok's tanks are full of fresh water even after every crew member has showered and washed clothes. No end of hard work on the *Nanok*. Even a holiday does not mean complete idleness. The galley never ceases to function, mess punks must work, bow, pilot house, and engine room watches must be maintained. A holiday usually means only if one has none of the above duties, he can sack-in, write letters, read, or whatever.

Two army weather specialists come on board. We push our way partly out of harbor so they can survey the icing situation firsthand. It is as expected. Very bad.

Clark is on a rampage. He demands a rating elevation from Maggie. I wish him luck. He is without a doubt the best pot-trundler in the entire Greenland Patrol and Wooden Shoe Fleet.

November 5, Thursday; Angmagssalik.

With the two army weathermen on board, we up-anchor early in a.m. with intention of hauling them to Comanche Bay. Turned back, however. Skipper felt that should we manage to get out of Angmagssalik Harbor, we may never be able to get back in through the ice. The two army men are put ashore.

In the p.m., we pull *Ozark*'s fresh water scow off the rocks in cold, heavy wind. We managed but almost at the cost of the life of several *Nanok* crew members.

Violent argument brews between Jenner and Brill. Almost fisticuffs. Maggie plans to make a wild attempt to get out of here on the 'morrow.

November 6, Friday; At sea.

Early in a.m. we leave Angmagssalik for last time this year, we hope. It has usually been requiring several hours to inch through the near-shore ice field. Today it requires nearly ten hours. I estimate we had gotten twenty-five to thirty miles out to sea and were still encased in the ice field.

The *Northland* is nowhere in sight. She must have broken free of the ice. Scuttlebutt has it that Maggie received orders to hole-up in Angmagssalik for the winter, but instructed radiomen not to acknowledge receipt of the message. They simply smile broadly and say they believe the skipper wants to be stateside for Christmas.

The freighter *Margaret Lykes* followed us out through the ice field, but we soon lost sight of her. The *Ozark* was to tag along also. Never saw her at all.

Darkness falls. I am bow-watch lookout. Jonesy is at the wheel. Sea is rough. Wind is full and biting cold. As usual, I lash myself under the breach of the three-inch gun.

The sea grows insane! It scales the bow and attempts to crush me. I try to think of home and warmth without success. We strike many ice cakes. Their arrival becomes known in total darkness when waves carry them over the bow and they bang down onto the gun deck, and again after they bounce from gun deck to main deck.

Many cakes strike atop the cannon under which I sit. One cake must have been traveling horizontally for it strikes me on my right shoulder. Then it is gone, washed overboard from whence it came. My shoulder aches with pain and breath has been knocked momentarily from me. I gasp for air and inhale a mouthful of salt water that makes me retch. I curse loudly but the wind shrieks in laughter, or so it seems.

The *Nanok* runs her head through a cluster of ice cakes and reverberates with a staccato of sharp bangs. Again rivulets creep through the neck area of my parka, down my belly and onto my privates. If this is the way to fight a war . . .

We hear Nazi General Erwin Rommel's latest attack on Egypt has ended yesterday after only sixty-six days. Better for him to die in Egypt than to face the wrath of Hitler.

November 7, Saturday; At sea.

Plowing through ice cakes and skirting bergs, the *Margaret Lykes* is astern once again. We are to escort her to a rendezvous with the trawler *Natsek*. Seas are rough as hell. Bergs pitch and toss like large chunks of potatoes in a witch's cauldron of stew.

I made ten dollar bets with both Roach and Comer that we will arrive in Boston prior to Christmas. I don't really think so, but the bets are something for us to joke about. If we don't get to the States before Christmas, I won't mind losing because I won't be needing the money.

We lose the *Lykes* in mid-day and relocate her toward evening? She needs us like she needs three legs. Theory is, should we contact the enemy and one vessel or the other is sunk, hopefully there will still be at least one Allied vessel afloat to assist in the rescue of other ships' survivors.

Maggie is throwing another temper tantrum. Apparently irritation is not limited to the forecastle termites. This time he curses the *Lykes'* skipper for her "now you see me, now you don't" appearances. Of course, the *Nanok* shares no portion of the fault.

Very bad news today, one of our bombers has crashed on the Ice Cap or into the sea in our vicinity. [32]

November 8, Sunday; At sea.

Been hove-to all night. Too dangerous to travel the night in total darkness through an ocean of icebergs. Morning comes and there is no *Margaret Lykes* or *Natsek*. Skipper foams at the mouth in anger because of their absence. At ten a.m. the *Lykes* comes out from behind a giant berg. The *Natsek* peeks out from behind another. *Natsek* escorts us to a suitable anchor area. We drop hook and the *Natsek* ties alongside.

The *Natsek* crew is loaded with dollars so we go on board to gamble. In jig-time we are taking her crew broke again. Radioman Charles Jensen and Yeoman Robert Repucci have soon lost all but their jock straps. Stakes are as high as one hundred dollars per roll of the dice. Many of the *Natsek* swabbies are going home broke for Christmas.

The freighter *Belle Isle* is here too. Some of her crew comes on board and the *Nanok*'s crew [wins] much of their folding money too. The Nanokians are extremely lucky.

To speed things up, bets are being made on one roll of the dice. One guy bets another that his roll of the dice will produce a higher number count than that of his opponent's roll. Others bet among themselves on the outcome of the original two betters. One guy rolls the dice and rolls an eight. The other guy rolls a nine and is therefore the winner. All of the others who made side bets among themselves win or lose accordingly.

A seaman on board the *Natsek* claims to have been in the service two years and is still only a seaman 1/c. Perhaps I am pushing for coxswain too hard?

November 9, Monday; Unidentified fjord.

We leave the *Lykes*, *Natsek*, and *Belle Isle* at anchor. We search for and locate a small bay and enter it. Maggie blows the *Nanok*'s whistle again and again, hoping to attract members of the downed bomber that is supposedly in our vicinity.

Robbins is pissed off at me. I was having chow when he hollered down into the galley that the anchor had to be catted. Being only part-way through my meal, I did not respond to his call because Jones, Stan, and Connors, who had all finished eating, did respond. Very rarely do more than half the crew turn-to when called for anchor catting. As matter of fact, the worst "gold bricks" are often among those being praised for duties they never performed.

Hook is later dropped in a tiny alcove of this remote, unidentified fjord.

November 10, Tuesday; Unidentified fjord.

Up-anchor and out to sea, back and forth, north and south, searching for that lost bomber. Maggie hangs onto the ship's whistle until I feel my nerves thinning out from the horrible sound. In evening we heave-to awaiting the arrival of the *Lykes, Natsek,* and *Belle Isle.* They arrive and we all drop our hooks some distance from one another.

It grows dark. Connors sights a green light while on pilot house watch. The light is challenged with our blinker. The light disappears. It is suddenly doused. Was it an enemy sub? A foreign vessel? Those who try to sleep are fully dressed including life jackets.

November 11, Wednesday; At sea.

Armistice day! Hooray!! For what?!!!

What are we doing here??

World War I was the war to end all wars, right?!

While the shroud of darkness still prevailed, skipper tried to fire the flare gun but it malfunctioned. Numerous hand-held flares are lit instead. Still in hopes of finding the bomber.

Margaret Lykes claims she saw red flares last p.m. The day is spent searching and again we anchor for the night.

Maggie orders all deck and other lights to be lit. We resemble a glowing Christmas tree. It is a bold and daring thing to do. If any enemy submarines are in the vicinity, they might well be afraid to attack us, fearing the lights to be a decoy and some major trap. How could they guess we are a puny trawler?

If the bomber crew is within 2,000 miles of the *Nanok*, they surely must have seen our glow. We are a man-made aurora borealis. No fireworks display could be more elaborate or colorful.

Word is that the British have landed at Algiers. Where is that?

November 12, Thursday; Prince Christian Sound.

The *Nanok* has been underway most of the night. No *Lykes, Natsek* or *Belle Isle.* Morning finds us southbound in very rough seas. I am so seasick I stagger as if drunk. Clark is pitifully seasick. He vomits traces of blood. For the first time he is too ill to prepare lunch. All must do for themselves. Very few want food today.

By four p.m. we enter shelter of Prince Christian Sound, quite near to Cape Farewell. It is calm here. We drop hook in over fifty fathoms of water.

The *Natsek* does not respond to our radio call. We receive message that another plane is down on the ice cap.

While there is relatively less ice here than at Angmagssalik, it is sure to flow this far south soon. We could still freeze-in for the winter. Rumors are that we have yet to assist in building another weather observation station.

Supposedly, planes have located the downed bomber.

November 13, Friday; Prince Christian Sound.

Bad start today. Began by cleaning Maggie's overflowing toilet. Then Roach falls down the ladder with Maggie's lunch. The skipper's teeth are bared again!

Up-anchor and at mouth of the fjord near the open sea we drop it again. Wind over the one hundred mile per hour mark. Both hooks hold fast. *Natsek* and *Belle Isle* appear and anchor nearby.

The weather station we are to help build and haul supplies to, is high up the side of a mountain.

Robbie and I are on good terms again. I stuck out my right hand and he shook it. Still hoping to be home for Christmas. Lots of time still left.

Wow!

Nazis have reached Marseille, France!

Will we live long enough to see Germany defeated?

Marseille yesterday; London tomorrow??

November 14, Saturday; Prince Christian Sound.

We tie up to the *Natsek* that is tied to the *Belle Isle*. In afternoon we cross around to the starboard side of *Belle Isle*. They load us with fifty barrels of shark livers which we lash on deck with cable.

We cross around and retie to the *Natsek*. I have a long, interesting bull session with cook Chester Benash. I try to finagle a polar bear uniform patch to sew onto my dress-blue uniform's sleeve. We are entitled to do this as recognition for crossing the Arctic Circle. Although he has several, he will not part with any at any price. Says that when he gets back to the States, he wants to look "slick." I would too.

The arrival of the trawler *Aklak* is anticipated. Whenever I hear this name, I associate it with the sound of something soft and foul-smelling striking the ground.

I practice blinker light signaling with Henry Schwencki, *Nanok*'s signal-man. In evening, a Natsekian comes on board with a fine guitar. He plays and we drown him out with our lousy singing.

By the time we finish gambling with the *Natsek* crew they won't have a dollar left in their coffers. It is a bad luck bunch of guys.

November 15, Sunday; Prince Christian Sound.

Sunday chicken dinner was lousy for the first time. Cookie Clark did not put his heart into it, nor any other good ingredient.

It blows up one hell of a cold, strong wind so we tie to the solidly anchored *Belle Isle*. Young Mister Hollingsworth is on board so we chat.

Aklak arrives and brings mail and packages from home. I receive a letter from Lucille post-marked August eight! Holy moley! I also receive a box of homemade cookies, nuts, gum, and even hard candy. The box has been beaten to hell. Though damp, the cookies are intact. I devour eight and give the rest to Clark to dry in the oven. I leave to do several chores and when I return, all but two of the cookies have been eaten! I do my version of an Indian curse dance!

Latest news is that four new trawlers have arrived at BW 1 from the U.S. As soon as the missing bomber and crew have been accounted for, the *Nanok* is to return to BW 1, then to the States. (Sez hoo??)

Nanok's crew busy themselves separating the *Aklak*'s crew from their money via the galloping cubes.

November 16, Monday; Prince Christian Sound.

We leave the other vessels and run up the fjord to find a fresh water supply. A suitable waterfall has been found but Maggie decides the wind and waves are too great to risk using dories to boat the water. Instead, he decides to drop one hook in mid-fjord and detach the other from its chain. Slowly, then, he will back the vessel up until her stern is close to shore. The cable and chain will be boated ashore and secured to huge boulders. Slack on the cable will be taken up until both cables are taut. One end of the fire hose would be taken ashore and its other end would be secured to our pump on board ship. A short length of hose would be attached to the pump's other side and would lead into the *Nanok*'s water tanks.

We get the cable ashore, secure it, and draw it taut. Unfortunately, Maggie had not considered how he would keep the *Nanok* from swinging sidewise like a pendulum in a horizontal position.

Heavy wind does indeed cause the vessel to swing like a kite attached to two separate kite strings. In the end we have to unfasten the cable from the bolder and reattach it to the other anchor. The cable is damn near ruined by kinks formed in it when it was drawn tight around the odd shaped boulder. It is not the skipper's best display of seamanship. Had I been the one who did the job or even suggested it, I could expect to remain a seaman 1/c for the rest of my life. But when you are a skipper . . . what the hell. No one would dare to even hint that the idea was a bad one.

We hurry now to fill the tanks for the day grows short. Because of great waves, we can only boat a half dory full at a time. The chore is endless. I am pretty well soaked to the skin with seawater. My body is numbed with cold. My legs are stiff. It becomes very dark and Maggie decides the *Nanok* will stay put for the night.

November 17, Tuesday; Prince Christian Sound.

Maggie has the *Nanok* tied to the *Belle Isle*'s starboard side. The *Natsek* is tied to her port side. A giant iceberg drifts along and tries to scrape the *Nanok* off the *Belle Isle*'s side. The *Nanok* has her engine "full ahead," trying to wedge her bow between the *Belle*'s side and the berg. No luck! The *Natsek* scampers around the *Belle*'s stern to come to *Nanok*'s assistance. The *Natsek*'s bow joins that of the *Nanok* and both skippers order "full ahead."

Ever so slowly the giant berg is pushed forward. It then scrapes the bottom of the fjord and stops. Both small vessels push as hard as possible but the berg does not tear loose from the fjord bottom! But it begins to capsize backward, away from the two trawlers. Finally it flops over backward and pulls away from fjord bottom. Both vessels continue to push the berg ever farther away from the *Belle Isle*. In the process, *Natsek* nearly scrapes some of her depth charges overboard. This presents a number of hair-raising moments. Dillon tries to photograph the goings-on, but it has grown too dark for his camera.

Dillon has been told that he has been elevated from ensign to lieutenant (j.g.). I am happy for him.

November 18, Wednesday; Prince Christian Sound.

During the night the giant iceberg broke loose from the fjord bottom again. It began pushing the *Nanok* backward toward the mountain's rock wall. The berg is at least five stories high and rather than continue to argue with it, we move to a safer location and drop hook.

Early in a.m. we up-anchor and patrol the coast back and forth most of the day, still searching for the grounded bomber. Late in day we enter a rather large fjord off Prince Christian Sound.

Behold! There is the *Aklak* at anchor! Actually, this fjord is simply a crack in the sky-scraping mountains that encase these fjords. The sides of the crack rise straight up and bend inward toward one another. The crack is wide enough to accept the width of several large houses and deep enough to enclose a tandem truck. Into one side of the crack is another, but much narrower, crack. It rises to the sky. Somewhere near the top of this smaller crack is a weather observation station. From the station, a net attached to the end of a rope is lowered. It is filled with supplies by the *Aklak*. The net is then hoisted up and disappears high up into the narrower crack. Someone up there empties the net and it is lowered again and again to be refilled. Looking straight up I can see only the narrowing of the crevasse, but no humans. It is a weird feeling in this remote, God forsaken place.

We tie to the *Aklak*. She is loaded chock-a-block full with food stuffs. Cookie scrambles on board to talk the *Aklak* cook out of some goodies. I help to transfer them to the *Nanok*. He acquires six turkeys, three geese, fourteen chickens, a lot of soap and a large can of hard candies.

For my effort, Clark gave me a pocket full of the candy. Won some poker money from Elmer and Abe Brill but stay even with Guns. Overall, not a bad day.

Yesterday's war activity? U.S. smashes a large part of the Japanese Fleet in the Solomon Islands. Twenty-three ships sunk and seven others damaged! Shouldn't this be some sort of a record? I hope all is true, but since we get information that is second, third, fourth and fifth-handed, it's difficult to be sure.

November 19, Thursday; At sea.

We leave the area with three army men and mail for the *Northland*. *Northland* was to be at fjord's mouth, but as usual, her whereabouts [are] elsewhere. The sea is rough and many are seasick including Maggie.

Northbound, we come across the *Northland* far at sea. There are no handy nearby fjords so Maggie decides to attempt the transfer at sea, by dory. Two trips are made from *Nanok* to *Northland*. Very dramatic and dangerous. It was like watching a motion picture. Foolhardy too, methinks.

Robbins performs the act masterfully. Thank heaven for his great strength and determination and ability to bend oars. The wind and sea does not cooperate. I have never seen greater fear in men's eyes than that in the eyes of Robbie's two army passengers.

A number of two to three hundred pound chunks of ice are tossed onto *Nanok*'s deck by mischievous waves. Other, friendly waves wash them back overboard, otherwise we would have had to chop them into smaller pieces in order to lift and toss them overboard.

Darkness falls before we can locate a friendly fjord so we heave-to for the night.

November 20, Friday; At sea.

Seas are so rough it feels like the *Nanok* is airborne again. Most of the crew is seasick. I am not and wonder why.

We are southbound through bow-tossed flying chunks of ice and small bergs that perform like ballet dancers atop wave crests. Wave tops fly and splash across *Nanok's* decks, freeze, and glaze them with crystal ice. Even when hanging onto the lifeline stretched from forecastle to pilot house aft, it is impossible not to slip and fall many times en route. Rain and sleet impairs vision so again we heave-to for the night.

We are to rendezvous with the *Ozark* and a troop transport that was with the vessel *Reuben James* when the *James* was sunk. It is so rough I am unable to stay put in my sack! [33]

November 21, Saturday; Unidentified fjord.

Landmarks are unfamiliar so I kiddingly suggest we have missed our intended fjord at Julianehåb's harbor. Fairbanks and Connors laugh themselves sick at my dead-reckoning suggestion. Amazingly enough, that's exactly what happened! Maggie is much amused at my judgment. He states we are some sixty miles north of Julianehåb.

A navy PBY Catalina flying boat circles overhead to inform us of our actual location by means of blinker light.

Late in evening we enter a nearby fjord and anchor for the night. We are to drop off the fifty wooden barrels of shark livers at Julianehåb that were foisted upon us by the *Belle Isle* on the fourteenth. In return, we are to receive a load of stinking, frozen, dog food fish. Also, we are to escort a number of vessels to Julianehåb.

November 22, Sunday; Unidentified fjord.

We now have been ordered to await the freighters *Brooklyn Heights* and *Ozark*, but they do not appear. Instead, the U.S.C.G. cutter *Modoc* appears, escorting a rusting, nondescript freighter. [34] We enter fjord early enough for Clark to create a super magnificent turkey dinner with all the compatible wrappings.

After chow, out of fjord to once again await the arrival of ghost ships. It's God-a-mighty-damn rough!! Despite this, Talledo and I fish for cod. He latches onto a giant catfish that scares hell out of me with its wide, laughing mouth and snake-like whiskers. I catch a good-sized cod and as soon as I remove it from the hook, Quick snatches it from me and disappears somewhere on deck.

We reenter fjord for the night.

November 23, Monday; Julianehåb fjord.

Again out to sea, searching for the elusive *Brooklyn Heights* and *Ozark* that do not appear.

Petrenko continues his fight against the world. He and Dreams have a snarling match. Of course Connors must eventually back off, but then, most of the crew have, at one time or another, had to do the same.

Talledo and I get along very nicely these days and I am glad. Robbins is more moody than ever before. He talks aloud to himself quite often. I dislike mentioning homesickness because it covers the *Nanok* like a fog.

Into Julianehåb fjord and drop hook.

November 24, Tuesday; Julianehåb.

Leaving the fjord we scan the horizon. If any ships are out there, they are invisible. Reentering the fjord we go all the way to Julianehåb, which, surprisingly, is not very far, arriving approximately 2 p.m.

Not seeing the place since the fifth of September, it is like a homecoming. In offloading the wooden barrels of shark livers, I operate the starboard boom to hoist them out of our deep cargo hold. The lift line is fouled around the slowly turning winch-drum. I have to quick-yank it free before it becomes hopelessly entangled. Yanking the line free causes a sudden, short drop of the barrel that was high above *Nanok*'s main deck. The barrel tumbled out of its chain sling, falls to the bottom of the hold, and breaks into many pieces. Shark livers, like giant anchovies, go slithering all over the place as though they were alive! Stench rises to the high heavens. Some men gag but I vomit. Jonesy and Stan shovel the giant, sickly gray anchovies into large garbage cans. Stomachs quiver all day. It is said that shark liver oil is many times more beneficial than cod liver oil. I prefer to perish before consuming either.

Lindsay Jordan, Vacar, Dexter, and Charlie Rollston are coming less and less often to chit-chat in the forecastle. Roach says he hopes they all stay aft. By the same token, few, if any, of the forecastle gang bother to visit aft unless it is necessary to do so. We seem to be growing worlds apart, separated by invisible emotional barriers.

At one time or another, minor conflicts have taken place between every two members of the crew. I was not present to witness every happenstance, [but] it is just obvious by looking at eyes and listening to tiny snatches of conversations between one another. Conversations lack spirit and substance. Everything we know to say has been said again and again and has become boring. In Jenner's face and tight smile it is apparent many inner thoughts plague him. Perhaps he has mailed his spirit home. I know I have sent mine some time ago.

Jenner is a very strong person both physically and mentally. Therefore he is my comparison gauge. Whatever he seems to be feeling, I feel justified in feeling similarly.

November 25, Wednesday; Julianehåb.

John Goncalves, "Balboa" of the black gang, bears a grudge against the Eskimos in general. They have overcharged him, traded inferior items and have even taken payment for goods never delivered. Balboa is determined to "get even."

A number of Eskimos paddle their kayaks out to the *Nanok* at anchor to trade. Balboa begins to dicker with one of the natives. He is attempting to trade a highly-polished pair of army shoes for a bundle of exquisitely carved, bone trinkets. There is much heat in the bargaining process. Johnny demonstrates a marked improvement in his ability to bargain. He is gaining on the Eskimo. The native is obviously desperate to acquire the shining shoes with the new laces.

A deal has been struck!

Goncalves gets a firm hold on the trinkets before relinquishing his vise-like hold on the shoes. The moment exchange has been made, Goncalves quickly disappears below deck.

The Eskimo affectionately fondles and closely examines his newly-gotten treasure. He grins broadly, turns the shoes upside down, and bellows like a sick seal!

Voila! There is a hole the size of a half dollar in each of the shoe soles! As a cry of anguish pierces the air, I too disappear below deck.

Later, Maggie has the hook lifted and heads the *Nanok* toward the open sea and BW 1. The swindled Eskimo circles round and round the *Nanok* in his kayak. He is wailing to beat hell! The *Nanok* almost runs over him several times. Maggie is mad as hell at the Eskimo and shouts something at him in Norwegian. The Eskimo shakes a violent fist at the skipper and holds up the pair of holey shoes for the old man to see. Thank goodness the skipper does not understand.

Hours later we arrive at BW 1. The base is a riot of activity. The *Nanok* receives much mail. In addition, I receive three pay checks: $95.76, $3.03, and $14.07. I have no way of knowing whether the payments are right or wrong or what they are supposed to represent. There is no complaint department in Greenland. One letter states sister Joann has moved into her brand new $5,200.00 home (*expensive!*), and Lucille misses me as much as I miss her.

Trawler *Arluk* is here and guess what? Old boot camp buddy "Sick, Lame, and Ivy" is on board! He is a sight for lonely old eyes! In Algiers, Louisiana, boot camp, for morning hospital call, we were required to stand at attention while our company "V" commander Armstrong would shout: "sick, lame, and lazy . . . fall out" for hospital. Ivy had some medical problem every single day and was ever in need of some minor medical attention, from heel blisters to nostril infections. It got so that Commander Armstrong changed his morning call to: "sick, lame, and Ivy . . . fall out!"

Some take movie liberty ashore. Fairbanks gives me a chocolate bar to stand his pilot house watch, so I do, and write letters home.

November 26, Thursday; BW 1.

Thanksgiving Day! Thanks for what!? That we're still alive? For strangers out there who want to kill us? We have to kill whoever they are first, right?

Rumor: Rear Admiral Edward Hanson Smith is to come on board for a visit today. They say it was he that talked his good friend Magnus Magnusson into taking this Greenland duty.

The east coast of Greenland is the coldest in the Arctic but is the ideal area for weather observation outposts. Monday's weather in Denmark Strait is the North Sea's weather on Wednesday—priceless information for both Allies and enemy.

Iceberg Smith is at a disadvantage. The most accurate charts available for Greenland's east coast and countless fjords are in Oslo, [Norway], and Germany controls Oslo.

No matter. As U.S. Coast Guard trawlers perform their usual duties, they also help correct the existing hand-drawn Eskimo maps. Too, his flagship *Northland* also helps.

I decide to have some fun with the crew. I hurry down the ladder to the forward crew's quarters and shout: "Attention men, the Admiral has arrived!" I expected everyone to snap to attention and salute. I was to laugh fiendishly and inform them that I am joking.

The joke is on me!

The Admiral, several of his staff, and Maggie, were having coffee at the crew's mess table!! The Admiral looked at me as if I were demented. I believe I am also. My face must have resembled a red, portside running light. Being totally flustered, I salute awkwardly, poking my thumb into my eye, do an about-face, fly up the ladder, and fade away.

Clark presents a magnificent Thanksgiving dinner. Variety of food is so great I cannot sample it all.

I run into Schafer ashore. He looked great and has put on some weight. He hopes to transfer on board a large C.G. cutter bound soon for the States. Hope he gets his wish.

Skipper says we may be on the way to the States by the twelfth of December. He's said many such nonsensical things before, but just in case he is right this time, I vow to gamble no more so I can be sure to afford train fare home.

November 27, Friday; BW 1.

Poker bets are running as high as one hundred dollars per roll.

Petrenko, Jones, Fairbanks, and I go ashore to see the base dentist for routine check-up and cleaning. I have several cavities so I receive an appointment for December third for a repair job.

We later stomp on down to crabby-ass Paymaster Levin for whatever balance of pay we may be entitled to. When Pete asked for our pay, Mister Levin's face turned purple as he screamed: "No!!!!!" without giving a reason for his refusal. He only said: "tell that damn, dumb skipper of yours to etc., etc., etc., etc." So we told our skipper "etc., etc., etc., etc.," as Levin instructed us. Pete and Fairbanks embellished Levin's refusal with a few nasty etceteras, etceteras of their own. Maggie promises that we will witness Mister Levin's castration.

November 28, Saturday; BW 1.

Washed all my soiled clothing this a.m. in anticipation of possibly heading stateside soon. Contrary to the promise I made to myself, I roll a few dice in a very small stakes game, and a bit of nickel, dime, and quarter poker. I had five bucks to lose and quit, but after a few rolls of the dice, I had twenty or so dollars of someone else's. "What the hell!" I thought, "I'm playing with someone else's loot now so why quit!?" Soon Roach owes me thirty dollars, Pete owes seven, and Robbie nine. The only one reluctant to pay off is Robbie.

A large freighter pulls in to tie up just forward of the *Nanok*. She flies in too swiftly and misses scraping the *Nanok*'s paint off by 27/32 of an inch!

Clark goes to dentist at ten a.m. and does not return until eight p.m. As usual, his excuses are sensational and as usual Maggie does not believe them. This time Maggie restricts Clark from leaving the *Nanok* ever again until after we arrive stateside.

We load the hold with cargo destined for a place called Gamatron, wherever or whatever that is. [35]

November 29, Sunday; BW 1.

We finish loading food-stuff and other cargo for Gamatron. Everyone is gambling. Stan and Rollston are winning heavily.

Good fried chicken even though Clark is brooding over his loss of shore leave.

Rusty the dog slipped ashore somehow and has disappeared. Talledo hunts him. He wants to keep him permanently.

November 30, Monday; BW 1.

We onload portable barracks panels and a large scow-like pontoon, probably for use as a floating dock, and shove off for Gamatron. Skipper is too irritated and impatient for some reason and does not allow the deck crew time to cat the anchor. He has done this several times in the past. It hangs over the side just above the water line. Rough waters slam it back and forth against the bow, making one hell of a racket inside the fo'c's'le head!

Talledo found Rusty late last evening hiding under an upside-down dory ashore. In gratitude the dog slides about in the head while busy unloading excrement. I can now say with experience that a ship without a guillotine is no place for weak-stomach dogs.

December

Maggie decided both vessels would proceed together in the semi-darkness even though visibility was barely marginal. Nature had other plans. Snow soon thickens and the Natsek *blends into it. To verify the* Natsek's *proximity, Maggie heaves-to and sounds two long blasts of* Nanok's *horn. The only reply is a single flash of white light. We wait in hope of additional signals but none are forthcoming. The* Nanok *proceeds slowly, cautiously, and alone.*

December 1, Tuesday; Gamatron.

For cryin' out loud!! Here it is December and we're still not heading south! What's this?? Maggie was about to go ashore alone. At the gunwale he stopped, turned around, and with a grin, said, "'ski, come along for the ride." I felt embarrassed and thought he was joking, but he was not. Ashore he conferred as to how to offload our cargo. Stan had rowed us ashore and rowed us back to the *Nanok*. Maggie talked my leg off but spoke not a word to Stan. Without asking I knew Stan's feelings by the beet-red of his face. I would have felt the same.

We towed the loaded scow ashore and offloaded it as per instructions, took it back to the *Nanok*, and repeated the chore. Later it was tied alongside and we knocked off for chow. The *Nanok* is backed into a short, deadend fjord off a larger, main fjord. The fjord is surrounded on three sides by mountains that rise straight up. The forth side has a small, narrow beach onto which we offload. An anchor has been dropped forward of the ship and a line from the stern has been taken ashore some seventy feet away. This seems to be quite a common tie-up arrangement in short, dead-end fjords.

It looked like a big blow coming up so Maggie wanted a second stern line tied ashore. To do so, we must first shift location of the first line. It had been fouled around large rocks by vicious but small waves. There is no end of trouble disengaging it. In the end an ax had to be used to chop some of it away. When settled, another scow load is offloaded ashore and we knock off for the day.

I am cold and wet as I relieve Jones on pilot house watch. I was just in time to get stuck with depth sounding around the *Nanok*'s perimeter. I never before had occasion to use a lead line but had no difficulty reading the markers as I had memorized them in boot camp. I find depth enough to float a battleship.

December 2, Wednesday; Gamatron.

Moved last scow of cargo ashore, secured the *Nanok* and hurried back to BW 1. Heading north we pass a trawler and the cutter *North Star* southbound. The *Arvek* is here from Iceland. We hear the *Atak* with boot camp buddy Clare Boike is frozen-in solid for the winter somewhere far north of us.

We receive additional pay—all in stacks of one hundred single dollar bills! Paymaster Levin grins fiendishly as he tells us that single dollar bills are all he has. There is now more cash on board the *Nanok* than the tub's value.

I am smitten with melancholia and cannot even stir myself into writing home. I don't want Lucille to feel as bad as me. Even feel like destroying dear diary but don't know how. I can't burn it in the galley stove, and if I threw it overboard it would float too long and someone would surely retrieve it. I search for something small and heavy to tie it to and then toss it overboard. While I search, someone suggested a game of craps and I put aside my emotions.

December 3, Thursday; BW 1.

Surely, if we are to be stateside by Christmas, we should be on our way by now. I am deep in gloom but not alone. Many others mention similar feelings to one another.

Crap game continued all night and is still underway. It is a great outlet for pent up emotions and steers the mind away from homesickness and loneliness. The small amount of recreation and entertainment in Greenland is insufficient. If that is the reason why officials mostly ignore the gambling, then they are aware of its necessary evil. Only Maggie, Dillon, Talledo, and McClay choose not to play today.

Nick Vacar, John Goncalves, Wilbur Owens, Carroll Jenner, Jack Dexter, Norman Comer, and Macon Roach were all officially promoted several days ago. I am bitterly disappointed but do not say so aloud to anyone. *C'est la vie.*

Late rumor: the *Nanok* and *Natsek* are to head stateside with cutter *Bluebird* as escort! How can this be possible when neither *Natsek* nor *Bluebird* is here and no one seems to know their whereabouts!? I gave Mister Dillon another hundred and thirty-five dollars to lock in the ship's safe, just in case the rumor has merit. I now have a total of two hundred and twenty bucks, more than enough for the round trip home.

Went to dentist late today. Little did I know the dentist is an apprentice. He alternates reading a book on dentistry and grinding my cavities.

Wind is blowing droplets of ice that sting the face.

Bob Hollingsworth comes on board for a while to chit-chat. Says he is to leave for the States on the *Dorchester* soon.

The U.S.C.G. cutter *Mojave* arrives. [36] We offload barrels of fuel oil while tied alongside the freighter *Tintagle*. They tell us the trawler *Aivik* has already gone stateside. Away we go to Gamatron, dump the oil, and zip back to BW 1.

Fairbanks makes the observation that December is colder than winter. Everyone laughs and he wonders why. It is so damned cold I find it near impossible to warm up. I'm reluctant to stand bow watch anymore but have no choice. Ugly *Nanok* goes on and on without complaint. Why doesn't she collapse?

I review the months gone by on board the *Nanok* and conclude this is the way things will always be, war without end. In sleep I dream we are to remain in the earth's rectum for the duration. If we are to go anywhere, we must do it soon. Ice fields are becoming almost impenetrable and cake ice forms between blinks of the eye. More rumors that we will be home for Christmas. I don't believe a word but my heart beats a little faster. Maggie will not confirm or deny. Everything we are ordered to do now seems spurred by a secret urgency for speed. No one knows why. Suddenly too, there are a multitude of minor tasks to be performed.

> Quickly, quickly, man-jack fly,
> Let me see but backside's eye,
> Show your brawn and not your brain,
> Ignore snow and driving rain.

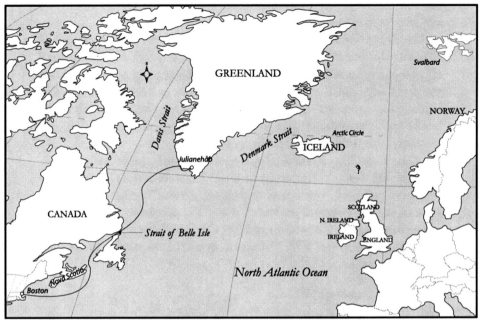

The route of *Nanok* from Greenland to Boston, December 1942.

December 4, Friday; BW 1.

Blowing a gale all day. Winds screech through rigging. I hate to leave the comfort of the forecastle for any reason. Bets fly heavy on "yes" and "no" on being in Boston for Christmas.

Bad news. We learn that the personable Lieutenant Demorest fell into a crevasse on the Ice Cap while on one of the motor sleds we brought here. It happened during a bizarre chain of events. A plane flying from Iceland to Greenland crashed on the Ice Cap. A second plane, a [Boeing B-17] Flying Fortress bomber sent out with other searchers, also crashed in the Comanche Bay area. The crew was all injured, one seriously. For nine days they were imprisoned in the cabin of the bomber. The radio operator managed to get their damaged radio operating well enough to tap out an S.O.S. His message was picked up and the plane's position pinpointed. Help was soon on the way.

A plane from Sondrestrom Fjord located the wreckage and dropped supplies. About the same time a party of scientists who were studying Arctic conditions in the area dispatched Lieutenant Max H. Demorest on motor sled. Demorest actually first reached the plane on foot. When he attempted to bring up the sled, he crashed through a thin snow bridge and fell to his death at the bottom of the deep crevasse. He was a very fine gentleman we will all miss very much.

The cutter *Northland* sent up its small amphibian plane under command of Lieutenant John H. Pritchard, Jr. He landed safely and managed to carry off two of the bomber's injured men. The following day the weather had worsened. He landed again and picked up one man but then crashed in a swirling fog and snow squall. The wreckage of his plane was later found but he and his passenger were never to be seen again. It is assumed they wandered away and perished in the snow. [37]

In the meantime, a fifth fatality happened during the rescue attempts. While trying to reach the coast by motor sled (the second of the two we had taken to Greenland), with one of the injured, Private C. Wedel suffered the same fate as Lieutenant Demorest. Colonel Bernt Balchen then suggested rescue using a large [Consolidated PBY] Catalina flying boat and the navy cooperated. Lieutenant B.W. Dunlop in three trips succeeded in rescuing all remaining men.

December 5, Saturday; BW 1.

The *Nanok*'s booms were rigged out in preparation to onload a shit-house-full of barrels of fuel for Gamatron again! This was not supposed to be our duty but someone higher up changed many plans.

Had one hell of a chin-fest with Petrenko. I ended up threatening his life. Lucky for me the giant always backs down.

December 6, Sunday; BW 1.

I'm convinced that the wind and the devil are one and the same.

Traded a carton of cigarettes for a handful of Danish coins with Toby on board the vessel *Tintagle*. Wanted to see the movie at the army base but decided not to face the rotten weather.

December 7, Monday; Gamatron.

First anniversary of Pearl Harbor day! This day too shall live in the annals of infamy! Onloading ever more drums of fuel oil. *Nanok* is all but sinking under the weight. Robbie says the ship is a blivet, two pounds of crap in a one pound sack. The hold is full of drums and the deck is stacked high on every single available square yard of space. Loaded, we waddle down the fjord to Gamatron. We anchor in total darkness. I'm so tired I can hardly hold my fountain pen.

I open letters and package received at last minute before leaving BW 1. Sister Joann has sent me two single dollar bills. Also received a small carton of hard candy from Dodge Brothers work mate Maffie Roman. Good. Letters are infested with homesickness worms. It is getting to be more like a plague and has tainted every long-term Greenland vessel. Must be an epidemic!

December 8, Tuesday; Gamatron.

Gamatron's base commander estimates it will take at least a week to offload our cargo. Maggie says if it takes that long we will miss whatever opportunity remaining to return stateside before a solid freeze-in.

As in the past, the *Nanok* backed into the short, dead-end fjord. Mooring lines were taken ashore and secured. One from each side of the bow and the same from the stern. The *Nanok* holds steadily in mid-fjord as if in the center of a spider web.

The small scow is no longer here. It has been taken away by some other vessel for use elsewhere. Our offloading problem is therefore increased. I suggest to the skipper a wild idea for offloading the drums. As I explain, his face turns from an "OK, tell me" look to a purple-faced "you stupid ass!" look. By the time I finished, he wore a "that's not too dumb an idea" look. As I began telling my plan, my mind started with a "why didn't I keep my stupid mouth shut!?" then I continued with "there goes my last chance for a coxswain's rating!" then on to "he may at least spare my life."

Since the *Nanok* was already spread-eagled in the fjord's center, why not anchor a single block (pulley) ashore and another on board the *Nanok*. Then reeve a sort of continuous clothes-line loop through block on ship and through block ashore. Much like a tenement house clothes-drying line from one building to another. It is well known that drums of fuel are light in the water and will therefore float. Why not lash the drums several feet apart, onto the continuous clothes line, using short, thin line pieces of rope?

I could see somewhere inside Maggie's eyes that he might go for the idea and he did so. To my surprise, the idea worked like a charm! We tied and individually lowered the drums over the ship's side and into the water, pulled on the loop of clothes line and shuttled the drums ashore. Ashore the drums are untied and the short lines are retied to the clothes line for a return trip to the *Nanok* for reuse.

Most of the crew work ashore. Someone there spawns a similar good idea. Instead of wrestling each individual drum up the high, snow- and ice-sided hill, a large, hand operated winch is anchored at the top of the hill. From the winch's spool they unwind a pencil-thin cable and lead it down hill to the water's edge. As each drum reaches shore, it is untied from the clothes line and onto the cable's end. Hand-turning the winch-crank, the drums are swiftly pulled uphill, untied, and rolled away. The end of the cable is coiled and tossed back down to the beach for reuse. We work swiftly all day and a good part of the night using a minimum of lighting. Two hundred and forty drums are ashore; sixty more to go.

The base commander comes on board and praises Captain Maggie for the feat in my presence. Maggie's face appears very pink. He tells the commander that the clothes line was my idea. This gets me a strong handshake and a profuse compliment.

"What's your rating son?" the commander asks. I tell him that I am a seaman 1/c. He is quite surprised and chides Maggie about my low rating. It is embarrassing to me as well as to the skipper. I must admit I felt a warm feeling somewhere deep in my gut.

December 9, Wednesday; BW 1.

I go ashore to pull juke suit duty. In jig-time we offload the remaining sixty drums and return to BW 1.

Oscar Dillon went ashore for our pay records and whatever mail that arrived. This is interpreted to mean that the *Nanok* is to leave the Greenland area shortly. Not necessarily for the States, but surely somewhere south. Ice conditions will render the *Nanok* useless here soon.

Thirty to fifty drums of diesel oil come on board. Thirty are stowed in the hold for ballast. Twenty are lashed with cable on deck. Grapevine has it that the fuel is to guarantee a non-stop trip to Boston.

Neither the *Natsek* nor *Bluebird* appear but our fresh water tanks have been topped off. If we are to indeed reach Boston before freezing in solid for the winter, then, damn it boy!, we had better get our collective asses in gear soon!! Ice is forming before one's eyes! It is ever more threatening.

December 10, Thursday; BW 1.

We have given the *Nanok* a sponge bath and dusted her entrails. She is as fresh as a southern breeze. The old tub needed a lesson in personal hygiene.

Roach and I were sent ashore for some paper work. On the way we run into one of my old *Sea Cloud* shipmates. He claims the *Cloud* has been credited with the sinking of a submarine. I doubt it. I told him the *Nanok* would never be cited for anything but her garbage-dumping or for sinking a few kayaks.

Clark is pissed-off at me for failing to light his galley stove early in the a.m. Bought a box of cigars. Can't understand why we can now purchase all of the PX crap we care to.

December 11, Friday; BW 1.

No *Natsek*! No *Bluebird*! Skipper orders all rigging to be stripped from the lower falls of the booms. The uppers are left in place. I feel all boom rigging should remain in place just in case it would be needed to lift dories over the side in an emergency. Ah! The answer comes. Maggie orders both booms to be restrung with newer, less worn rope. As soon as we finish, the *Nanok* is ordered to transfer two giant lumps of molded concrete from one small vessel to another. Who in hell do you suppose ordered such lumps of concrete, and for what possible use!? I was so tired my pooper stuck out far enough to slice washers off it. What a life! I'm froze to death! Almost.

December 12, Saturday; BW 1.

Hah!

The *Natsek* has arrived. The *Bluebird* is expected tomorrow. Deck is secured for sea once again. New lashings were made up to secure lifeboat dories in their deck cradles.

Received much mail today. I am sure it has been more than a month since I have written home. Damned if I know why. Don't know what to write about. Lucille must be worried sick.

Not too sure I care to leave for the States at this time. The last two nights in succession I have had nightmares about drowning in a juke suit.

We visit on board the *Natsek* and yak-yak for quite some time. *Natsek* crew is electrified at the possibility of getting home for Christmas. Her skipper, Lieutenant (j.g.) Thomas S. La Farge teases that the rumors are just that, nothing more. Skipper Tom is said to be closely related to John La Farge, the world famous artist known for his sensational murals. [38]

A stranger comes on board late in the day. He gives each of us a sack of candy and four packs of gum. He gives me the creeps with his never-smiling sad look. Said he is army but he is dressed civilian. No one seems to know who he is or why he came on board. Robbie decides to question him but he is gone.

December 13, Sunday; BW 1.

Awake to a special surprise! The *Bluebird* is here! At last!

The *Tintagle* moved from dockside so the *Nanok* can move in to refuel and re-top our fresh water once again. The *Natsek* replenished next.

Captain Magnusson breaks the news! We are going home!! He wanted to shove off today but the powers that be said "nix." We are to leave in the a.m. tomorrow. Maggie estimates the trip will take nine days, thirteen hours, and thirty-six minutes before we either drop the hook or have one of our mooring lines hit shore. Others estimate lesser and greater amounts of time and each contributes to what is called the "anchor pool." Whoever estimates closest to the actual time becomes winner of the pool. On battleships, anchor pools amount to thousands of dollars.

Talledo says Maggie, La Farge and Lt. Commander James F. Baldwin, U.S.N.R., have met and decided our three vessels would travel in a column. Since the *Bluebird's* skipper is senior officer, and probably because the *Bird* is the largest and best-armed vessel, she will lead our miniature flotilla.

The crew is alive once again! Everyone is in the highest of spirits. It is as cold as setting on a cake of ice with a bare ass but it does not cool our spirits. No one cares to argue about anything. Things are nauseatingly peaceful. I thought I saw Petrenko sneering, but he was really smiling. We have shed loneliness as one sheds a frayed garment. A half dozen of us have a community sing-along. We sound like meadowlarks.

December 14, Monday; At sea.

I awaken very early. Not because of excitement, but because of another nightmare about drowning in a juke suit. I was bathed in cold perspiration. I feel uneasy that our voyage may not go well.

Robbie slaps my back as he rarely does. "Cheer up, 'ski!" he says, "we're going home buddy! Home!!" I choose not to dampen his spirits with my stupid nightmare.

Bluebird and *Natsek* left earlier this a.m. We had to wait (impatiently) for several passengers to board, and for mail remnants to arrive.

Cast off!! We are on our way! So-long BW 1, Narssarssuaq, on Skov-fjord!

Part way down the fjord we come across the *Bluebird*, *North Star*, and *Natsek*. They are hove-to and conducting some sort of business. I expect the *Nanok* to heave-to and await outcome of *Bluebird's* business, praying it would not be orders to return to BW 1 and further work duty. If we were to return to BW 1 at this date a stateside trip would be impossible this year because of the now constant heavy weather and great iceberg masses in motion.

We delay one half hour and receive one more passenger, a young army weatherman. We lucked out! The *Bird* did not require the *Nanok* to wait for her so *Nanok* and *Natsek* head for the open sea. Either the *Bird* will catch up to us or we will proceed to Boston without her. In either case, who gives a rat's ass?!

We push through miles of icebergs of all sizes. Some look like large, white and blue islands. Our travel is very slow and arduous. *Nanok's* bow is gently eased against one giant iceberg after another. Push, push, push, and ever so slowly the monsters move aside for the *Nanok* to pass. One berg replaces the other, ever larger and more towering and threatening. Fortunately the seas are flat calm. Winds are in hiding, ready to pounce at their discretion.

Almost at the moment we enter open sea, a great ground swell develops and wind makes its hiding place known. It bites the cheeks, gently at the beginning, then intensifying like an arousing lover. Near day's end, swells become monumental. Waves and wind become unbridled fury.

It occurred to me that had the ground swell began while we were still amidst the icebergs, they would have become giant grinding blocks that surely would have reduced both vessels to pulp.

I experienced mixed emotions. The ominous rolling of iceberg fields had me wishing we had been unable to penetrate their density. We would then have returned to the safety of BW 1's bosom. On the other hand, I would feel totally crushed not to be able to leave Greenland's frozen hell-hole before the spring of 1943, perhaps not even then. Having successfully penetrated the ice fields, it would be totally impossible to return through them. For better or worse, we are on our way home. Lord willing, we will get there safely. The *Natsek* is nearby and rides the heavy seas nicely. All is well.

Bluebird has not yet made an appearance. Snow is falling and visibility decreases. For all we know our escort vessel may well be nearby. We cannot check by radio because of the imposed silence we are ordered to maintain.

December 15, Tuesday; At sea.

Sea and wind are very high and rough. Snow falls intermittently. Looking in any direction, the view is similar, either boiling mountains of water or white walls of falling snow.

The young army weatherman is uncanny. He is able to accurately predict weather changes hour by hour. His predictions anger Stan and Fairbanks and some of the Black Gang crew. Whenever we experience somewhat of a weather calming, he delights in stating the condition is only temporary. And he is always correct!

There is an area some twelve foot square on the portside forecastle that is leaking seawater into the forward bilges. The forecastle was damaged September seventh, when we collided with the corner of the scow in tow. Chips had patched the damage quite well, but after much sea and iceberg beating the patch is losing integrity. Our two bilge pumps are used alternately so as not to damage them, but we are barely able to keep pace with the incoming water.

Accumulated water in the forward bilges causes the *Nanok's* bow to assume a permanent downward dip. This makes steering more difficult than usual. We of the forecastle may be forced to sleep in the engine room if the dip worsens. Sleeping up forward would be dangerous if we should have to abandon ship. It could prove impossible to exit the forecastle hatch. Captain Magnusson has given permission to sleep aft whenever we choose to. We would have to sleep in bunks of others while they were on watch, or curl up on the engine room's steel deck.

Ice accumulates and thickens on the forward, starboard, weather side and the *Nanok* lists heavily to starboard.

I am not knowledgeable about the dangers of heavy icing conditions. Maggie shows no visible concern so it must not be too worrisome. Chief Talledo, on the other hand, displays some anxiety. There is definitely an unspoken fear in the eyes of much of the crew. I too begin to feel something stirring uneasily inside of me. We no longer dwell upon the fancy foods we had been longing for. Instead we speak of wives and sweethearts and family.

On board the *Nanok*, ice chopping is continuous around the clock. On board the *Natsek* on our port beam, there is no visible ice chopping. I am encouraged by the apparent strength of the *Nanok*. Her heart never throbbed so rhythmically before, faster too. She wants to fly. She seems to be in good humor and giddyantics. The *Nanok* does not feel quite so clumsy anymore. I find myself beginning to enjoy her company. She is still an ugly duckling, true, but she does demonstrate spunk and determination. Admirable tributes for a brow-beaten lady.

Do I imagine it, or does the wind continue to increase in velocity? I am sure it is growing ever colder. My teeth chatter uncontrollably as I chop ice away. I am sneezing, my eyes burn, and I am catching a cold, dammit! Many of the others have colds. I find it difficult to relax. The ship pitches and rolls heavily. This must be the reason for my uneasiness; a blasted cold!

December 16, Wednesday; At sea.

Is it morning or is it night? Have I slept some or do I imagine it? My body does not feel rested. There is an odor of coffee. Clark is more than a genius in providing it. It must be morning. Forecastle noises are loud.

I heard the wind even before going topside. The deck is a wonderland of wet, packed snow, and ice. The *Nanok* carries almost twice the ice she carried yesterday. It clings mostly to her forward half and to its entire starboard side.

Talledo, per skipper's orders, has instructed the crew to continue chopping away the ice formation in period lengths of two hours off instead of the usual four hours on and eight hours off. Since heavy seas and rolling vessel did not permit more than short snatches of fitful sleep, it is just as well to continue chopping as long as one is awake.

The *Nanok* reminds me of a puppy dog sliding forward on his chin and chest. Giant waves assault the bow and explode into expanding curtains of shimmering, sparkling globules of mercury. Airborne firecrackers on the Fourth of July.

There is very little ice chopping equipment on board. We have two fire axes, paint-chipping hammers, a meat cleaver, butcher knives, and a number of marlin spikes. One wonders why we haven't a crate full of axes and hatchets. Men are at work chopping everywhere.

The skipper has owned and operated many fishing trawlers for more years than I have been in existence. He must know all there is to learn about North Atlantic icing conditions. Today there is a seriousness in his white-rimmed eyes that I have never seen before. Lines around his mouth are drawn tight. I don't imagine this because Lindsay and Dexter share my observation. I hope Maggie does not know something that the three of us do not.

Maggie has not mentioned our escort *Bluebird*. When Talledo mentioned the name to Maggie, the skipper snarled and hissed: "piss on the bastards! Piss on 'em!!"

The skipper's attitude does not suggest any difficulty the *Bluebird* might be having. My personal feelings are that the *Bird* can go straight to hell and forget about the *Nanok* and *Natsek*. I have much more confidence in Maggie's seamanship know-how than that of the *Bird's* skipper. At any rate, no escort vessel of any size could successfully execute a rescue in these violent seas should we find it necessary to abandon ship. As matter of fact, it would be impossible to abandon ship. The lifeboat dories lie frozen beneath thick ice. So is the large, rigid cork-bodied life raft frozen to the pilot house portside. All an escort vessel's crew could do is to wave goodbye as we

plunge into Davy Jones' coffin. I hear Talledo tell Maggie that the aft superstructure is no longer water-tight . . . whatever that means.

It is near impossible to stand upright even with legs spread wide. Many
are seasick, but not Sullivan Jones. Davy's wide grin is very reassuring to
me. His years of sailing [around] Martha's Vineyard have conditioned him.
He should already be ranked coxswain. Abe Brill is too seasick to stand
watch. He tries hard but sailing is not his forte and never will be. Stan has
periods of total unconcern. He can sit, stand, lie on his back, or stand on his
head, and still manage to read comic books.

Clark has an awful time at the galley stove. That old seahorse will never
give up. He battens down his damn pots and pans and goes on cooking.

The cannon and two, twenty millimeter anti-aircraft guns on the forecastle's
head are frozen under mounds of ice. They are of less use than sling shots.

More problems!

The *Nanok*, down at the bow and with a frightening starboard tilt, causes
fuel oil to escape from the ship's boiler and starts a fire aft! The Black Gang:
McClay, Vacar, Petrenko, and others, luckily extinguish the blaze before it
has opportunity to seep flaming oil into the *Nanok's* bilges. It is touch-and-
go for a frightening eternity. If it remains unsafe to relight the boiler while
the *Nanok* remains tilted, there will be no heat from now on.

From the sky both *Natsek* and *Nanok* must appear as two cockroaches
scaling mountain peaks and skiing down the opposite sides.

Clark appears wretched. His color is that of dirty snow. Stan, Jones, and
Delaney are soaked through to the goose pimples. I fare somewhat better.

Did I stand watch or not? I am too tired to remember. Perhaps I should
have mailed some letters home before leaving BW 1. My arms and legs are
cramping from chopping ice. My throat is sore and my left ear is infected. I
have either contracted a cold or have the flu. A number of the crew is having
similar problems.

The *Natsek* is riding heavily and deep in the sea. She is still abeam of our
portside, beyond shouting distance. If anyone on board her is chopping ice,
they are not visible. La Farge may believe the weather will clear and ice will
melt. *Natsek* is supposed to lead the *Nanok* because *Nanok's* fathometer is
not operable. *Natsek* wears a blanket of white much like her sister.

There is no let-up on ice chopping. Talledo should not work so hard. He
sets an impossible example for the crew to follow. As nightfall approaches, I
notice ice accumulation has kept pace with ice removal efforts.

Delaney and I each have a half bowl of stew. We wedge our asses in between lockers in the forecastle head. It is the only way to maintain stability enough to avoid missing the mouth with a spoon. It is like dinner on a roller coaster.

Dear diary is to be transferred and hidden in rear of Comer's filing cabinet aft because I plan not to sleep forward again until the danger of capsizing is diminished.

Chief Talledo finds me putting the diary away and becomes furious when he learns what it is. He had asked me what the book is and I told him. Why should I not!? Like old times, Talledo screams at me!

"Do you know you could be dishonorably discharged for keeping a diary!?"

"No! Why!?" I scream back at him. "It's just a journal of our experiences in Greenland!"

"Yes! God damn you, and if we were to be taken by the enemy, it would tell them everything they might want to know about locations and the activities of our army and navy in all of Greenland you dumb ass!"

His truth strikes me as lightning might! Yes! Of course, he is right! At that moment I could not recall any specifics that could be of value to the enemy, but I felt sure there were many. A recollection ran through my mind. Everywhere in Boston there were posted placards that read: "Loose Lips Sink Ships." At the time I thought such slogans were silly and of no importance. Now, I instantly realized their great importance.

The chief raved on and I handed him the diary with shaking hand. He snatched it from me and was about to tear it to pieces but stopped short.

"Didn't Mister Dicastro take away your camera a long time ago and lock it in the ship's safe?! Or do you still have it?"

"No sir," I reply. "We were told that we were not allowed to have or use cameras until the war's end."

"Why do you suppose he did that!?" asks Talledo.

"Because, we were not allowed to photograph any army or navy or weather base, equipment, machinery, ships or planes," I reply.

Talledo is calming down. His face turned from deep purple to pink.

"Of course," he said, "so that the pictures would not fall into enemy hands. Weren't you told to surrender all diaries?"

"No sir," I reply truthfully. "We were not!"

I now realized the seriousness of keeping a diary during wartime . . . too late!

"There goes my coxswain's rating," I say dejectedly.

"Yeah," says Talledo, "and maybe your ass in the brig for a few years, too!"

"Oh my God, NO!"

"Yeah, ya damn betcha!" says Talledo.

He is silent for a few moments, studying my fearful face.

"Look," he said, "as soon as we get to Boston, get rid of that damn thing. I want you to take it home and stash it somewhere. Don't show it to anyone until the damn war is history! Don't bring it back! Understand?!"

I was shocked! He shoved the diary back into my hands.

Talledo turned and left. Over his shoulder he said: "I never saw it! You get me?" I couldn't reply. He was gone.

My first reaction was to destroy the diary page by page, but I did not. I wondered why he gave it back to me. The only rationale I could come up with was that he did not have the heart to see me punished. Or possibly more important, he did not want me to fail being promoted. When we first became friendly, I had confided in him that if I could prove to myself that I was capable of climbing up the rating ladder, I would strongly consider making the Coast Guard my career. Whatever his reason, I was grateful.

No one, not even my closest buddies knew of the diary's existence. I always made my entries into it sometimes at two or three day intervals while lying on my side in my sack so no one would notice. If they had, they may have thought I was writing letters. Whenever I finished an entry, I slid the diary between my two, thin mattresses. I kept its existence secret not because I knew it was prohibited (which I did not know), but because I knew my shipmates would poke fun at it and embarrass me. Too, I wanted no one to peek into it when I was not around. I kept the damned thing simply because I felt my wife and family might enjoy reading it one day. I purchased it from the Coast Guard small stores at the Algiers, Louisiana, boot camp. Why in hell were they selling them? I wondered how many other swab jockeys purchased them. I knew buddy Clare Boike had one.

As soon as I reach Boston I will mail the book home. Or, if I am fortunate enough to get a leave of absence, I will carry it home. I tire of keeping it anyway.

With the *Nanok* pitching and tossing, I find it difficult to lie still in my sack. I have changed into dry clothing and try to have a restful sleep. The day has been too eventful to allow me to rest.

December 17, Thursday; At sea.

At approximately 0100 this morning the Belle Isle Strait light was sighted.

The strait is a narrow body of water that connects the Gulf of Saint Lawrence to the Labrador Sea, and separates the great island of Newfoundland from the mainland. Our course is southbound through the strait.

At approximately 0215 snow begins to fall and obscures the light.

Later we close-haul the *Natsek* so Maggie and La Farge can shout back and forth to one another. Not being on the scene at the time, I do not learn the true state of *Natsek*'s icing condition. Others, however, say *Natsek* is an iceberg.

Maggie decided both vessels would proceed together in the semi-darkness even though visibility was barely marginal. Nature had other plans. Snow soon thickens and the *Natsek* blends into it. To verify the *Natsek*'s proximity, Maggie heaves-to and sounds two long blasts of *Nanok*'s horn. The only reply is a single flash of white light. We wait in hope of additional signals but none are forthcoming. The *Nanok* proceeds slowly, cautiously, and alone.

I arrive at the wheel at 0400 and learn all that transpired during the night as Mister Dillon and the skipper discuss the events. From the tone of their voices, I grow apprehensive and fearful of a disaster in the making, or of a disaster that may have already taken place.

We lay-to until approximately 0645. When Captain Magnusson is satisfied with his calculation of our position, and that the *Natsek* is beyond communicative distance, he gives orders to get underway again. We proceed into the Belle Isle Strait. There is much conjecture in the pilot house regarding the situation. Was the flash of light a flare? It was doubted because of its short duration.

Could it have been an explosion? Hardly, no sound. Could it possibly have been a blinker light? Possibly, but if so, more should have followed. I began to wonder if a light had been sighted at all. But it must have been, a number of others claimed to have seen it.

My fear grows that all is not well. It is inconceivable that an enemy surface craft or submarine could be active in these waters and, if they were, the constantly ragged seas would not allow them to board and capture. What then, is amiss!? My flesh prickled beneath damp clothing. Is it possible that the flash of white signaled the death of a wooden shoe?

If others were experiencing fear for the safety of the *Natsek* crew as I, it is indeed evident. As for the skipper, I know him well enough to know when he is deeply concerned as he is now. He shuffles back and forth, peering often into the dark mist through binoculars. He mutters much in Norwegian, punctuated with an occasional, choice American cuss word. When this stanchion of a man is moved enough to demonstrate such concern, it is time to be fearful.

Nature has provided us with much Arctic phenomenon. She now displays another. We are supposedly abeam of Point Amour light. We again heave-to. Skipper does not explain why. Weather is momentarily calm. No wind, no waves, and very little ground swell. Fog has settled close on the water. It lies but three to six feet in height. It is possible to see across the top of it. As far as the eye can see the ocean surface is frosted. A witch's wand gently stirs the frosting into slow motion. It twists ever so slowly and rises into a field of small, thin pinnacles of white that retain their shape. To Jonesy and Robbins it all appears to be an early morning cemetery scene from a horror movie. The graveyard is strewn with tombstone-like pinnacles protruding upward through a graveyard mist that is hugging the earth and the bodies below. One can almost hear strains of *The Sorcerer's Apprentice*.

The mist thins out and soon it is gone.

There is a groan from the engine room and our rusted giant springs to life. We are underway once again.

Wind begins to sigh-in from the west. In slightly over an hour it reaches gale force. It is a banshee that has gotten its second breath. The *Nanok* bows its nose.

Maggie is most concerned that I keep the *Nanok*'s bow pointing head-on into the wind. Therefore, in order to head toward Boston to the south, I must aim the *Nanok*'s bow southwest. In a sense, we are traveling sidewise toward Bean City. Should the *Nanok*'s bow be turned directly south, great west winds and sea would strike the vessel on her heavily ice-laden starboard side and possibly cause her to capsize.

For the most part I was quite successful. Whenever a large wave struck even slightly starboard, I automatically turned the large wheel as far right as possible so as to compensate for any misalignment caused by such waves.

At 0800 no one came to relieve me. I didn't ask why. I was content to fight the wheel rather than be on deck soaking up sea water and chopping ice. The pilot house is covered with ice at least six feet thick. Somehow the skipper has managed to drop open a shutter just to the right of my wheel-tending position and just a few feet to the front of me. In the beginning, ice formed across the entire pilot house front. After a period of time, the warmth inside the pilot house melted the ice that was on its surface. This is what made it possible for Maggie to drop open the shutter.

With the shutter out of the way, he still faced a solid wall of ice. He used his toilet plunger to punch-open a one foot diameter hole through the ice.

As the ice thickened, he used a boat hook to keep punching open the hole. Through the hole, Maggie had a limited view of the forecastle and the men chopping ice off it. Whenever I chose to, and the skipper was not in front of me, I was able to peek through the tunnel too. I chose not to do this often. Airborne waves often fly into the pilot house through the tunnel and strike my chest and face. Ice would form on my brow and eye lashes. Removing it tore away both the brow and some lashes.

The pilot house is a mountain of ice. Inside visibility is minimal. The only light filters in through the ice and the portside hatch glass.

At 1400 hours there is still no relief. I am very cold and experiencing chills. I would ask for relief but fear Maggie might consider it a seamanship shortcoming which I cannot chance. Getting a rating has indeed become an obsession with me. Too bad I was stupid enough to tell Lucille I already had the rating. I have grown so tired of trying to please Maggie, Dillon, and Talledo that I would like to tell them to cram the rating up their respective asses. I cannot afford the privilege. Too much at stake.

Quite suddenly I feel the starboard bow being struck by a quick succession of three large waves. I instantly turn the wheel full right to compensate for the blows. The compass shows a swift movement southward.

Another hard blow!

Bow of the *Nanok* turns ever more southward, exposing her ice-laden starboard to the smashing waves

"Full right wheel!" Maggie shouts at me.

"Full right, sir," I respond.

I had the wheel full right already, but try to turn it even more. Many more great waves strike the starboard. The vessel began rolling ever more.

"Full right! Full right, God damn it!" the skipper screams.

"She is full right!" I yell back.

Each wave slides the *Nanok* evermore southward and rolls her more and more onto her starboard side. The deck tilts. My legs slide out from under me and I fall to the deck on my left side. Maggie is now standing with one foot on what had been the starboard bulkhead and one foot on the deck. He reaches, grasps, and pulls at one spoke of my wheel.

Now I am on my back, partially under the great wheel, pushing up on its spokes. The *Nanok* is at an impossible angle, down at the bow and almost lying on her starboard side. Because of the angle and giant wave combinations, flying wave-tops spray into the smoke stack! The diesel engine falters, and then dies completely!

"There she goes!" yells the skipper. I too feel we are capsizing.

More great waves strike the ship mercilessly. We are wallowing hopelessly. Maggie grabs the handle of the ship's telegraph and signals full speed ahead to the engine room. For an eternity there is no response! (We were to learn later that as the *Nanok* wallowed, solid green waves of water cascaded down the stern ladder, through the Black Gang's companionway and on into the engine room. Most of the Black Gang believed the *Nanok* was sliding beneath the sea and were trying to fight their impossible way up through the heavy water and up, onto the deck.)

All had left the engine room with the exception of Petrenko. As tall as he is, salt water had risen to his waist by the time he received Maggie's order for full speed ahead. Pete stood his post and blasted air into the diesel until she quit coughing and finally fired. Accidentally or on purpose he raced the engine so fast it felt as if the ship would tear into pieces.

In the pilot house the skipper and I were ecstatic! Nothing on earth could sound as beautiful as that racing diesel engine!

Wallowing as she was, the *Nanok* often found herself atop a large wave with both her bow and stern out of water. Whenever this was so, the propeller, without resistance, was free to gather sudden speed and scream like a stuck hog running amok. The entire ship would tremble and vibrate horribly! It seemed like five minutes before the prop would take hold again and bite into solid water, even much longer before the vessel began to move foreword once again, and still longer before she began to turn right, face the wind head-on, and right herself.

I was on my feet once more. Only now did I fully realize the danger we had been in. I don't believe it was fear I felt but I had never experienced the same sensation before. At first my legs felt a weakness in them and I was unable to hold my body still and steady. My knees wobbled a bit and I looked down at them. They wobbled more and more until they reminded me of someone doing the old Charleston dance. Knees were swinging swiftly inward and outward. This struck me as being very funny and I began to laugh aloud. The captain stared at me with a strange look in his eyes. He probably thought I had gone out of my mind. The expression on his face caused me to laugh even louder as my knees wobbled out of control. Try as I would, I was unable to stop them. A few select cuss words from Maggie brought me back to earth. I sobered and my knees stopped flapping.

I felt a severe chill and needed to urinate as I had so many times this day. As usual, Maggie took over the wheel long enough for me to use the head inside Maggie's quarters just behind and adjacent to the pilot house. Then the captain hurried into his quarters to do his business. When he returned, he brought with him two cans of beer. He popped one open, gave it to me, and told me to "hurry up and drink some."

I was happy to cooperate. When I had removed a couple of gulps, he replaced them with a large slug of dry gin. I could not steer with only one free hand while drinking, so the skipper assisted me. He stood to the right of the wheel and grabbed hold of one of the spokes with his left hand as he downed his beer with the other.

Talledo fought his way up the port side and into the pilot house. He informed Maggie that so far we had not lost any of the crew, and the *Nanok* suffered no serious damage. He did mention that the afterstructure was seeping some seawater between it and the main deck. He hoped the seepage could be taken care of by the two bilge pumps. Both he and McClay and Robbins examined the areas as best they could. They all agreed that greater seepage was not likely to occur.

It is cold and very windy as I am relieved of wheel watch by Jonesy at approximately 2100 after seventeen straight hours at the wheel. Jones takes over and I lay below to find some food. I am overtired and have a fever. I lay sprawled out on the engine room deck plates. Not all of the black, oily water has been pumped out of the stern bilges. Some of it washes into my clothing. A large portion of my parka that I lay in is somewhat of a mess. I have no other parka.

We are west of Rich Point wherever that is.

Just before my feet had gone out from under me in the pilot house, I recall a quick look through Maggie's ice tunnel and saw Dreams, Fair, Rollston, Robbins, and Jones sliding off the gun deck toward the ship's starboard side. I am elated to learn they are all well, now that I can actually see them again.

I sleep in fitful snatches, warmed by the thought that thus far I had no reason to think of myself as a coward.

December 18, Friday; At sea.

Ice chopping continues at a frantic pace. No further chopping orders are given or needed. Every man-jack in the crew is aware of the need, urgency, and existing danger. Whenever anyone is not on a specific assignment or on watch, he is chopping ice. Many more are ill. Young Mister Dillon does his share of de-icing. The only tool available to him is a butcher knife. He has learned to do quite well with the blade. Chips of ice fly continuously from his spirited onslaught. His determination is a thing to behold. His hands bleed from a number of tiny blade cuts, as a wall of seawater breaks over the deck. Oscar is lifted from his seated position, carried a short distance away, and deposited, still in a seated position. His chop-chop doesn't miss a stroke.

Normally, climbing a ladder is simple. But with the *Nanok* climbing mountains, then skidding into deep valleys, climbing becomes a chore. When the *Nanok* begins a downward plunge, I become weightless on the ladder that drops away from under me. The *Nanok* ends her downward plunge and begins to climb upward again. Gravity pulls at my body so strongly that ladder climbing is near impossible. I seem to weigh tons!

Pelting drops of airborne seawater is stripping the *Nanok* of her paint. It is just as well that the dories are frozen beneath mounds of ice. At least they won't be washed overboard. Knowing you have dories on board is supposed to instill a sense of security, but truthfully, when one's situation is such that a lifeboat is required on a small vessel, it is likely to be at a time when a small boat is grossly inadequate.

Weather is unchanged. Its fury plagues us and is of endless endurance. It simmers down for very short periods and the crew becomes hopeful the remainder of the trip will be smooth sailing.

The army weatherman's predictions are damnably accurate! Robbins thinks the guy is a sorcerer, a bad luck piece, or worse, and tells him so . . . close-up. The man is unflustered and grins as he tells us the weather will shortly become horrible once again, and it does! His predictions are often contrary to the barometer's indication. He even accurately tells us the amount of time it will require for the weather to change. Rain, snow and heavy winds arrive according to his time table. He points out the fact that it is not his fault the weather does not remain placid.

Cables securing the drums of fuel oil to the deck have given way and drums roll and tumble and pound one another before they bounce, one by one, into the sea and disappear.

More sea water enters the forecastle through the old patched-up hole in the port bow. Some dribbles into Stan's bunk. He is mad enough to bite himself. We could use two more bilge pumps. It is still possible to sleep in the forecastle but few choose to do so. Some alternate between engine room and forecastle when the need to sleep in comfort exceeds the fear of the *Nanok* sinking.

At times I am near despair. All seems so hopeless!

Are the *Bluebird* and the *Natsek* on the ocean's bottom?

My legs tremble and I am weak. I feel ill, am constantly wet and cold. Some men about me are hardly more than zombies, robots that go about their business as if programmed. There is a world somewhere but we have lost contact. Everyone appears to be as bad or worse off than I.

There is nowhere to run as a blue-black wave comes after me. It carries me across the slippery deck and slams me against a wall of ice. I recover and grab desperately at one of a number of lifelines strung across the deck. I catch the line and fall into a seated position. My legs refuse to lift me so I rest a while. I eat soda crackers and drink the fluid from a can of peas and eat the peas. They feel like mashed ball-bearings going down my sore throat. We help ourselves to some army rations in the hold. Hard tack and canned ground meat that has been given many unprintable names.

At day's end I quietly say prayers for the *Bluebird* and *Natsek*. At least I know the *Nanok* is still afloat.

December 19, Saturday; At sea.

Weather conditions unchanged. This must be hell for hell too is eternal.

We continue to chop ice like there is no tomorrow and possibly there may not be. Wind and waves beat at us. Snow is intermittent. The army weatherman's predictions are devastating. Barometer is useless, weather changes so swiftly.

Flu-like symptoms prevail. Men move silently. Weariness takes its toll. Conversation is an effort.

The anemometer high on the yardarm records maximum speed, then jams. Later it tears away from the yardarm, falls into the sea, and is lost. Finally, the yardarm is ripped from the mast and the mast splits. Rope lines that had been left strung and secured are torn loose. They fray and snap in the wind and must be chopped away. I am stricken with the worst sea sickness experienced to date. My retching ceases after I spit some blood.

The radio antenna strung from fore to aft masts has flown away. It is now impossible to send S.O.S. or Mayday should such an emergency arise. It will be great if we should have no such need.

Maggie and the aerographer are in the pilot house as I take over the wheel. Water sprays into the pilot house through the skipper's old peep hole. It splashes onto clothing and becomes ice crust. The skipper speaks kindly to me. No sarcasm or impatience. As many times in the past, he asks many questions, mostly about my home life, my family, friends, and hobbies. He grins broadly when I tell him I am the second youngest of twelve children. I tell him my oldest brother Ben served in World War I, while brothers Joe, Ray, and Ed are serving in World War II. Ben, the oldest, is thirty-one years older than Ed, the youngest. Ben has a son older than I am.

Conversation keeps time moving along. Maggie tells me much more about himself. I believe we have become shipmates.

Maggie's glances return again and again to my cold hands. I'd forgotten to bring along my waterproof mittens. Maggie disappears into his cabin and returns with a heavy pair of woolen socks and pulls them onto my hands. He pours both of us several ounces of dry gin. Mine burns its way to my stomach. It is stimulating and I am grateful.

The rudder becomes ever more difficult to control because my strength is not up to par. The wheel is necessarily large to provide leverage enough to move the giant rudder. My first Coast Guard vessel, the *Sea Cloud*, was equipped with electric motors that provided the necessary muscle. Not so the *Nanok*. *Nanok*'s rudder shaft is topped with a quadrant strung with heavy chain that leads through a series of pulleys, into the pilot house. There, the chain-ends are led-in from both port and starboard sides and are fastened to cable ends. The cable itself is wound around the axle of the ship's wheel. Controls of this type are powered solely by man's muscle. It is all one can do to steady the wheel as the seas whiplash the rudder. My arm muscles cramp and I pound the arm against the wheel to alleviate muscle constriction while I steer with the other. My teeth chatter constantly and I wonder why they don't shatter. My knees quiver again with cold. According to the adjustment holes in my belt, I have lost much weight and several inches of girth.

December 20, Sunday; At sea.

We are in a witch's cauldron. Mountainous waves, howling wind, and skin-searing airborne wave-tops. Either the waves are growing ever higher and more vicious, or my mind is on its way elsewhere!

The *Nanok* zombies move more slowly and seemingly in jerky movements, like a motion picture gone awry. Hair and beards are long and matted with bilge grease. Head hairs are tangled mops.

I cannot believe the *Nanok* is making any headway. It feels as if we are at a standstill. *Nanok*'s paint is almost all scrubbed away. Depth charges have been torn loose and lost in the sea. Some remnants of rigging flap in the wind. I am the only person left alive in my world of loneliness.

An average sea is estimated to be one hundred and fifty feet from peak of one wave to that of the next. The *Nanok* is only one hundred and twenty feet overall and does not reach from one peak to the next. She is also quite narrow, twenty-three feet five inches maximum beam, and only a twelve foot draft. She is, therefore, forever balanced atop of a wave, or down in a valley between two peaks. She struggles as she climbs to a wave-top, only to have the wave pass by. Her bow then plummets swiftly downward, barely contacting any part of the wave's hind side.

Flying swiftly downward, the vessel is unable to follow the exact contour of the wave's valley. Instead, she runs straight downward. Reaching the valley bottom, she continues downward and drives her nose into the bottom. At this point, buoyancy takes over and the bow pops backward out of the depths and begins to climb the leading side of the next oncoming wave.

"This voyage can't last much longer," I tell myself. I wonder just how far from Boston we still are.

I am astounded! Robbins comes to see me and is in tears. He tells me he is scared to death! He says he is homesick and lonely and feels a compulsion to destroy himself!

"Good god man!" I say. "Everyone is as scared and as lonely as you are."

He does not believe me.

"But they don't have the problems I do."

"Like what, Robbie?" I ask sympathetically as possible. "We're almost home, fella!"

"That's the trouble," says Rob. "I'm scared to go home, I know what I'll find."

"Bob," I say, "your wife and mother will just hug you to death."

"Think so? Look, 'ski, I never told anyone this before. As you know, I once held the rating of surfman for more than fifteen years. Then the rating was eliminated and they rated me boatswain's mate 1/c. As soon as he came on board and found out I was a boatswain's mate who had never served on board a large vessel, Maggie came down on me. He never gave me a chance, 'ski! You know how asinine he can be."

Yes, I knew.

"I don't think the old man knows the purpose or importance of our periodic achievement reviews. I've carried a perfect 4.0 rating throughout my career and Maggie knocked me down to a two point something!"

"Oh my God!" I say. "How bad does that make things for you?"

"My entire career is ruined, 'ski!" he sobbed. Tears streamed down his cheeks.

"Did I tell you about my mother and my wife?" he asked.

"I remember you telling me about your mom being ill and your pregnant wife having to walk a long distance every day to help her. Weren't we still in

Boston at the time? Come to think of it, you never did say if or when the baby was born. How come?"

Bob's teeth were grinding and he told me the worst. Shortly after leaving Boston, his mother suffered a stroke and was left partially paralyzed. Robbie's wife continued to look after her as often as she could despite her advanced pregnancy. Late one evening on her way home she was viciously raped. She lost the baby and narrowly escaped death herself.

"Did you tell the skipper?" I asked.

"I wouldn't tell that bastard anything that might make him think I wanted favors! I wouldn't ask him to hand me a life jacket if we were going under!"

"Oh! Bob!" I said. "I'm sure he would have sent you home and had you transferred to shore duty."

"After what he has done to my career and my retirement pension I can't even look at him without wanting to tear him apart! I know damn well he's never had any formal Coast Guard training when he came on board in civilian clothes during wartime. He didn't know from shit what performance ratings meant! He, without knowing, had the guts to mark me down as incompetent, when it was he that was, and is, incompetent! He could have asked Talledo for advice, but no, that would have indicated he was less than perfect!"

Even though tears streaked his face, he managed to display a sardonic smile.

"Later, when Maggie learned from Mister Dillon that he ruined my career, he apologized! Can you imagine him being so nice!? He apologized!!"

And Robbins spit on the floor in contempt and anger.

What could I say? I wrapped an arm around the poor guy's shoulders and swallowed a lump in my throat.

I said: "I didn't believe the skipper had any formal training either, but he came on board at a time when competent, well-trained men were either scarce or non-existent. The old man had very special talents and sea experience that the Coast Guard needed desperately. Maybe Admiral Smith conned Maggie into enlisting, who knows? They were said to be close friends for a long time."

No doubt Maggie was a super seaman, but he had some serious shortcomings, too. I never felt more anger toward the man than I did after listening to Robbin's story.

I am on wheel watch alone with Maggie in the pilot house. Robbie runs through my mind. I feel sure I will never get my coxswain's rating. But I don't want to go down as silently as Robbie did. In a not-too-calm voice I blurt out: "Captain, am I ever going to get a coxswain's rating? If I don't get it in time to go home with it, I don't want it ever. You promised it to me a long time ago, but you seem to avoid discussing it with me."

I can't believe I said it! I'm sure there was anger in my voice. I thought he would tell me to go to hell. Instead, without turning around to look at me he asked: "What is your rating now?"

"For cris'sake!" I thought, "don't give me that crap again that you don't know my rating!" Instead, I try to answer calmly.

"I'm a seaman, first class, sir."

"Well, we'll see."

God, I was raging inside!

"Captain," I said in desperation, "I believe I have proven myself equal to the rating and I want it on my sleeve for Christmas."

"We'll see," he said, and spoke no more for the balance of my watch. Neither did I. I had run out of words. I wanted to yank a spoke out of the wheel and hit him with it. It was the longest watch I ever stood. I just knew I would get the same crap as Robbie had.

The sea calms a bit, wind just whispers. We sight for the first time several American vessels heading in opposite directions. Temperature is eighteen degrees below zero. My eyes feel frozen in my head. My cold, or whatever it is, has settled in my chest, making breathing painful. Fever and chills alternately hamper my activities. Legs and back feel weak. Ice chopping continues but not as urgently as before. Much less ice shrouds the *Nanok*.

Elmer Comer, our feather merchant, comes running. He grins broadly and is very excited. "Sew the crow on your sleeve buddy, the old man has rated you coxswain!"

I am overwhelmed! The achievement is so very dear to me. I suppose it is because I had to earn it from a most demanding master. A man who refuses to acknowledge mediocrity? (Hah!)

December 21, Monday; At sea.

Where in hell are we!? It's not possible to miss Boston, is it?! The wind whistles but with much less gusto. Temperature has risen notably. Many vessels are sighted, going every which way. Thick ice on deck is being loosened by the rising temperature. It has become much easier to chop larger chunks loose and we hoist them over the side. There is hardly a foot-thick wall of the stuff still clinging to the face of the pilot house. With luck the decks may be cleared in short order. Forward bilges are being pumped out.

Without the smashing waves we are shipping less seawater. The *Nanok* is not so far down at the nose anymore. The starboard list has lessened considerably. The worst may be over.

The sun pops out and shines brightly. It appears as a Christmas tree ornament with a frosty halo surrounding it. As we proceed, the sun moves toward the western horizon. The sky is exceptionally beautiful. It turns from orange to red with wide, purple beams that unsuccessfully try to penetrate low-hanging haze hugging the flat, green-black carpet of the sea.

December 22, Tuesday; Constitution Wharf, Boston.

Wind and some ice are still with us but hardly. The *Nanok* is now at a stable, even keel. Forward bilges have been drained. The *Nanok* has practically no paint left.

As the day wears on, the wind becomes a gentle breath and the seas are asleep or at least napping. A low-lying mist lies close to the water and through it we see snatches of landfall.

There is a yell from a dozen voices. I exit the forward hatch and am elated to see the entrance to Boston Harbor. The thrill of seeing it defies description. From somewhere inside the harbor there is a blinker light's Morse code being directed toward the *Nanok*. Robbins is responding with blinker from atop the pilot house. He relays the received message to the skipper in writing. As Maggie reads, his face begins to redden, and the veins in his forehead bulge. He breaks loose with a violent stream of Norwegian profanity, punctuated by several "God damn's" and "sons of bitches" in the American language.

"Damn if we're going to stay out here for the night!" he shouts.

We have been ordered to drop hook and lay-to for the night outside the harbor for quarantine purposes. There are giant nets woven of cable that are suspended deep in the waters and held in a vertical position, suspended from buoys floating on the water's surface. The nets are laced with anti-submarine depth charges. Should an enemy submarine attempt to enter the harbor during the night, it would become entangled in the cable-net and, upon contact, would trigger an explosion of one or more depth charges.

Every morning, two tug boats tow open the center of the net/gate to permit American and other friendly vessels to enter and/or depart. In the evening the process is reversed. The gate is closed to all traffic for the night.

We temporarily wallow in the sea outside harbor. The two tugs are in process of pulling the gates closed in front of the *Nanok*. The skipper shouted to no one in particular, that we are hungry, and sick, and cold, and we are entering the harbor with or without official permission!

He slams the ship's telegraph to "Full Forward" and heads for the net's opening. As we draw near, both tugboat skippers become aware of what we are attempting to do. They blast warning whistles that can possibly be heard as far away as Chicago.

Both tugs were full-speeding the net closure to thwart the *Nanok*'s entry. The tugs loomed ever larger as we approached one another. It occurred to me that both tugs and *Nanok*'s path were about to terminate at precisely the same point of the harbor's entrance!

The tugboat skippers had a task to perform, and just because the *Nanok* was a relatively small American vessel they had no way of confirming we were genuinely American, nor what our cargo might be.

Some of the crew was shouting: "We'll never make it! We'll never make it!" Others shouted: "Look out!" Others only mouthed: "Oh, God!"

The *Nanok*'s bow was at its normal height and her gun deck was higher than the bow of either tug. I leaned far over the portside gunwale to see the one tug almost directly in front of us. She was about to try ramming our port bow in hope of pushing us aside. We were trying to outrace the tug and pass in front of her. We were gaining but not fast enough. The *Nanok* curved to the right, trying to pass without being struck.

We were about to collide! Like a fool I stood transfixed, unable to move away from the gunwale. Instead I braced for impact and held fast to the inboard side of the gunwale.

There was a loud, dull thud and a boom and a screech of timber and steel being forcefully ground against one another! The grinding vessels threw off acrid smelling smoke and some sparks as friction burned them. Miraculously, we moved past the tug. Some of her crew was screaming profanities at us.

I remembered the other tug!

From starboard, tug number two is bearing full speed toward *Nanok*'s bow! A collision seems certain! Crew members grasp whatever secured object is available to them to brace themselves against impact.

It happens!

Another great ear-punishing "Thump!" Then the grating, tearing, screeching sound of wood and steel grinding against one another forcefully. Smoke and odor from friction is terrible. *Nanok*'s bow has contacted the tug's starboard just beyond her bow. The blow is a glancing one but staggering in severity. Both vessels rebound in opposite directions. The *Nanok* is inside Boston Harbor!

From shoreward a siren screams. The *Nanok* heaves-to as a large speedboat pulls alongside *Nanok*'s starboard. Several captain of the port details scramble angrily on board. They are ushered hastily into the skipper's cabin. Muffled sounds of loud, angry voices emanate from the small, closed cubicle. There is a short, heated debate regarding the *Nanok*'s quarantine directive. Health inspection outside the harbor had been ignored. The captain of the port detail leaves in a greater hurry than they had arrived.

Maggie is more furious than I have ever seen him. His reddened face was about to explode. He stomped heavily behind the departing men. They too are red-faced and furious! They sped shoreward without a backward glance, heading toward the shipyard. We follow them. The tugs have completed closing the gates behind us.

Every man that is not on watch stands silent and shivering along the portside gunwale, looking shoreward, wondering about what has yet to happen. It is bitter cold. We glide slowly and silently into a slip for tie-up. The port detail is nowhere about.

Customarily a crew tries to look their best upon arrival at a port after a long voyage. The *Nanok* crew is at their worst! Below the knee-length khaki parkas, clothes are ragged and torn and coated with black oil. The warm bodies inside seawater-dampened clothing give off a frosty vapor. Red eyes stare from inside black rings. Long, matted hair and beards are as dirty as the parkas. All is silent except for Captain Magnusson's commanding voice ordering bow, breast, and stern lines cast ashore for mooring.

Scores of late-working shipyard office personnel flock to the *Nanok*. The vessel's physical appearance is as shocking as her crew on deck. In moments a milling throng fills the pier like extras in a silent movie.

Women with horrified expressions whisper to one another as they point fingers at zombie-like crew members. One woman mutters a long, almost inaudible "Oh my dear God!" and begins to sob, and then cry loudly. It is as if one of her children has been struck by an automobile.

We appear as though we survived some disastrous sea battle. *Nanok*'s paint all gone. Shredded lines and rigging hanging loose. Antenna gone, some shutter glass beaten out, and a very large patch on our portside bow. It occurred to me that this could have been a great moment to recruit new Coast Guardsmen from among the men ashore. Who or whatever it was that damaged a United States vessel so badly, the men appeared ready to destroy. Their obvious concern was gratifying to witness.

Deck hands ashore refused to secure our lines despite Maggie's shouted orders. Obviously the captain of the port has ordered them not to. Maggie is enraged. His jutting, stubborn jaw juts angrily forward. His face muscles quiver and his bloodshot eyes flash! He orders our lines to be withdrawn and backs the *Nanok* out of the slip. Civilian workers ashore are about to attack the deck hands for not securing our lines.

It is deliriously wonderful to be safely back stateside after so long a time away. Yet I feel heartsick for some reason. What have we accomplished? We are not even welcome home!

Nanok is put about and is aimed at our point of origin, Constitution Wharf. Arriving at the wharf we find it devoid of any vessels or human activity. Its building is dark and foreboding. Night is falling swiftly now. Many of our men leap ashore as pirates boarding a prize frigate. Lines are secured on the dock. Pent-up emotion takes hold of half dozen men. Even before the lines were secured, some race through the near-empty cavernous interior of the long building. Perhaps they are fearful the *Nanok* will be turned away again. Several stumble and fall in their haste through the darkness. Out the front of the building they fly! Across Atlantic Avenue and up Hanover Street toward Scollay Square. I choose to remain on board even though I am tempted to run.

In minutes, Elmer Comer, our feather merchant, becomes very busy typing leave of absence papers for many of the crew including me. Those of us who had not fled ashore were ordered to round-up those who had. Most were easy to locate. Every tavern that housed one or more of the ghoulish crew is surrounded by an unbelieving, curious crowd of civilians.

What scenes there were!

I find three of our men in a tavern. One has his parka open, his shirt stuffed with fresh fruit and a carton of ice cream that is melting and oozing out, over the front of his dungarees. He holds a large portion of a layer cake in one hand and a bunch of green onions in the other. How and from where, especially [in] so short a time had he acquired all this?! He alternated eating mouthfuls of each, washing them down with long drafts of beer. He laughs wild and fiendishly behind an oily, matted beard. I feel sure it is Goncalves, but he does not answer to the name. His bloodshot eyes shift quickly back and forth across the ring of civilians who, not too closely, surround him. He seems fearful that some may interfere with, or take away, his banquet. Woe to anyone who might be foolish enough to try! This guy is of steel and lignum vitae.

Civilians are greatly amused at the loud, mad scene. Another crew member, Petrenko, has a table top covered with hot pastrami sandwiches. He devours them with three bites each, using a tumbler of whiskey as a wash. The third crew member (who later asked not to be identified) is piss-assed drunk and experiencing a laughing jag for the first time in his life (so he was to later say). He has (supposedly) always been a teetotaler or thereabouts. He rocks precariously back and forth in uncontrollable laughter. The unusual and amazed expressions of onlookers had set him off and he couldn't stop. Every face strikes him as hilariously funny. He points at each of them, even the bartender. Each point creates its own burst of laughter. Somehow we manage to herd them all back down Hanover Street to the *Nanok*. We are trailed by civilians much as the Pied Piper had been by other followers.

From somewhere in heaven the Salvation Army has heard of the *Nanok's* arrival and is at the wharf to tend to our needs. No one who has ever been to war will ever forget the Salvation Army. They have chosen their name perfectly. If I were to describe them, I would say the Salvation Army is the mother of all those of heavy heart. God bless her.

I have been granted a ten-day leave of absence. I could begin immediately, but I choose to squeeze every ounce of pleasure out of this hard-earned Christmas. I decide to wait until Christmas Eve before catching a train for Detroit. I want to arrive there on Christmas morning to sweeten the thrill of coming home.

Lucille has not heard from me for several months. I have written a number of letters to her but never mailed them. I was stupid enough to believe I would be stateside a long time ago, so I mailed nothing.

It is difficult to restrain myself from not even making a phone call home. The family and Lucille must imagine all sorts of horrible things happening to me. I wonder if folks will easily recognize me with my very thin face and body. I am six foot two inches tall and now have about a thirty-four inch waste. I have lost nineteen pounds and had to hastily sew wedges in the backside of my dress blue trousers. The *Natsek* is not here yet, but she is sure to arrive tomorrow.

After an extremely long and red-hot shower and a few cups of coffee, I feel less tense and nervous. My chest still hurts and my eyes feel hot. I am weak and head-achy. The thrill of going home is a very effective medicine. It is very late and dark but I choose to go ashore alone. I walk slowly without any particular direction. It is refreshing and very satisfying just to walk on solid ground. I feel like a rural stranger in a large city for the first time. Every passing face seems beautiful to me, what little I see of them in semi-blackout. I want to talk to everyone I see. From out of the darkness a loud-speaker emits Christmas carols. Organ music and a children's choir sounds so beautiful that I weep as I walk. I am happy that no one is with me to witness my emotion. Thoughts and visions of all I hold dear pass through my mind. I experience an unusual inner warmth and at the same time a horrible sadness. I believe I weep for every member of the *Nanok*'s crew as if they were family. I know of their courage and strength first-hand. My mind reviews many of the trying times we've experienced together.

I feel a special affection for the *Nanok* herself. Her durability is a tribute to the men who built her. She survived the onslaught of an ocean gone mad. Though stripped of her trappings, she lays at rest in the place of her voyage beginning and where the proud vessel Old Ironsides once lay. The tiny lady *Nanok* carried us safely home and I'm grateful.

I now know better the men who sail in ships and the affection they demonstrate for the sometimes rusted hulks they travel in. Ships are most often referred to in the feminine gender for they comfort and protect those within their keep. There is a certain something that every sailor leaves with his ship. Perhaps a certain portion of his loneliness, a bit of laughter, a coat of paint, a repaired yardarm, some pain or illness, or perhaps a frightened heartbeat or two. All such things mold a ship into a lady.

Protection from all hostile elements. A home away from home.

Ships are more than steel and wood
And heart of burning coal,
For those who sail upon them know
That some ships have a soul.

December 23, Wednesday; Constitution Wharf.

The *Natsek* has not been heard from.

Deep concern shows in every face. I refuse negative thoughts. She must be crippled and holed-up in some remote fjord or bay in Newfoundland, experiencing engine problems or such. What else could have befallen her? No one need be a sea captain to realize no enemy vessel could have challenged her in the type of weather we came through.

Comer was unable to type my coxswain's rating paper work because he lacked the proper forms. Since I've long had the cross anchors and eagle sewn onto the upper right arm of my winter blue jumper, I had no intention of removing same. I intend to wear it home no matter what. I have done a rather good job of cross-stitching the "crow" onto the sleeve. What a beautiful bird the American eagle!

Forms were obtained from a Coast Guard cutter nearby and I do not leave Elmer's presence until he has completed typing them.

Finally! I am a coxswain!!

I complete many small chores. My uniform has been pressed automatically. As per common practice, it had been turned inside out and has lain between my two, thin mattresses. When turned right-side out, the pants and jumper appear ironed.

Elmer, Jonesy, and I go into town, enjoy a great meal, goodies, and brew, and return to the *Nanok*. It is almost deserted. The crew has fled in all directions.

December 24, Thursday; En route home.

Fear for the *Natsek*'s safety is now official.

I know all of her crew and it is very difficult to accept the premise that all is not well. The thinking now is that she may have capsized under heavy ice as the *Nanok* almost had. This scenario is of course possible. Skipper La Farge is known to be a most competent sailor but only with sailboats and sport sailing. Supposedly he had never sailed as far north as Newfoundland. From actual observation, I know for fact that his crew did not chop ice as fast or effectively as the *Nanok* crew. He possibly did not know the full danger of heavy icing conditions.

Maggie certainly knew.

The crew members still on board the *Nanok* are raucous with excitement. So am I, except I feel an occasional tug of guilt because the *Natsek* is not here to share. I pray for her and her crew.

Signals are crossed. Elmer and I were to go to the rail depot together. While I was showering, someone told him I'd already left. So he left also. He was gone about an hour before I became aware of his absence. Even though he was bound for Danville, Indiana, and I for Detroit, Michigan, we were to lunch together and have a few shells of beer before boarding our respective trains. They may have proven to be one and the same for at least part of the way.

Arriving at the depot I learned that I had several hours before my train time. I purchased my ticket and decided to walk away my waiting time in the busy downtown Boston area. On an obscure little side street I came across a very small barber shop. It had but one chair and of course only one barber. I decided to have my shoulder-length hair sheared. Since the barber was surprised at my hair's length, I told him I had just returned from over-seas and had had no time for a professional haircut. He said that about an hour before my arrival, another Guardsman dropped in to have his ex-tra-long mane sheared. He had also just arrived from overseas and in his haste to catch a train, he forgot and left his eyeglasses at the barber shop. Could it have been Comer?!

"Can I see the glasses please?" I asked.

"Sure" he said and showed them to me.

"By God! I can't believe this!" I say. "Those are my shipmate Elmer's glasses!" I knew them well because of several small, unusual kinks in the left earpiece, and their not too common-shaped gold frames. Both barber and I marvel at the unbelievable coincidence of Elmer and me selecting the same, small, obscure shop!

"Could you see to it that your friend gets these glasses?" asks the barber.

"But I will not see him again for almost two weeks," I reply.

"I'll probably never see him again," counters the barber. I agree to take the glasses along with me. Hah! Elmer always said he is as blind as a bat without his glasses! His vision problem must be, at least in part, imaginary. . . . Otherwise, how did he manage to leave without them? The barber said Elmer appeared to be quite intoxicated and amused the barber with his very dry humor.

On the train I sat alongside a happy civilian who had a small, black leath-er satchel containing several bottles of liquor. We two proceeded to drain them. The trip was jolly. Passengers all join into singing Christmas carols. My friend disembarked long before Detroit.

December 25, 1942, Friday; At home, Detroit, Michigan.

I nap on and off until the conductor passes through crying: "Detroit, next, Michigan Central Depot, end of the line, remember your baggage, please."

A Checker Cab carried me from the southwest side of downtown to the farthest northeast boundary of the city, Eight Mile Road, and Gratiot Avenue. Home is my sister Joann at brother-in-law Walter Kluza's house on Hickory Street.

Joann cries when she answers the doorbell and finds me standing on her porch. Husband Walter's face wears a broad smile, but where is Lu-cille!? Joann informs me Lucille had decided to spend the holidays with her sister and family. Joann phones the sister and uses some excuse why Lucille must return immediately.

She soon returns and is obviously irritated for having to do so. As she enters the house, Joann and Walter step aside to allow her to see me. She is shocked! She trembles and falls in a dead faint but I manage to catch her. I tell her how much I love her and how much I missed her. In return I am smothered with kisses.

We go about enjoying the best Christmas of our lives.

Editor's Epilogue

The night of December 16, 1942, was a particularly rough one off the coast of Newfoundland. Yet, it is probable that the men returning to Boston from wartime Arctic patrol preferred it that way. Submarines were unlikely to be lurking in heavy weather: icebergs, blizzards, and heavy seas conspired to keep submarines away. More attacks were made by subs in calm or moderate seas than in a rough sea, and rough seas, all believed, could be conquered; submarines could not. Writes historian Samuel Eliot Morison: "The men actually began to pray for dirty weather." On the night of December 16, such prayers were answered. The *Nanok* and the *Natsek*, two of ten 120-foot fishing trawlers hastily converted by Edward Hanson "Iceberg" Smith into emergency Arctic cutters, clawed their way from Narsarssuak to Boston through the Strait of Belle Isle, an area of shoalwater famous for ripping the guts out of far sturdier ships. Interviewed after the war, the commander of the *Nanok*, Magnus G. Magnusson, remembered that he had watched his young crew fight "cold weather, ice, fog, snowstorms . . . [at times] stand[ing] in water up to their armpits . . . water that had a temperature of 34 degrees . . . I saw them hang on with one hand and break ice with the other, 20 out of 24 hours, in a 65-mile-per-hour gale, with the ship on her beam ends, and the temperature at five degrees below zero." [39]

More than sixty years ago, an hour past midnight in the early morning of December 17, *Nanok*'s sister ship *Natsek was* on her beam ends, and her crew was in their seventeenth hour of chipping ice and shouldering the sea. At that moment the Strait of Belle Isle came into view. At a quarter past two in the morning, as a heavy snowfall obscured Belle Isle Light, Magnusson hailed his counterpart on the *Natsek,* and the two decided to proceed through the darkness of the strait so long as their positions were known. The *Natsek* took the lead, sounding its way through the strait after the

Nanok's fathometer died. Before long, snowfall intensified, and Magnusson lost sight of *Natsek*. He gave two blasts on *Nanok*'s horn, calls answered by a flash of white light from *Natsek*. That was the last he ever saw of her.

For the commander of the *Natsek*, it was not supposed to end this way. For him, the Second World War should have been the start one of those stories so familiar from his besieged generation: a young artist yearns for time at sea, for wartime adventures at far-off coordinates to fill notebooks full of colorful anecdotes and scenes; all capped by a triumphant return to write and paint his way into history. It later worked precisely that way for so many writers, from Norman Mailer to Joseph Heller to James Jones to Alex Haley, all of whom returned from the war to create the bulk of the memorable postwar literature. But the story was very different for another artist, the painter T. S. La Farge.

According to the official U.S. Coast Guard history of the Second World War—and in an unself-consciously ironic phrase typical of World War II—Thomas Sargent La Farge joined the Coast Guard "to paint, while performing regular war duties."

Beyond his commission qualifications as a "yachtsman and lover of ships," La Farge had already acquired an impressive reputation as a painter, and his murals, stained glasses, frescoes, and mosaics could be found at New York Hospital and the New York World's Fair, and at Trinity College and St. Matthew's Cathedral in Washington, D.C. [40]

At a quarter to three on that December night, as Magnus Magnusson blindly laid *Nanok* to for about four hours to find out where he was, perhaps on board *Natsek* La Farge was remembering what Iceberg Smith had told his ten newly commissioned fishing vessel skippers as they set out for Greenland. "Your first command. Your first great chance. It is hard, responsible, vital duty. War duty. Don't fail your country or your ship or me."[41] It was perhaps too much to ask of a "yachtsman and lover of ships" to bring a less-than-heavy weather trawler against and through thirty-foot seas amidst a Newfoundland blizzard. In the next hours, the through-bolts bearing against washers that secured the deckhouse structure gave way, ice accumulations listed the ship heavily, and the *Natsek*, the Inuit word for fjord seal, began to sink.

Some of what La Farge and his twenty-three men must have experienced before they all went down together came from Magnusson's own experiences later that morning and through the next week. After *Nanok* cleared the Belle Isle Strait, twenty-four hours after leaving Greenland, and as she came abeam of Point Amour Light, the weather cleared and the wind hauled from the west, reaching gale force in less than an hour. The wind fired bullets of spray at the ship, forming a canopy of ice the crew had to fight for five seemingly endless days, breaking ice chip by chip from the deckhouse structure until *Nanok* passed south of Cape Sable on December 22. As Ted Novak writes, they reached Boston in time for Christmas.

The *Nanok* and the remaining Arctic trawlers were sent home permanently as soon as the U.S. Coast Guard could procure adequate cutters to replace them toward the end of the war. After a second cruise to Greenland in 1943, the *Nanok* itself was decommissioned in July, 1944. Ted Novak was unable to be on board for that second cruise. Suffering a back injury as he was scheduled to report, he was medically discharged from the service.

After the war, Ted Novak returned to Michigan, where he worked for the state and built a life with his beloved Lucille. He sent his diary to the U.S. Coast Guard Historian's Office in 1994, three years before his death in Macomb County, Michigan.

In 2003, a widow of one of the *Natsek* sailors found the diary posted on the Historian's Office website. Her husband had been a radioman, and together they had had a daughter, before war separated them forever. As she wrote, "after sixty years, Mr. Novak's eyewitness account of events surrounding *Natsek*'s disappearance afforded us an unexpected measure of closure and finality." [42]

Air and land searches found no trace of *Natsek* in the Strait of Belle Isle, nor has any trace been located to this day. Nevertheless, a memorial to the crew does exist, in a sense. In a small chapel in St. Matthew's Cathedral near the corner of Connecticut and Rhode Island Avenues in Washington, D.C., you can light a candle, as I did a decade ago, beneath a large mosaic depicting the Resurrection. In the lower right-hand corner is the name "T. La Farge." Resting among the whispers of the devout, only these silent creations on the walls of St. Matthew's remain as reminders of twenty-three men and their captain, a young painter whose dreams of combining service and art were overwhelmed by the "regular war duties" of a small ship in a December gale.

Appendix

Units of the Greenland Patrol, 1940–1945

Task Force 24.8, CinClant

USS *Active* (WSC-125)
USS *Aivik* (WYP-164)
USS *Aklak* (WYP-168)
USS *Alatok* (WYP-172)
USS *Albatross* (AM-71)
USS *Algonquin* (WPG-75)
USS *Amarok* (WYP-166)
USS *Arluk* (WYP-167)
USS *Arundel* (WYT-90)
USS *Arvek* (WYP-165)
USS *Atak* (WYP-163)
USS *Bear* (AG-29)
USS *Big Horn* (AO-45)
USS *Bluebird* (AM-72)
USS *Bowdoin* (IX-50)
USS *Cactus* (WAGL-270)
USS *Cayuga* (WPG-54)
USS *Citrus* (WAGL-300)
USS *Comanche* (WPG-76)
USS *Eastwind* (WAG-279)
USS *Escanaba* (WPG-77)*
USS *Evergreen* (WAGL-295)
USS *Faunce* (WSC-138)
USS *Frederick Lee* (WSC-139)

USS *General Greene* (WSC-140)
USS *Laurel* (WAGL-291)
USS *Manitou* (WYT-60)
USS *Modoc* (WPG-46)
USS *Mohawk* (WPG-78)
USS *Mojave* (WPG-47)
USS *Nanok* (WYP-169)
USS *Natsek* (WYP-170)**
USS *Nogak* (WYP-171)
USS *Northland* (WPG-49)
USS *North Star* (WPG-59)
USS *Raritan* (WYT-93)
USS *Sorrell* (WAGL-296)
USS *Southwind* (WAG-280)
USS *Storis* (WAGL-38)
USS *Tahoma* (WPG-80)
USS *Tampa* (WPG-48)
USS *Travis* (WSC-153)

USS *SC-527*
USS *SC-528*
USS *SC-688*
USS *SC-689*
USS *SC-704*
USS *SC-705*

Weather Station #2
USS *Sea Cloud* (WPG-284/IX-99)
USS *Monomoy* (AG-40/WAG-275)
USS *Muskeget* (AG-48)
USS *Manhasset* (AG-47)

Air Unit

VP-6 (12 PBY-5A Catalina Flying Boats)

Source: U.S. Coast Guard Historians Office
* Sunk, torpedoed
** Sunk, iced-up and capsized, all hands lost

Notes

1. As of December, 2004, only three *Nanok* crew members were still alive. These are Bernard "Chips" Delaney, Russell C. "Cookie" Clark, and John "Balboa" Goncalves. All are in their late 80s. The editor spoke with both Clark and Goncalves in late December, 2004, and it was Clark who provided the photograph of *Nanok* that appears in this volume. Previous to this, the U.S. Coast Guard possessed no image of this Arctic trawler.

2. The *Sea Cloud* (WPG-284) had a brief service in the U.S. Coast Guard. Commissioned into service on April 4, 1942, it was transferred to the U.S. Navy on April 9, 1943. For part of this time, the vessel was operated as an integration experiment, with part of its compliment of officers and men being African-American. The *Sea Cloud* operates to this day as a sail cruise ship in the Mediterranean and the Caribbean. See Scheina, *U.S. Coast Guard Cutters*, 10.

3. According to U.S. Coast Guard and other government records, George Talledo was born in San Francisco in 1901. So when Thaddeus Novak met him in 1942, Talledo was hardly a "fuzz-faced chief boatswain's mate about sixty-two years old," although such an estimation gives the reader an idea of how old and worn a Coast Guard chief could appear to a twenty-one-year-old sailor. Talledo passed away in Richmond, New York, in 1973.

4. A native Icelander and thirty-year sea veteran, Magnus G. Magnusson served as Danish consul in Boston until the Nazi invasion of Denmark in 1940, whereupon he resigned his post and entered the U.S. Coast Guard. While Novak often refers to Magnusson as speaking Norwegian, he more likely spoke Icelandic or Danish. To American ears, all of these Scandinavian languages would sound similar.

5. Born on the island of Martha's Vineyard, Massachusetts, in 1889, Edward Hanson Smith descended from a family of island whalers. After a year at the Massachusetts Institute of Technology, Smith in 1910 entered the U.S. Coast Guard Academy at New London, Connecticut, when it was still known as the U.S. Revenue Cutter Service School of Instruction and classes were held on board the Revenue practice cutter *Itasca* at Arundel Cove, Maryland. He graduated and received his commission as an ensign on May 17, 1913, and earned the World War I Victory Medal for his work as navigator of the cutter *Manning* on escort duty between En-

gland and Gibraltar from August 1917 to January 1919. In November of 1919, Smith was assigned to the *Seneca*. When the *Seneca* left for International Ice Patrol (IIP) duty in the spring of 1920, E. H. Smith was on board as navigator and scientific observer. For the first time, a commissioned officer of the Coast Guard was detailed as scientific observer during a Coast Guard cruise, conducting experiments and observations for the furtherance of oceanographic knowledge. Smith made the most of his chance, transferring from ship to ship so that he could remain at sea conducting observations from the time the patrol began in February until its conclusion in July. The bulk of the remainder of Edward Smith's career in the Coast Guard, from 1920 until his retirement as rear admiral in 1950, would be spent studying the oceanography of the Arctic and the North Atlantic. By the early 1920s it became apparent that in order to successfully conduct its required duties, the International Ice Patrol required Coast Guard officers with professional training in oceanography. So in 1923 the Coast Guard established an oceanographic unit at Harvard University in Cambridge, Massachusetts, charged with providing support and conducting research for the IIP. From 1923 to 1931, the unit consisted of one civilian and one military oceanographer, plus five enlisted oceanographic technicians. The military oceanographer was E. H. Smith who, as a result of his annual IIP reports, was rapidly becoming known to his fellow officers as "Iceberg" Smith. In order to study ice more completely, Smith brought chunks of it back to Harvard University in the iceboxes of ice patrol cutters. He would place a piece of berg or pack ice retrieved from the North Atlantic on the deck of a cutter and look at it for hours. At meals, it was said that he would stir the ice in a pitcher of ice water and study the melting ice and the eddies in the pitcher. After his leadership of the *Marion* Expedition, among the most comprehensive American oceanographic expeditions to that moment, Harvard University awarded Smith the degree of Doctor of Philosophy in geological and oceanographic physics. He was apparently the first Coast Guard officer to earn such an advanced degree. The Woods Hole Oceanographic Institution was established in Woods Hole, Massachusetts, in 1930, and a year later the Coast Guard moved the oceanographic unit from Harvard to this small village of ocean scientists in the southwest corner of Cape Cod. In 1931, Smith served as navigator on board the German dirigible *Graf Zeppelin* on an 8,000-mile flight that took place from July 24 to August 1. Data was collected on terrestrial magnetism and atmospheric electricity above the Arctic Circle and on the geography of vast sections of the Arctic archipelago of Franz Josef Land. Iceberg Smith became the first Coast Guard officer awarded the Distinguished Service Medal for World War II service. "Under extremely difficult conditions, the forces of his command successfully operated patrols and escorts, maintained a system of weather stations, and provided full logistic and tactical support for the Army," reads in part his citation from James Forrestal. What the citation doesn't mention is that Admiral Smith also prevailed upon Army Air Corp bomber pilots to fly Christmas trees from Labrador to all of his outlying bases in treeless Greenland every December. In 1950, Iceberg Smith retired from the Coast Guard to take up a six-year tenure as director of the oceanographic institution at Woods Hole. He died in 1961. See Capelotti, "The Coast Guard and Oceanography."

6. *The Bluejackets' Manual* for U.S. Navy sailors had been published and revised ten times between 1902 and the start of the Second World War. It offered rudimentary and advanced instruction on a wide variety of maritime and maritime-related topics for the enlisted sailors. These topics included seamanship, gunnery, physical drills, inspections, and other basic subjects, through the perils of gambling and moral turpitude: "occasionally a person of immoral habits succeeds in joining the naval service." Eventually, five Coast Guard–specific chapters were published during the war, and then an entirely separate work, *The Coast Guardsman's Manual*, appeared in 1952.

7. This is perhaps the converted whaler *Belmont* (WYP-341) (ex-*Thorarinn*). *Belmont* was commissioned into the Coast Guard in 1942 and decommissioned three years later. It proved, according to Scheina (179), "a very crowded and wet craft."

8. At 769 feet overall length, the aircraft carrier *Ranger* (CV-4) would have dwarfed *Nanok* by nearly 650 feet. Its complement, 1,788 including 162 officers, was similarly massive.

9. The *North Star* (WPG-49), constructed in the 1930s for work in Alaskan waters by the U.S. Department of the Interior, was commissioned into the U.S. Coast Guard as an emergency acquisition on May 14, 1941. A wooden-hulled vessel with an ice-strengthened bow, she served alongside the *Northland* in northeast Greenland in September of 1941 during the seizure of the Norwegian sealer *Buskoe*, the first U.S. naval capture of the Second World War. In July of 1943, *North Star* survived an attack by a German aircraft off Jan Mayen Land. See Scheina, 11.

10. U.S.S. *Massachusetts* (BB-59) had just been commissioned in May of 1942. She was 680 feet long and carried 2,000 sailors. She received eleven battle stars for service in the Second World War. See U.S. Navy, *American Naval Fighting Ships*, vol. 4, 265–66.

11. Novak certainly means "*not* normal practice" here. The chain of command is perhaps the one and only constant of military life, and Magnusson's casual approach to it was an apparent source of frustration for his crew.

12. Such a title would normally only be applied to a warrant officer, but could occasionally be applied to a chief petty officer. It was perhaps Magnus Magnusson's experience in a merchant fleet that led him to call the chief the ship's boatswain, or, as Novak speculates, Magnusson's general disdain for rank of any kind.

13. Unfortunately, this pivotal martinet character in Novak's story remains forever anonymous. No officer by the name Dicastro served in the U.S. Coast Guard Reserve during the Second World War. Two officers with the last name DeCastro did serve, and it is possible Novak refers to one of them.

14. The U.S. Coast Guard cutter *Mohawk* (WPG-78) was a 165-foot light icebreaker. Stationed out of Boston during the Second World War, she was used as an escort in Greenland waters. See Scheina, 22. Built in 1928, the U.S.S. *Hydrographer*, originally a Coast and Geodetic Survey vessel, was commissioned as AGS-2 by the

U.S. Navy in April, 1942, and spent 1942 charting the approaches to the base at Argentia in Newfoundland. Starting in 1943, she shifted to the Pacific for charting work there. See *American Naval Fighting Ships*, vol. 3, 410.

15. As Novak writes, Gunnbjorn Ulfsson sighted Greenland around A.D. 900. The coastal feature he named for himself, the "Gunnbjornar Skerries," are thought to be near present-day Angmagssalik. His cruise was not followed up until Iceland was fully settled, around 978, by Snaebjorn Galti's failed east coast overwintering. The next reconnaissance, this time of the west coast, was conducted by Eirik the Red in 981–982. It was Eirik who named it "Greenland": in legend to attract settlers, in truth perhaps because in summer southwestern Greenland is brilliantly green, albeit in patches.

16. Brattahlid is the site of the farm that belonged to the Norseman Eirik the Red. The ruins of the farm can still be seen, and a reconstruction of Eirik's wife Thjodhild's small chapel was built in 2000. Today it is called Qassiarsuk and lies across a fjord from the airport at Narsarssuak, site of the original BW 1 airbase.

17. The disappearance of the Norse Greenland colony has been the subject of speculation and science for nearly three hundred years. It is the only European colony to vanish without leaving a written record behind of its fate. An excellent recent treatment of the subject can be found in Kirsten A. Seaver's, *The Frozen Echo*.

18. Hans Egede (1686–1758), a Norwegian missionary/colonizer, voyaged to Greenland in 1721, fully expecting to find Norsemen there. When he found Inuit instead of Norse, he founded a Greenland mission and began the Christian conversion and Danish colonization of Greenland.

19. The U.S. Coast Guard cutter *Comanche* (WPG-76), another 165-foot light icebreaker, played a pivotal role in the early prewar maneuvering for priority in Greenland. See Scheina, 21. It was *Comanche* in May, 1940, that transported an American consul—the first in Greenland—to Godthåb, where the first American consulate on the island was established. See Willoughby, 95 and U.S. Coast Guard, *Greenland Patrol*, 6. When the transport *Dorchester* was attacked and sunk by a submarine 150 miles south of Cape Farewell, Greenland, on February 3, 1943, *Comanche* combined with U.S. Coast Guard cutter *Escanaba* to rescue 225 of the 299 survivors of the original 904 on board *Dorchester*. See Willoughby, 105. The sinking gained international attention when four U.S. Army chaplains perished after voluntarily giving up their life jackets to other *Dorchester* survivors. Comanche Bay, Greenland, where the *Comanche* helped establish Ice Cap Station in the summer of 1942, was named for the cutter. See Scheina, 21.

20. According to the U.S. Coast Guard's official history of the war—and in an unself-consciously ironic phrase typical of World War II—Thomas Sargent La Farge joined the U.S. Coast Guard "to paint, while performing regular war duties." Beyond his commission qualifications as a "yachtsman and lover of ships," La Farge had already acquired an impressive reputation as a painter, and his murals, stained glasses, frescoes, and mosaics could be found at New York Hospital and the New

York World's Fair, and at Trinity College and St. Matthew's Cathedral in Washington, D.C. See U.S. Coast Guard, *Greenland Patrol*, 42. See also Capelotti, "Lost World War II Skipper Leaves Artistic Legacy."

21. For nearly a decade prior to the Second World War, the U.S. Coast Guard cutter *Escanaba* (WPG-77), another in the 165-foot *Algonquin*-class of light cutters and seasonal icebreakers, was stationed at Grand Haven, Michigan, on the Great Lakes. Assigned to the Greenland Patrol in 1941, *Escanaba* was used for escort duty in Greenland waters. On June 15, 1942, *Escanaba* rescued twenty from the U.S.S. *Cherokee*, and rescued 132 from the S.S. *Dorchester* on February 3, 1943. On June 13, 1943, while escorting Convoy GS-24 from Narsarssuak, Greenland, to St. Johns, Newfoundland, *Escanaba* blew up and sank in three minutes. Only 2 sailors of 103 on board survived. See Willoughby, 104, 201; see also Scheina, 21.

22. Novak means the U.S.S. *Bluebird* (AM-72) (ex-Maine). *Bluebird* was converted into a minesweeper and commissioned by the U.S. Navy in 1940. See U.S. Navy, *American Naval Fighting Ships*, vol. 1, 134. The 132-foot vessel was supposed to lead *Natsek* and *Nanok* south through the Strait of Belle Isle on the fateful night of December 17, 1942. See Willoughby, 102–3.

23. The issue of cameras and diaries is not a straightforward one. Although standing orders forbade both, conversations with surviving crew members, as well as Novak's diary, indicate that enforcement of these instructions was haphazard at best. Some crew members speak of carrying cameras, others of having them confiscated, and still others, like Novak, of being warned not to carry a camera until war's end. As a result, comparatively few photographs from the Greenland Patrol have found their way into the collection of the U.S. Coast Guard Historian's Office.

24. Julianehåb is today known as Qaqortoq (pronounced "kraak-ah-tok"). It was named for the Danish queen Juliane Marie. The modern Greenlandic name means "the white," and the modern population is a bit more than 3,000 citizens. It is a fishing, sealing, and canning port, with lately an influx of tourists centered around the Norse presence in Greenland.

25. Bernt Balchen (1899–1973), a twentieth-century aviation legend, was perhaps the greatest Arctic expert in the United States since Charles Francis Hall. Born in Norway, Balchen worked as ground crew on Roald Amundsen's 1926 airship flight to the North Pole. It was there, in King's Bay, Svalbard, that he came to the attention of Richard E. Byrd and subsequently came to the United States as a pilot for Byrd's transatlantic flight of 1927. Balchen was at the controls when Byrd reached the South Pole through the air on November 29, 1929. Prior to the attack on Pearl Harbor, Balchen joined the U.S. Army Air Force at the behest of General "Hap" Arnold and supervised the construction of and later commanded BW 8. Balchen's command of a secret Allied transport fleet of B-24 aircraft led to dramatic aerial resupply missions of the Norwegian Underground. After the war, Balchen refined his Arctic rescue techniques as commander of the 10th Rescue Squadron in Alaska. His books include an autobiography, *Come North With Me* (1958).

26. The U.S. Coast Guard cutter *Arundel* (WYT-90) was a 110-foot icebreaking tug on the Hudson River at the start of the war, when it was assigned to Greenland waters. Its complement was two warrant officers and fourteen crew.

27. The U.S. Coast Guard cutter *Algonquin* (WPG-75), another of the 165-foot cutters to see service in Greenland, was used for icebreaking along the Maine coast prior to the war. On March 21, 1943, *Algonquin* rescued twenty-two survivors of the S.S. *Svend Foyne* after it struck an iceberg. See Scheina, 21.

28. The British explorer Robert F. Scott attempted to use motorized sledges in Antarctica during his 1910–11 expedition to the South Pole. The American journalist Walter Wellman tested motor sledges for use at his airship base in Svalbard as early as the spring of 1906. See Capelotti, *The Wellman Polar Airship Expeditions.*

29. The U.S. Coast Guard cutter *Northland* (WPG-49), one of the service's most famous vessels, was designed in the 1920s as a replacement to the even more legendary polar cutter *Bear*. In the summer of 1940, *Northland* was ordered to duty on the Greenland Patrol. Under the command of E. H. "Iceberg" Smith, *Northland* cruised from New York to Greenland in the late summer of 1940, charting both eastern and western coastlines. On September 12, 1941, the cutter captured the Norwegian vessel *Buskø*. This ship, sent to northeast Greenland by the head of polar research in occupied Norway, Adolf Hoel, carried trappers, supplies, and a radio transmitter to Norwegian outposts in the area. While Norwegians such as Hoel apparently believed the Germans would look favorably on Norwegian claims to East Greenland following a German victory, the U.S. was equally determined that no German nor German-occupied country be allowed to keep or maintain weather outposts anywhere in the Western Hemisphere. See Barr, 205–8; Willoughby, 102–3; and Scheina, 31. *Northland* made eight cruises to Greenland during the war. On July 22, 1942, the cutter rescued twenty-five survivors from the forced landings of two B-17s and four P-38s on the ice cap; in November of that year in separate incidents, *Northland* rescued three Canadian airmen and two U.S. Army Air Force airmen downed on the ice cap. Two U.S. Coast Guard aviators, Lieutenant John A. Pritchard and Radioman Benjamin A. Bottoms, were lost during the latter rescue when they attempted to bring out a third army airman. For the remainder of the war, *Northland* patrolled from East Greenland to Jan Mayen Land, engaging German surface and submarine vessels on several occasions. See Willoughby, 96–98, 101–2, 105–10.

30. This was not a bad suspicion. Reserve officers in the Coast Guard during the World War II often earned their commissions on the strength of little more than a college degree and/or wealthy connections in yachting circles—either of which had little to do with the ability to command two dozen hard-bitten sailors in the Arctic. Thomas S. La Farge, captain of the *Natsek*, for example, became a lieutenant (j.g.) because he was a "yachtsman and lover of ships."

31. The U.S. Coast Guard cutter *Ingham* (WPG-35) was a 327-foot secretary-class vessel designed for multimission, high seas work. *Ingham* conducted escort duties during the Battle of the Atlantic, rescuing dozens of survivors of ship disasters

and sinking the German submarine *U-626* on December 15, 1942. Later in the war, *Ingham* operated in both the Mediterranean and Pacific theatres. See Scheina, 13–14.

32. The crew of this bomber, three Canadian airmen, was rescued in late November by searchers from the *Northland*. These rescuers were led by Lieutenant John A. Pritchard, who would lose his own life only a week later rescuing U.S. Army airmen whose plane had gone down on the ice cap. See U.S. Coast Guard, *Greenland Patrol*, 134.

33. The U.S. destroyer *Reuben James* (DD-245) was torpedoed on the morning of October 31, 1941, while escorting convoy HX-156. One hundred and fifteen of one hundred and sixty crew were lost. Folk singer Woody Guthrie penned a now-famous song, "Sinking of the *Reuben James*," after the incident, with a refrain that concluded, "did you have a friend on the good *Reuben James*?"

34. The U.S. Coast Guard cutter *Modoc* (WPG-46) was used on International Ice Patrol before the war and was assigned to the Greenland Patrol on July 1, 1941, and used as an escort. On March 21, 1943, *Modoc* rescued twenty-eight survivors of the collision between S.S. *Svend Foyne* and an iceberg. See Scheina, 33.

35. Gamatron was a radio beacon base, emplaced in a narrow cut in Skovfjord, across from Simiutaq. With difficult geographic conditions hampering both aerial approaches and radio direction finders at BW 1, the tiny base at Gamatron propagated a generally reliable radio direction beacon for aircraft attempting to locate BW 1 under instrument flying conditions. For a more detailed discussion of the geographic and physical challenges presented by flying over southern Greenland, see Chase, "Overview: North Atlantic Ferry Route."

36. The U.S. Coast Guard cutter *Mojave* (WPG-47) was stationed in Boston and used in Greenland waters from 1941 to 1944. On August 27, 1942, *Mojave* rescued 293 survivors from the army transport *Chatham*. See Scheina, 33.

37. On November 28, the cutter *Northland* received word that the U.S. Army had made contact with the crew of a B-17 Flying Fortress downed on the ice cap. Lieutenant Pritchard and his radioman, Benjamin A. Bottoms, took off from the *Northland* in a Grumman J2F-5 Duck amphibian pontoon aircraft and made a wheels-up landing on the ice cap, some four miles from the wreck of the B-17. Pritchard managed to shepherd the three injured survivors back to the Duck, where Bottoms was maintaining radio contact with *Northland*. The weight and take-off limitations of the Duck forced Pritchard to leave one of the airmen behind until the next day. After he and Bottoms returned and successfully retrieved the man, worsening weather apparently forced Pritchard off course. Bottoms' signals to *Northland* grew faint and then went silent. Five volunteers from *Northland* searched for Pritchard for a month without success. An army aircraft located the wreckage four months later, but no bodies were ever found. Both Pritchard and Bottoms were posthumously awarded the Distinguished Flying Cross. See U.S. Coast Guard, *Greenland Patrol*, 136.

38. Lieutenant LaFarge was the grandson of the artist John LaFarge.

39. *Greenland Patrol* (U.S. Coast Guard, 1945), 44.

40. Ibid., 42.

41. Ibid.

42. Elizabeth J. Millner to P. J. Capelotti, personal communication, February 10, 2003.

References

Balchen, Bernt. 1958. *Come North With Me.* New York: E.P. Dutton.

Barr, Susan. 2003. *Norway: A Consistent Polar Nation?* Oslo: Kolofon A.S.

Capelotti, P. J. 1997. *The Wellman Polar Airship Expeditions at Virgohamna, Danskøya, Svalbard. Meddelelser* No. 145. Oslo, Norway: Norsk Polarinstitutt.

———. 1996. "The Coast Guard and Oceanography." *Coast Guard Magazine* (August).

———. 1993. "Lost World War II Skipper Leaves Artistic Legacy." *Commandant's Bulletin* 93–92 (February).

Chase, Jim. 1999. "Overview: North Atlantic Ferry Route." http://members.aol.com/JCStott/chase/history.html.

Krietemeyer, George E. 2000. *The Coast Guardsman's Manual.* 9th ed., rev. Annapolis: Naval Institute Press.

Scheina, Robert L. 1982. *U.S. Coast Guard Cutters & Craft of World War II.* Annapolis: Naval Institute Press.

Seaver, Kirsten A. 1996. *The Frozen Echo: Greenland and the Exploration of North America, ca. A.D. 1000–1500.* Stanford: Stanford University Press.

Smith, E.H. 1931. *The Marion Expedition to Davis Strait and Baffin Bay Under the Direction of the U.S. Coast Guard, 1928. Scientific Results, Part 3: Arctic Ice, with Especial Reference to its Distribution to the North Atlantic Ocean.* U.S. Coast Guard Bulletin No. 19. Washington, D.C.: GPO.

Tilley, John A. "The Coast Guard and the Greenland Patrol." http://www.uscg.mil/hq/g-cp/history/h_greenld.html.

U.S. Coast Guard. 1945. *Greenland Patrol.* Vol. 2 of *The Coast Guard at War.* Washington, D.C.: U.S. Coast Guard Historical Division.

U.S. Navy. 1969. *Dictionary of American Naval Fighting Ships.* Vol. 4. Washington, D.C: Department of the Navy.

———. 1968. *Dictionary of American Naval Fighting Ships.* Vol. 3. Washington: Department of the Navy.

———. 1940. *The Bluejackets' Manual.* Annapolis: U.S. Naval Institute.

Willoughby, Malcolm F. 1957. *The Coast Guard in World War II.* Annapolis: Naval Institute Press.

Index

P.J. Capelotti retired in 2012 as Master Chief Petty Officer in the U.S. Coast Guard Reserve, after 24 years of service to his country. Recalled to active duty five times, his work documenting the Coast Guard's response to the 9/11 attacks earned a decoration with the Meritorious Service Medal in 2003. He twice received the "best book of the year" award from the Foundation for Coast Guard History (including for *Life and Death on the Greenland Patrol*) and his edited volume *The Whaling Expedition of the Ulysses* (Florida, 2010) was also nominated for the award. He teaches anthropology at Penn State University.

CPSIA information can be obtained at www.ICGtesting.com
Printed in the USA
BVOW03s0635160514

353553BV00009BA/111/P